D Cookbook

Discover the advantages of programming in D with over 100 incredibly effective recipes

Adam D. Ruppe

BIRMINGHAM - MUMBAI

D Cookbook

First published: May 2014

Production Reference: 1190514

Published by Packt Publishing Ltd.
Livery Place
35 Livery Street
Birmingham B3 2PB, UK.

ISBN 978-1-78328-721-5

www.packtpub.com

Cover Image by Dennis Ruppe (dennis.ruppe@gmail.com)

Credits

Author

Adam D. Ruppe

Reviewers

Andrei Alexandrescu

Brad Anderson

Maxim Fomin

Kai Nacke

Commissioning Editor

Sam Birch

Acquisition Editor

Sam Birch

Content Development Editor

Sriram Neelakantan

Technical Editors

Krishnaveni Haridas

Monica John

Edwin Moses

Shiny Poojary

Copy Editors

Alisha Aranha

Roshni Banerjee

Mradula Hegde

Project Coordinator

Amey Sawant

Proofreaders

Simran Bhogal

Paul Hindle

Indexer

Priya Subramani

Production Coordinators

Manu Joseph

Nitesh Thakur

Cover Work

Manu Joseph

Foreword

There is an immediacy and a delicious sense of urgency running through Adam's book that makes the very notion of its foreword almost offensive. "Let's go implement some great ideas", the book seems to rejoice at every page; "I know you don't have the patience but read me first, this may help." I wouldn't want to hold you much with a fluffy, needless opener for a book that in turn frames itself as a prelude to many enjoyable hours of spinning code. I'll try to keep this short and to the point—much in the spirit of the book itself.

D Cookbook aims at enabling you to get work done using D, and it is written from the perspective of one who's clearly walking the walk. I know that Adam has leveraged D for years in his consulting gigs, but even if I didn't, I would have inferred this easily. He writes in the factual, no-nonsense tone of the senior engineer who wants to bring a n00b up to speed so they can get good work done together. Adam's use of "you" and "we" nicely orients himself and the reader toward solving a problem together. He's not coy to just tell the reader what to do to accomplish a task, but never comes across as patronizing. Simple explanations pepper the recipes, and there's always an implied "here's something I tried and works well, you may find that useful" lurking in the subtext.

The book covers a variety of topics that appear to be only loosely connected: what do (to quote a few consecutive chapter titles) "Ranges", "Integration" (with platforms and other languages), "Resource Management", and "Wrapped Types" have in common? Usefulness, that's what. Such topics, and everything else that the book sets out to explain, are likely to be important in real-world D applications. Of these, a few are "canon". At the other extreme there'd be borderline apocryphal stuff such as the *Kernel in D* chapter. Finally, the bulk of it is annotated folklore (idioms and patterns known by D's early adopters but not yet by the wider community), mixed with the author's own insights for good measure. Such a collection of relevant, high-impact topics is difficult to find collected, let alone in book format. You should read this book if you want to ramp up to using D in industrial-strength applications.

Adam's style is refreshing for someone like me; I've been involved in a mix of language design and language advocacy for years now, both fields of considerable subjectivity and fervor. Adam's dispassionate take on language advocacy is a breath of fresh air. His passion is expended on building great systems, and the language is but a means to that end. If Adam likes a language feature, he does primarily because he can use it to good effect, and proceeds to illustrate that. If, on the contrary, he finds a shortcoming, he simply discusses possible workarounds; that, and the missing lamentations, wonderfully imply that the point of it all is to get work done. "There is one disadvantage", Adam notes in a sidebar, "to operator overloading being implemented with templates, though: the operator overload functions cannot be virtual." Before even finishing that sentence, I've evoked in my mind enough pros and cons for a lively talk show debate. He's unfazed: "To work around this, write the overload implementation as a final method which merely forwards the request to a virtual method."

Last but not least, I took pleasure with the varying "zoom level" of the book. Like a philosopher who also knows his way around a welding machine, Adam can discuss esoteric code generation topics and show code disassembly, sometimes within the same chapter (see for example, "Code Generation") and all in style, while illustrating a good point. Wherever you dwell on the high-level/low-level continuum, it's likely you'll find ways to expand your range by reading *D Cookbook*.

Many years ago, while in the military, I learned to shoot the famed Kalashnikov AK47. I was bad at shooting from the hip (which is odd because everybody in the movies is great at it) until one day I learned a trick that was doing the rounds—wrap the weapon's strap tightly around the left arm at the elbow. The extra tension increases hand stability. That hack worked great; yet it was not to be found in any doctrine or manual, and in fact I couldn't find much about it today on the Internet. *D Cookbook* reminds me of that hack—it contains advice that's hard to find in the official documentation, and of immense practical utility. If you want to work in D, you'll find this book a great companion.

Andrei Alexandrescu, PhD

Research Scientist, Facebook
Author of *The D Programming Language*
San Francisco, CA, 12th May 2014

About the Author

Adam D. Ruppe is a professional software developer living in Watertown, New York. He started programming PCs in high school, writing assembly language, and later C and C++, using the Digital Mars compiler to build programs based on MS DOS on a hand-me-down computer. Programming in the DOS environment with the slow computer gave him early practical experience in low-level and efficient code—skills he carries on developing today.

After finishing school, he started doing web programming—initially with PHP. While he'd make it work, he often found himself longing for the good old days. One day, he decided to check back with the vendor of his old compiler and discovered the D programming language (well before it reached 1.0!).

He was enamored with it and used it to write some games, and then started writing web libraries to use it for work too, to replace PHP. He found success in this endeavor in early 2009.

Combining his pioneering spirit with his blend of low-level and high-level programming experience, he was able to forge ahead with D, taking it to places many people didn't believe possible.

About the Reviewers

Andrei Alexandrescu coined the colloquial term "modern C++", which is used today to describe a collection of important C++ styles and idioms. His book on the topic, *Modern C++ Design: Generic Programming and Design Patterns Applied* (Addison-Wesley, 2001), revolutionized C++ programming and produced a lasting influence not only on subsequent work on C++, but also on other languages and systems. With Herb Sutter, he is also the co-author of *C++ Coding Standards: 101 Rules, Guidelines, and Best Practices* (Addison-Wesley Professional, 2010). He has garnered a solid reputation in both industrial and academic circles through his varied work on libraries and applications, as well as research in machine learning and natural language processing. From 2006, he worked on the D programming language together with Walter Bright, the inventor and initial implementer of the language. He co-designed many important features of D, authored a large part of D's standard library, and wrote the book *The D Programming Language* (Addison-Wesley Professional, 2010). Andrei holds a PhD in Computer Science from the University of Washington and a B.Sc. in Electrical Engineering from University Politehnica of Bucharest. He works as a research scientist for Facebook.

Brad Anderson is a computer programmer living in Salt Lake City. He has been writing software professionally for over 10 years and is currently a Lead Developer at Phoenix Project Management Systems.

Maxim Fomin is a programmist who is currently living and working in St. Petersburg, Russia. Coming with a background in other languages, he quickly recognized D programming language for its convenience, efficiency, and power synthesis. He helped a company to apply D language in writing software in an area of his professional interest—Finance.

I would like to thank my family for helping and encouraging me in times of difficulties and pessimism. I would also like to thank all the mentors that I've had over the years. Without their assistance, I would not have acquired knowledge and skills that I possess today.

Kai Nacke is the current maintainer of LDC, the LLVM-based D compiler. He has a strong interest in compiler construction and is also a contributor to the LLVM framework. In 1998, he received his Master of Computer Science degree. He is an IT architect at IBM and has over 10 years of experience in architecturing solutions and developing custom applications.

www.PacktPub.com

Support files, eBooks, discount offers, and more

You might want to visit www.PacktPub.com for support files and downloads related to your book.

Did you know that Packt offers eBook versions of every book published, with PDF and ePub files available? You can upgrade to the eBook version at www.PacktPub.com and as a print book customer, you are entitled to a discount on the eBook copy. Get in touch with us at service@packtpub.com for more details.

At www.PacktPub.com, you can also read a collection of free technical articles, sign up for a range of free newsletters and receive exclusive discounts and offers on Packt books and eBooks.

http://PacktLib.PacktPub.com

Do you need instant solutions to your IT questions? PacktLib is Packt's online digital book library. Here, you can access, read and search across Packt's entire library of books.

Why Subscribe?

- ▶ Fully searchable across every book published by Packt
- ▶ Copy and paste, print and bookmark content
- ▶ On demand and accessible via web browser

Free Access for Packt account holders

If you have an account with Packt at www.PacktPub.com, you can use this to access PacktLib today and view nine entirely free books. Simply use your login credentials for immediate access.

Table of Contents

Preface

The D programming language's popularity is growing rapidly. With its seamless blending of high-level convenience with low-level power and efficiency, D is suitable for tackling almost any programming task productively. This book comes out of years of experience of using D in the real world and closely following the language and libraries' development. It will also help you get up to speed with this exciting language and burgeoning ecosystem.

What this book covers

Chapter 1, Core Tasks, will get you started with D and cover the tasks you can perform with D's core language features that differ from other popular programming languages.

Chapter 2, Phobos – The Standard Library, introduces you to the standard D library to perform common tasks, including generating random numbers, writing a network client and server, and performing type conversions.

Chapter 3, Ranges, covers the range concept, which is central to D algorithms. Ranges allow you to write and consume generators, views on various collections, and perform generic transformations of data.

Chapter 4, Integration, explores integrating D with the outside world, including creating Windows-based applications, using C libraries, and extending C++ applications with D.

Chapter 5, Resource Management, discusses how to manage memory and other resources in D, including tips on why, when, and how to use the garbage collector effectively.

Chapter 6, Wrapped Types, dives into the world of user-defined types, showing you how to extend and restrict types via cheap wrapper abstractions.

Chapter 7, Correctness Checking, shows how to use D's bug-hunting features such as testing, assertions, and documentation, and the correct way to do conditional compilation.

Chapter 8, Reflection, teaches you about the rich introspection capabilities D provides, including tips learned through years of experience which stretch the limits of the language.

Chapter 9, Code Generation, demonstrates several techniques to automate the creation of new code to write efficient, generic, and specialized code, including a primer on creating your own mini languages inside D.

Chapter 10, Multitasking, introduces you to the options D offers for concurrency and parallelism.

Chapter 11, D for Kernel Coding, will get you started with writing bare metal code in D, stripping out the runtime library to say hello directly through the PC's video hardware and then handling interrupts sent back by the keyboard with D's low-level features.

Chapter 12, Web and GUI Programming, showcases some of the libraries I've written over the years that show how to make a dynamic website and desktop graphics windows while discussing my practical experience from writing these libraries, which will give you a leg up when you write your own code.

Appendix, Addendum, briefly shows how to use D on ARM processors, including systems without an operating system, and other small topics that didn't fit elsewhere in the book.

What you need for this book

You need to have a Windows or Mac PC that is capable of running the DMD compiler, which is available at `http://dlang.org/`.

Who this book is for

This book is for programmers who want to continue their professional development by learning more about D. Whether you are looking at D for the first time or have used it before and want to learn more, this book has something to offer you.

Conventions

In this book, you will find a number of styles of text that distinguish between different kinds of information. Here are some examples of these styles, and an explanation of their meaning.

Code words in text, database table names, folder names, filenames, file extensions, pathnames, dummy URLs, user input, and Twitter handles are shown as follows: "Add a struct to `test.d`, which uses `alias this` to activate subtyping."

A block of code is set as follows:

```
import project.foo;; // disambiguate with project.foo
import bar; // you can disambiguate calls with the name bar
```

Any command-line input or output is written as follows:

```
coffimplib myfile.lib
```

New terms and **important words** are shown in bold. Words that you see on the screen, in menus or dialog boxes for example, appear in the text like this: "Running the program will print **Hello, world!** in green text on a red background."

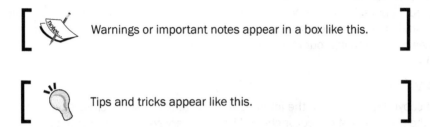

> Warnings or important notes appear in a box like this.

> Tips and tricks appear like this.

Reader feedback

Feedback from our readers is always welcome. Let us know what you think about this book—what you liked or may have disliked. Reader feedback is important for us to develop titles that you really get the most out of.

To send us general feedback, simply send an e-mail to feedback@packtpub.com, and mention the book title via the subject of your message.

If there is a topic that you have expertise in and you are interested in either writing or contributing to a book, see our author guide on www.packtpub.com/authors.

Customer support

Now that you are the proud owner of a Packt book, we have a number of things to help you to get the most from your purchase.

Downloading the example code

You can download the example code files for all Packt books you have purchased from your account at http://www.packtpub.com. If you purchased this book elsewhere, you can visit http://www.packtpub.com/support and register to have the files e-mailed directly to you.

Errata

Although we have taken every care to ensure the accuracy of our content, mistakes do happen. If you find a mistake in one of our books—maybe a mistake in the text or the code—we would be grateful if you would report this to us. By doing so, you can save other readers from frustration and help us improve subsequent versions of this book. If you find any errata, please report them by visiting http://www.packtpub.com/submit-errata, selecting your book, clicking on the **errata submission form** link, and entering the details of your errata. Once your errata are verified, your submission will be accepted and the errata will be uploaded on our website, or added to any list of existing errata, under the Errata section of that title. Any existing errata can be viewed by selecting your title from http://www.packtpub.com/support.

Piracy

Piracy of copyright material on the Internet is an ongoing problem across all media. At Packt, we take the protection of our copyright and licenses very seriously. If you come across any illegal copies of our works, in any form, on the Internet, please provide us with the location address or website name immediately so that we can pursue a remedy.

Please contact us at copyright@packtpub.com with a link to the suspected pirated material.

We appreciate your help in protecting our authors, and our ability to bring you valuable content.

Questions

You can contact us at questions@packtpub.com if you are having a problem with any aspect of the book, and we will do our best to address it.

1
Core Tasks

In this chapter, we will get started with D and explore some of its core features. You will learn the following recipes:

- Installing the compiler and writing a "Hello World" program
- Adding additional modules (files) to your program
- Using external libraries
- Building and processing arrays
- Using associative arrays to translate input
- Creating a user-defined vector type
- Using a custom exception type
- Understanding immutability
- Slicing a string to get a substring
- Creating a tree of classes

Introduction

The D language borrows from several other programming languages, including statically typed languages such as C, C++, and Java, as well as dynamic languages such as Ruby, Python, and JavaScript. The overall syntax is very similar to C; the use of curly braces to denote blocks, declarations in the form of typename initializer, and more. In fact, a lot of, but not all, C code will compile in D too.

D also is aimed at convenience, productivity, and modeling power. These principles can be illustrated with D's type inference feature. Type inference means you can write code without explicitly thinking of and repeating a variable's type. This gives the convenience of using a dynamic language, without sacrificing the compile-time checks of static typing. You'll use type inference throughout your programs. Any variable declared without a type (typically, the keyword `auto` is used to declare a variable without an explicit type) has an inferred type, where the type is automatically determined by the right-hand side of the assignment. D is one of the fastest compiling languages available, and it gives quick edit-run cycles that help rapid development in dynamic languages. Modeling power comes in the form of D's rich code generation, introspection, and user-defined types, which you'll start exploring in this chapter when you look at structs and classes.

Installing the compiler and writing a "Hello World" program

You're going to create your first D program; a simple "Hello World" program.

How to do it...

Let's execute the following steps to create your first program:

1. Download the DMD compiler from `http://dlang.org/download.html`.

2. If you use a platform installer, it will install. If you use a ZIP file, simply unzip it and use it in place of the platform installer. The binaries for each operating system are found in `dmd2/your_os_name/bin`. You may choose to add this directory to your `PATH` environment variable so you do not need to use the full path each time you run the compiler.

3. Create a file with your favorite text editor with the following content and name it `hello.d`:

```
import std.stdio : writeln;;;
void main() {
    writeln("Hello, world!");
}
```

4. Compile the program. In your command prompt, run the following:

   dmd hello.d

5. Run the program as follows:

   hello

You should see the following message appear:

Hello, world!

Downloading the example code

You can download the example code files for all Packt books you have purchased from your account at `http://www.packtpub.com`. If you purchased this book elsewhere, you can visit `http://www.packtpub.com/ support` and register to have the files e-mailed directly to you.

How it works...

The DMD compiler is the key tool needed to use D. Although IDEs exist, you won't be using them in this book. So, you'll learn how to use the compiler and be better equipped to handle problems encountered during the build process.

D source files are Unicode text, which are compiled into executable programs. The DMD compiler, by default, generates an executable file with the same base name as the first file passed to it. So here, when you called `dmd hello.d`, it created a file named `hello.exe` on Windows or `hello` on Unix systems. You can change the output file with the `dmd -of` option, for example `dmd -oftest hello.d` will create a file named `test.exe`. You'll learn more about the options of `dmd` as and when they'll be required.

Next, let's look at each of the lines of `hello.d`, beginning with the following `import` statement:

```
import std.stdio;
```

A D program is composed of modules. Each module is a file, but unlike C or C++, where you use textual `#include` directives, D uses a symbolic `import`. When you import a module, its public members become available for use. You can import the same module multiple times without any negative effect, and the order of top-level imports does not matter.

In this case, you're importing the module `std.stdio`, which is a part of the standard library that provides input and output functions, including the `writeln` function you'll use later in the code. Next, let's discuss the following `main()` function:

```
void main()
```

D programs typically begin execution at the `main()` function. D's `main()` function can optionally take command-line arguments of type `string[]`, and they may return either void or integer values. All forms are equally valid.

It is possible to write D programs that start somewhere other than `main()`, which allows you to bypass D runtime initialization. You'll see this in *Chapter 11, D for Kernel Coding*.

Here, you're returning void because you aren't returning any specific value. The runtime will automatically return zero to the operating system upon normal termination, and it will return an error code automatically if the program is terminated by an exception. Now, let's look at the following output function:

```
writeln("Hello, world!");
```

Finally, you'll call the function `writeln` from the `std.stdio` module to say **Hello, World!**. The `writeln` function can take any number of arguments of any type, and it will automatically convert them to string for printing. This function automatically adds a newline character to the end of the output.

There's more...

Here, you used the DMD compiler. There are two other major D compilers available: GDC and LDC. You can learn more about these at `http://gdcproject.org/` and `http://github.com/ldc-developers/ldc`, respectively.

Adding additional modules (files) to your program

As your program grows, you'll want to break it up across multiple files. D offers a way to do this that is similar, but not identical to other popular programming languages. D source files are also called D modules.

How to do it...

Let's add modules to your program by executing the following steps:

1. Create an additional file.

2. Put the `module` declaration in the other file with a package and module name. These names should be meaningful for your project and this specific file, respectively, as shown:

   ```
   module yourpackage.yourmodulename;;;
   ```

3. Import it in the existing file to use it. Import works in different ways—it does not have to be at the top of the file and may appear more than once in the file. The `import` statement should always match the full name given in the `module` statement in the file being imported, as shown in the following code:

   ```
   import yourpackage.yourmodulename;
   ```

4. Use the functions, disambiguating with the full module name if required.

5. Compile with all files listed on the command line using the following syntax:

   ```
   dmd file1.d file2.d
   ```

6. This will produce a single executable file out of the passed files. The name of the executable is, by default, the same as the first file passed. So here, the executable file will be named `file1`.

How it works...

In D, code is organized into modules. There is a one-to-one correspondence between files and modules—every D source file is a module, and every D module is a file. Using a module involves importing it into the current scope, accessing its members in code, and adding it to the build command when compiling.

 If you forget to add a module to the build command, you'll see an error such as `cannot find module of name NAME` or `undefined symbol _D6module`.

Modules are conceptually similar to static classes with a single instance; they can have constructors, destructors, fields, and so on. Each declaration inside a module may have attributes and protection qualifiers. In D, unlike C++, modules (not classes) are the unit of encapsulation. Therefore, any code can access any entity within the same module (regardless of the entity's protection qualifier).

Modules have logical names that do not need to match the filename. This is set with the `module` statement, which must appear at the top of the file. The `module` statement is not strictly required. If you leave it off, it will default to the filename. However, it is strongly recommended that you write it, including a package name, (the first part of the dot-separated full name) in every module that may ever be imported, because relying on the default module name will cause trouble if you organize your code into directories. The common error module `foo.bar` must be imported as the `foo` module is caused by a missing `module` statement in the imported module. The typical organization of modules into packages mirrors the source files' directory structures. You are to match package and module names with directory and filenames, but doing so will help other users and build tools understand your project layout.

The `import` statement may appear at any point. In module scope, it may appear anywhere and any number of times without changing anything. It can also be used in local scopes, where it must appear before the member is used and visibility is limited to that scope.

Names of members in a module are not required to be unique among all the modules that make up a program. Instead, when necessary, they are disambiguated at the usage point or at the `import` statement by the module identifier, as shown in the following code:

```
import project.foo;; // disambiguate with project.foo
import bar; // you can disambiguate calls with the name bar

project.foo.func(); // call project.foo.func
bar.func(); // call bar.func
```

The compiler will always issue an error if a reference is ambiguous so that you can specify your intent.

 You can also rename modules when you import them. The statement, `import foo = project.foo;` will then allow you to use `foo` to disambiguate a name instead of having to write out the full `project.foo` name every time.

There's more...

The `dmd` distribution also includes a program called `rdmd`, which can recursively find dependent modules and compile them all automatically. With `rdmd`, you only have to pass the module that contains `main`.

See also

▶ The module documentation at `http://dlang.org/module.html` details how D's module system works, including a list of all the forms of the `import` statement and information about symbol protection

Using external libraries

D can use external libraries written in D, as well as other languages, with direct access to C functions, such as those provided by the operating system or the wealth of code written in C that can perform a variety of tasks. Here, you'll learn how to use an external library in your D program.

How to do it...

Let's use external libraries by executing the following steps:

1. Create or download bindings, a list of function prototypes, and a data structure definition from the library.

2. On 32-bit Windows with dmd only, get or create an `import` library (`.lib` file).

3. If you have a `.lib` file, you can use `coffimplib`.

4. If you only have a DLL file, you can use `implib`.

5. Import the binding by using the following statement:

   ```
   import package.module.name;
   ```

6. Compile with the library. For Linux, pass `-L-llibname` to dmd. On Windows, pass the `.lib` file to `dmd` when compiling your program. This will link the file with the generated executable, producing a working program.

How it works...

D is binary compatible with C, but not source compatible. This means you can link directly to C libraries, including most operating system libraries, without any wrapper or invoker code. You do need, however, to port the header files, the function prototypes, and the variable declarations, to D. This process is called binding.

While you can use a library by only providing the prototypes for the functions you need, being minimally type-safe, the recommended way is to port the C header as closely as possible. This will minimize bugs and maximize the ease of use for programmers who are familiar with the usage and documentation of C.

In your code, using the library is the same as using any other module; you import the module, call the functions, and disambiguate the names by using fully-qualified package and module names.

When compiling, the `-L` flag to dmd passes the rest of the argument straight to the linker. On 32-bit Windows, using an existing library may be difficult because dmd uses an old library file format called OMF that is incompatible with the newer and more common COFF format. This is where `implib` and `coffimplib` come into play—these programs generate the format that the linker, `optlink`, expects from the more common formats available. The `implib` command creates a `.lib` file that you can use with D directly from a `.dll` file. The `implib` command's invocation format is as follows:

```
implib /s myfile.lib myfile.dll
```

The `coffimplib` command converts the more common COFF `.lib` format to the format D requires. The `coffimplib` command's invocation format is as follows:

```
coffimplib myfile.lib
```

These programs can be separately downloaded from Digital Mars, the small company behind the D programming language and DMD compiler. They are not necessary when building 64-bit Windows programs, or programs on any other operating system.

There's more...

The DMD compiler supports `pragma(lib, "name");`, which will automatically handle the linker flag while building, if you pass the module to dmd's command line. This pragma is not fully supported on GDC, but it doesn't necessarily hurt either. It will issue a warning about an unsupported pragma.

You can also create D interface files for D libraries, the extension `.di` is used traditionally. The `.di` files can be automatically generated with the `dmd -H` option. The D interface files are similar to header files in C or C++; they list the interface definitions, but omit function bodies. The use of D interface files is optional.

See also

> ▸ Sometimes, using other libraries isn't as simple as calling their function, or you want to improve upon the API somehow. *Chapter 4, Integration*, explains how to address these issues.

> ▸ Deimos (`https://github.com/d-programming-deimos`) is the official repository for translated bindings and common C libraries. It makes no attempt to change the API; it is simply a collection of ports of C library headers that can be used in D, saving you the trouble of recreating the prototypes yourself.

> ▸ Dub (`http://code.dlang.org`) is the semi-official D package manager, and `code.dlang.org` lists community libraries that are available through it. This includes C bindings as well as pure D libraries.

> ▸ If you are developing for 32-bit Windows, the Basic Utilities Package from Digital Mars (`http://digitalmars.com/download/freecompiler.html`) contains the `implib` tool as well as others to build advanced Windows `.exe` files.

> ▸ The directory `dmd2/src/druntime/import` in the dmd's ZIP file has various D interface files for the D runtime library and the C standard library.

Building and processing arrays

D has three types of arrays built in: static arrays, with a set length known at compile time; dynamic arrays, with a variable length; and associative arrays, which are similar to hashmaps or dictionaries in other languages. D's arrays and array slices are a very flexible and easy-to-use tool used in almost all D programs. Here, you'll look at some of their capabilities by building a list of integers and then finding the sum of the contents.

How to do it...

Let's use the following steps to build and process arrays:

1. Declare an array variable by using the following statement:

   ```
   int[] arr;
   ```

2. Append data to it as shown:

   ```
   arr ~= 1;
   arr ~= [2, 3];
   ```

3. Create a function that takes a slice and does some processing on it, as shown in the following code:

   ```
   int sum(in int[] data) {
       int total = 0;
       foreach(item; data)
           total += item;
       return total;
   }
   ```

4. Pass a slice of the array to the function, as shown in the following code:

   ```
   // Dynamic arrays can be passed directly. Static
   // arrays can be sliced with the [] operator..
   writeln("The sum of ", arr, " is ", sum(arr));
   ```

How it works...

D types are always read from right to left. The `int []` array is an array of integers. The `string* [] *` pointer is a pointer to an array of pointers to string. The `int [] []` array is an array of an array of integers; a staggered array.

There are two kinds of arrays in D: static and dynamic. A static array is a value type that represents a solid, fixed-size block of memory (this corresponds to an array in C). A dynamic array is conceptually a struct with two members: a pointer to the data and the length of the data. Thus, unlike a static array, dynamic arrays and slices have reference semantics. You can access the pointer and length components with the `.ptr` and `.length` properties, respectively. In the example here, you used a dynamic array, which has the same syntax as a slice.

There are three major operations on an array: appending, indexing, and slicing.

▶ **Appending**: This is done with the `~=` operator. There's also the binary `~` operator (not to be confused with the unary `~` operator, which inverts bits), which concatenates two arrays to form a new one. You can append an individual element or another static or dynamic array of compatible type.

▶ **Indexing**: This is done with the `[expr]` operator, for example, `arr[0]`. This is very similar to C, but a key difference in D is that arrays know their own length, enabling automatic bounds checking. If you attempt to access an out-of-bounds index, you will see a RangeError.

▶ **Slicing**: This is done with the `[]` operator, for example, `arr[]` or `arr[0 .. 2]`. This is done to get a view into an array starting at the left-hand index (inclusive) and ending at the right-hand index (exclusive, which means you can use the array's length as an ending bound, which also has a shorthand syntax $). `[] [] []` gets a slice into the whole thing, and it is useful to pass static arrays or user-defined array types to functions expecting slices or dynamic arrays. Slicing is a fast, constant-time operation.

You can iterate over an array or slice using the `foreach` loop. You put the iteration variable, then a semicolon, and then the variable you want to iterate over. You do not have to explicitly name the variable's type, for example, `foreach(item; array)` or `foreach(int item; array)`.

In the example code, the function parameter is defined as an `in` variable. The `in` variable is shorthand keyword to give the parameter the storage classes of `const` and `scope`. What this means in practice is that you must not modify the array or its contents (this will be a compile error), nor should you keep a copy of or return a reference to the passed array.

There's more...

D also supports array vector operations like the following:

```
arr[] = arr[] + 5;;;
```

This code will add five to every element of the array. You can also create array copies this way: `arr2[] = arr[]`. This will copy `arr` into `arr2`. For this to work, the lengths of the two arrays must already match. To do an array copy without matching lengths, you can write `array.dup`.

See also

▶ `http://dlang.org/d-array-article.html` for details of array memory management and the difference between a dynamic array and a slice.

▶ `http://dlang.org/arrays.html` for a more complete listing of what D's arrays can do.

▶ The *Creating an array replacement* recipe in *Chapter 5, Resource Management*. This will show you how to create a new array type that has the same capabilities as the built-in arrays, with custom behavior or memory allocation strategies.

▶ The *Avoiding the garbage collector* recipe in *Chapter 5, Resource Management*. This will discuss the built-in array's memory allocation habits and what to avoid if you don't want to use the garbage collector.

Using associative arrays to translate input

D also has associative arrays, sometimes called maps or dictionaries. An associative array maps arbitrary keys to values. Unlike a regular array, the keys do not need to be sequential and do not need to be integers. Here, you'll explore their functionality by creating a program that translates input strings to other strings.

How to do it...

Let's translate an input by using the following steps:

1. Declare the associative array with string keys and string values.

2. Initialize it with initial data.

3. Loop over input lines. If the line is in the array, show the value and remove it. If not, add this line with a replacement.

4. When you're done, loop over the array to show your changes.

The code is as follows:

```
void main() {
    import std.stdio, std.string;
    string[string] replacements =
    ["test" : "passed", "text" : "replaced"];
    replacements["foo"] = "bar";
    assert(replacements["test"] == "passed");
    foreach(line; stdin.byLine()) {
```

```
        line = line.strip(); // cut off whitespace
        // see if the given line is in the mapping…
        if(auto replacement = line in replacements) {
            // if yes, show the replacement, then unmap it
            writeln(line, " => ", *replacement);
            replacements.remove(line.idup);
        } else
{

            // if no, add it to the map
            writeln(line);
            replacements[line.idup] = "previously inserted!";
        }
    }
    foreach(line, replacement; replacements)
        writeln("Mapping ", line, " => ", replacement););
}
```

When the program runs out of lines to process, it will print out the current array contents, showing you what has been added and removed as you entered data.

How it works...

First, you declared your `main` function and then imported the `std.stdio` and `std.string` modules, which contain the I/O and whitespace stripping functions that you used later.

Next, you declared an associative array that maps strings to other strings. The syntax is `ValueType[KeyType]`, and both sides can be of any D type. You also initialized the replacements with an associative array literal.

It is also possible to use user-defined types as associative array keys. Using custom types as key types requires that they implement `opHash`, `opCmp`, and `opEquals`.

The syntax of an **associative array (AA)** literal is `[Key:Value, Key:Value, …]`. AA literals can have both compile-time constant and runtime data; `["foo":x]` is legal too.

Next, you can set a value outside the literal and check the value of a key, just for demonstration purposes. Associative arrays have similar syntax to regular arrays: you use the same bracket syntax to get and set elements.

Then, you can enter the replacement loop, reading the standard input by line and then stripping off whitespace and looking for the line in the replacements array. Let's look at this line in more detail, as follows:

```
if(auto replacement = line in replacements) {
```

On the right-hand side, you can use the `in` operator to do a key lookup. This operator returns a pointer to the element if it is found, and null if it is not found.

> You don't have to use the pointer returned by the `in` operator. `if(line in replacements)` works just as well. There's also the inverse of `in`, which is `!in`. The `if(line !in replacements)` statement is true if line is not in the replacements array.

On the left-hand side, you can declare and assign the variable right inside the `if` statement. This keeps the newly declared variable limited in scope. If the variable replacement is available, you can be certain that it is not null, since the `if` statement will not execute otherwise!

In the next example, you'll proceed into the `true` branch of the `if` statement. This branch uses the dereference operator, `*replacement`, to print out the value. The `*` operator is necessary because the `in` operator returns a pointer to the element rather than the element itself. Then you'll remove this key from the mapping by using the built-in associative array property `remove`. Next time you insert that line, it will not be replaced.

After that, the false branch of the `if` statement does not have the `null` pointer stored in the variable `replacement` available to use. Any attempt to access it will be a compile error. Instead, you can add the new line to the replacement map. The `.idup` property is required because associative array keys must be immutable, and `stdin.byLine` returns a mutable buffer. `Array.idup` creates a new, immutable copy of the data.

Finally, once the input has been exhausted, you can loop over the associative array with a `foreach` loop. The syntax is `foreach(index, value; array)`, and you can print out the current state. The `index` parameter is optional if you only need the values.

There's more...

You can also get a list of all keys and values with the `.keys` and `.values` properties on the associative array. The `std.traits.KeyType` and `std.traits.ValueType` variables can be used to do compile-time reflection of generic AA types.

Creating a user-defined vector type

User-defined types are used everywhere in D to group data, model objects, provide compile-time checks, and more. Here, you'll create a simple vector type with a length and direction to look at some basic capabilities.

Getting ready

Whenever you create a user-defined collection in D, the first decision to make is whether it should be a class, struct, mixin template, or union. Mixin templates are great for code reuse. They define code that can be copied (or mixed in) to another type, with parameterization. Unions are for the cases when you need the same block of memory to have multiple types, and are the least common in typical D code. Classes and structs are the backbone of user-defined types in D, and they have the most in common. The key difference is polymorphic inheritance; if you need it, you probably want a class. Otherwise, structs are lighter weight and give maximum flexibility. Using them, you can precisely define the layout of each byte with no hidden data, overload all operators, use deterministic destruction (the RAII idiom from C++), and use both reference or value semantics depending on your specific needs. D's structs also support a form of subtyping, though not virtual functions, which you'll see in *Chapter 6, Wrapped Types*.

Let's summarize as follows:

Struct	Class
This offers precise control over memory layout	This offers virtual functions and inheritance
This is ideal for lightweight wrappers of other types	This is always a reference type
This offers deterministic destruction	This is usually managed by the garbage collector

Since your vector type will not need virtual functions, it will be a struct.

How to do it...

Let's look at creating a vector type using the following steps:

1. Declare the `struct` variable with a name. This declaration can appear anywhere; but, in your case, you want it to be generally accessible. So, it should go in the top-level scope of your module. Unlike C++, there is no need to put a semicolon at the end of the `struct` definition, as shown in the following code:

```
struct Vector {}
```

2. Determine which data members are needed and add them to the struct. Here, you need a magnitude and direction, and they will be floating point types:

```
struct Vector {
    float magnitude;
    float direction;
}
```

3. Add methods that operate on the data to the struct. In this case, you want to be able to add vectors together and convert from (x, y) coordinates. The complete code is as follows:

```
struct Vector {
    // the data
    float magnitude;
    float direction;

    // the methods
    /// create a Vector from an (x, y) point
    static Vector fromPoint(float[2] point) {
        import std.math;
        Vector v;
        float x = point[0];
        float y= point[1];
        v.magnitude = sqrt(x ^^ 2 + y ^^ 2);
        v.direction = atan2(y, x);
        return v;
}}}
    /// converts to an (x,y) point. returns in an array.
    float[2] toPoint() const {
        import std.math;
        float x = cos(direction) * magnitude;
        float y = sin(direction) * magnitude;
        return [x, y];
    }
    /// the addition operator
    Vector opBinary(string op : "+")(Vector rhs) const {
        auto point = toPoint(), point2 = rhs.toPoint();
        point[0] += point2[0];
        point[1] += point2[1];];];

        return Vector.fromPoint(point););
    }
}
```

4. Use the new type as follows:

```
auto origin = Vector(0, 0);
import std.math;
auto result = origin + Vector(1.0, PI);
import std.stdio;
writeln("Vector result: ", result);
writeln(" Point result: ", result.toPoint());
```

It will print `Vector(1.0, 3.14)` and `[-1, 0]`, showing the vector sum as magnitude and direction, and then x, y. Your run may have slightly different results printed due to differences in how your computer rounds off the floating point result.

How it works...

Structs are aggregate types that can contain data members and function methods. All members and methods are defined directly inside the struct, between the opening and closing braces. Data members have the same syntax as a variable declaration: a type (which can be inferred, if there is an initializer), a name, and optionally, an initializer. Initializers must be evaluated at compile time. When you declare a struct, without an explicit initializer, all members are set to the value of their initializers inside the `struct` definition.

Methods have the same syntax as functions at module scope, with two differences; they can be declared static and they may have `const`, `immutable`, or `inout` attached, which applies to the variable `this`. The `this` variable is an automatically declared variable that represents the current object instance in a method. The following recipe on immutability will discuss these keywords in more detail.

Operator overloading in D is done with methods and special names. In this section, you defined `opBinary`, which lets you overload the binary operators such as the addition and subtraction operators. It is specialized only on the + operator. It is also possible to overload casting, assignment, equality checking, and more.

At the usage point, you declared a vector with `auto`, using the automatically defined constructor.

Finally, when you write the result, you use the automatic string formatting that prints the name and the values, in the same way as the automatic constructor. It is also possible to take control of this by implementing your own `toString` method.

See also

▶   *Chapter 6, Wrapped Types*, will show more advanced capabilities, including how to use structs to make a reference type and to use constructors, destructors, postblits, and so on.

- Inheritance and dynamic class casting will show how to make the most of classes.

- Visit http://dlang.org/operatoroverloading.html for the language documentation on operator overloading. It details all the operators available for overloading and how to do it.

Using a custom exception type

D uses exceptions to handle errors, just like many other programming languages. In D, exceptions are always implemented as classes that derive from the class Throwable, and they are differentiated by their type. So, it is best to generate a new exception subclass for different types of errors your code can generate. This way, users of your code will get the most information and control out of your exceptions.

How to do it...

Let's use a custom exception type by using the following steps:

1. Declare a class that inherits from Exception.
2. Make a constructor that takes, minimally, two parameters: string file and size_t line, with default values of __FILE__ and __LINE__, respectively.
3. Have the constructor forward the arguments to the constructor of Exception.
4. Use your exception.

The following is the code:

```
class MyException : Exception {
    this(string message, string file = __FILE__, size_t line = __
LINE__, Throwable next = null) {
        super(message, file, line, next);
    }
}

void main() {
    import std.stdio;
    try
        throw new MyException("message here");
    catch(MyException e)
        writeln("caught ", e);
}
```

How it works...

D uses exceptions to handle errors. All throwable objects inherit from either `Exception`, for recoverable events, or `Error` for unrecoverable errors, which generally ought not be caught. The common base class is `Throwable`.

Typically, a custom exception inherits from `Exception`, then declares, minimally, a constructor that forwards the functionality to `super()`. You may also store additional information specific to your use case.

The constructor of `Exception` (here, called with `super()`) takes four arguments: a string message, a filename, a line number, and optionally, a reference to another exception. The message, filename, and line number are used to construct a message for the user, which is printed to the console if the exception is not caught.

You don't have to specify the file and line number at the throw site; any default argument of `__FILE__` or `__LINE__` is automatically expanded at the function's call site. This is useful to make the error message more useful by showing exactly where the exception came from.

The fourth parameter, `Throwable next`, is used if an exception handler throws an exception. It references the exception that was being handled when this one was generated.

> To get full stack trace symbols in the printed exception, you may need to compile with the debug information enabled by using `dmd -g`.

There's more...

You should check error codes when using the C functions and turn them into exceptions. If it sets `errno` for error details, the `std.exception` module has a subclass called `ErrnoException` that is perfect for the following code:

```
import core.sys.posix.unistd; // for the low-level Posix functions
import core.sys.posix.fnctl // for more low-level Posix functions
import std.exception; // for ErrnoException
auto fd = open("myfile.txt", O_RDONLY);
// open() returns -1 if it was unable to open the file,
// and sets errno with error details. Check for that failure.
if(fd == -1)
    throw new ErrnoException("Couldn't open myfile.txt");
// close the file automatically at the end of the scope
scope(exit) close(fd);
/* read the file here */
```

See also

Scope guards, discussed in *Chapter 5, Resource Management*, are convenient for use with exceptions. They let you put clean-up or recovery code near the creation point in an exception-safe way. In the preceding example, you used a scope guard to ensure the file is properly closed when the function returns, even if an exception is thrown.

Understanding immutability

Here, you'll look at how to use immutability in your functions and data types. Immutability helps us to write code that is easier to understand and maintain because it limits the places where things can change.

Getting ready

First, write a function. Then, look at it and determine what it needs to do. Does it just look at the data passed to it? Does it store or return a reference to data passed in? We'll use these facts about how the function uses its arguments to determine the best-fit qualifiers.

How to do it...

The use of `const` and `immutable` is slightly different on free functions and object methods.

Writing functions

If you are accepting a value type, `const` and `immutable` aren't very important.

If you are borrowing a value—going to look at it, but not store it nor modify it—use the `in` keyword and, if it is a character string, use `char[]` instead of `string` (`string` is an alias for `immutable(char)[]`):

```
void foo(in char[] lookAtThis) { /* inspect lookAtThis */ }
```

If you are going to store a reference, it is best to take immutable data, if possible as follows:

```
void foo(immutable(ubyte)[] data) { stored = data; }
```

If you are going to modify the data, but not store it, use `scope`, but not `const` (`in` is shorthand for `scope const`), as follows:

```
void foo(scope char[] changeTheContents) { /* change it */ }
```

If you are not going to modify or store the contents, but will return a reference to it, use `inout` as follows:

```
inout(char)[] substring(inout(char)[] haystack, size_t start, size_t
end) {
    return haystack[start .. end];
}
```

If you are going to change the value itself (not just the contents it references), use `ref` as follows:

```
void foo(ref string foo) { /* change foo itself */ }
```

Writing object methods

When writing object methods, all of the preceding functions still apply, in addition to putting a qualifier on the `this` parameter. The qualifier for this goes either before or after the function as follows:

```
int foo() const { return this.member; } /* this is const */
const int foo() { return this.member; } /* same as above */
```

Since the second form can be easily confused with returning a `const` value (the correct syntax for that is `const(int) foo() { ...}`), the first form is preferred. Put qualifiers on this at the end of the function.

How it works...

D's `const` qualifiers is different than that of C++ in two key ways: D has `immutable` qualifiers, which means the data will never change, and D's `const` and `immutable` qualifiers are transitive, that is, everything reachable through a `const`/`immutable` reference is also `const`/`immutable`. There is no escape like the `mutable` keyword of C++.

These two differences result in a stronger guarantee, which is useful, especially when storing data.

When storing data, you generally want either immutable or mutable data—`const` usually isn't very useful on a member variable; although it prevents your class from modifying it, it doesn't prevent other functions from modifying it. Immutable means nobody will ever modify it. You can store that with confidence that it won't change unexpectedly. Of course, mutable member data is always useful to hold the object's own private state.

The guarantee that the data will never change is the strength of immutable data. You can get all the benefits of a private copy, knowing that nobody else can change it, without the cost of actually making a copy. The `const` and `immutable` qualifiers are most useful on reference types such as pointers, arrays, and classes. They have relatively little benefit on value types such as scalars (`int`, `float`, and so on) or structs because these are copied when passed to functions anyway.

When inspecting data, however, you don't need such a strong guarantee. That's where `const` comes in. The `const` qualifier means you will not modify the data, without insisting that nobody else can modify it. The `in` keyword is a shorthand that expands to `scope const`. The `scope` parameters aren't fully implemented as of the time of this writing, but it is a useful concept nonetheless. A `scope` parameter is a parameter where you promise that no reference to it will escape. You'll look at the data, but not store a reference anywhere. When combined with `const`, you have a perfect combination for input data that you'll look at. Other than that you have the short and convenient `in` keyword.

When you do return a reference to `const` data, it is important that the constancy is preserved, and this should be easy. This is where D's `inout` keyword is used. Consider the standard C function `strstr`:

```
char *strstr(const char *haystack, const char *needle);
```

This function returns a pointer to `haystack` where it finds `needle`, or null if `needle` is not found. The problem with this prototype is that the `const` character attached to `haystack` is lost on the return value. It is possible to write to constant data through the pointer returned by `strstr`, breaking the type system.

In C++, the solution to this is often to duplicate the function, one version that uses `const`, and one version that does not. D aims to fix the system, keeping the strong constancy guarantee that C loses and avoiding the duplication that C++ requires. The appropriate definition for a `strstr` style function in D will be as follows:

```
inout(char)* strstr(inout(char)* haystack, in char* needle);
```

The `inout` method is used on the return value, in place of `const`, and is also attached to one or more parameters, or the `this` reference. Inside the function, the `inout(T)` data is the same as `const(T)` data. In the signature, it serves as a wildcard that changes based on the input data. If you pass a mutable haystack, it will return a mutable pointer. A `const` haystack returns a `const` pointer. Also, an `immutable` haystack will return an `immutable` pointer. One function, three uses.

D also has the `ref` function parameters. These give a reference to the variable itself, as shown in the following code:

```
void foo(int a) { a = 10; }
void bar(ref int a) { a = 10; }
int test = 0;
foo(test);
assert(test == 0);
bar(test);
assert(test == 10);
```

In this example, the variable `test` is passed to `foo` normally. Changes to `a` inside the function is not seen outside the function.

If a was a pointer, changes to a will not be seen, but changes to *a will be visible. That's why `const` and `immutable` are useful there.

With the function `bar`, on the other hand, it takes the parameter by reference. Here, the changes made to a inside the function are seen at the call site; `test` becomes 10.

 Some guides recommend passing structs to a function by `ref` for performance reasons rather than because they want changes to be seen at the call site. Personally, I do not recommend this unless you have profiled your code and have identified the struct copy as a performance problem. Also, you cannot pass a `struct` literal as `ref`, because there is no outer variable for it to update. So, `ref` limits your options too.

Slicing a string to get a substring

D's strings are actually just an array of characters. This means any operation that you can do on arrays, also works on strings. However, since string is a UTF-8 array, there are some behaviors that you may find surprising. Here, you'll get a substring by slicing and discuss potential pitfalls.

How to do it...

Let's try to get a substring from a string using the following steps:

1. Declare a string as follows:

   ```
   string s = "▨▨▨▨ is some Japanese text.";
   ```

2. Get the correct index for start and end. You'll get the Japanese text out by searching the string for the first space, and slice up to that point by using the following code:

   ```
   import std.string;
   string japaneseText = s[0 .. s.indexOf(" ")];
   ```

3. Loop over the string, looking at the UTF-8 code units as well as the Unicode code points. So, you can see the difference in your string by using the following code:

   ```
   import std.stdio;
   foreach(idx, char c; japaneseText)
       writefln("UTF-8 Code unit at index %d is %d", idx, c);
   foreach(dchar c; japaneseText)
       writefln("UTF-32 code unit with value %d is %c", c, c);
   ```

The program will print out more code units in UTF-8 than in `dchars`, because the Japanese text is composed of multibyte characters, unlike English text.

How it works...

D's implementations of strings uses Unicode. Unicode is a complicated standard that could take up a whole book on its own, but you can use it in D knowing just some basics. D string, as well as D source code, uses UTF-8 encoding. This means you can paste in text from any language into a D source file and process it with D code.

However, UTF-8 has a complication; the length of a single code point is variable. Often, one code point is one character, though Unicode's complexity means graphemes (that is, what you might also call a visible character) may consist of more than one code point! For English text, UTF-8 beautifully maps directly to ASCII, which means that one code unit is one character. However, for other languages, there are too many characters to express in one byte. Japanese is one example where all the characters are multibyte in UTF-8.

So, while there are only four characters in your program, if you slice from `s[0 .. 4]`, you won't get all four characters. D's slice operator works on code units. You'll get a partial result here, which may not be usable.

Instead, you found the correct index by using the standard library function `indexOf`. This searches the string for the given substring and returns the index, or -1 if it could not be found. The slice `[start .. end]` goes from start, including it, to the end, not including that. So, `[0 .. indexOf (...)]` goes from the start, up to, but not including, the space. This slice is safe to use, even if it contains multibyte characters.

Finally, you looped over the Japanese text to examine the encodings. The `foreach` loop understands UTF encoding. The first variant asks for characters, or UTF-8 code units, and yields them without decoding. The second variant asks for `dchars`, which are UTF-32 code units that are numerically equivalent to Unicode code points. Asking for `dchars` is slower than iterating over `chars`, but has the advantage of removing much of the complexity of handling multibyte characters. The second loop prints only one entry per Japanese character, or any other character that cannot be encoded in a single UTF-8 unit.

There's more...

D also supports UTF-16 and UTF-32 strings. These are typed `wstring` and `dstring`, respectively. Let's look at each of these as follows:

- `wstring`: This is very useful on Windows, because the Windows operating system natively works with UTF-16.
- `dstring`: This eats a lot of memory, about 4 times more than strings for English text, but sidesteps some of the issues discussed here. The reason is that each array index corresponds to one Unicode code point.

Creating a tree of classes

Classes are used to provide object-oriented features in D. To explore how they work, you're going to write a small inheritance hierarchy to evaluate basic addition and subtraction operations.

Getting ready

Before writing a class, step back and ask yourself whether it is the best tool for the job. Will you be using inheritance to create objects that are substitutable for their parent? If not, a struct may be more appropriate. If you plan to use inheritance for code reuse without substitutability, a mixin template may be more appropriate. Here, you'll use classes for substitutability, and a mixin template for some code reuse.

How to do it...

Let's create a tree of classes by executing the following steps:

1. Create a class, with the data and methods it needs. For your expression evaluator, you'll create two classes: `AddExpression` and `SubtractExpression`. They will need variables for the left and right-hand side of the expression, and a method to evaluate the result.

2. Move common methods from substitutable classes out to an interface, and make the classes inherit from it by putting a colon after the class name, followed by the interface name. In both `AddExpression` and `SubtractExpression`, you will have an evaluate method. You'll move this function signature, but not the function body, to the interface, called `Expression`.

3. If there is still a lot of code duplication, move the identical code out to a mixin template, and mix it in at the usage point.

> If you want to use most, but not all, of a mixin template, you can override specific declarations by simply writing your own declaration below the `mixin` statement.

4. Functions should operate on interface parameters, if possible, instead of classes, for maximum reusability.

    The following is the code you have so far:

```
interface Expression {
    // this is the common method from the classes we made
    int evaluate();
}
mixin template BinaryExpression() {
```

```
        // this is the common implementation code from the classes
        private int a, b;
        this(int left, int right) { this.a = left; this.b= right; }
    }
    // printResult can evaluate and print any expression class
    // thanks to taking the general interface
    void printResult(Expression expression) {
        import std.stdio;
        writeln(expression.evaluate());
    }
    class AddExpression : Expression { // inherit from the interface
        mixin BinaryExpression!(); // adds the shared code
        int evaluate() { return a + b; } // implement the method
    }
    class SubtractExpression : Expression {
        mixin BinaryExpression!();
        int evaluate() { return a - b; }
    }
```

5. Let's also add a `BrokenAddExpression` class that uses inheritance to override the `evaluate` function of `AddExpression`:

```
class BrokenAddExpression : AddExpression {
    this(int left, int right) {
        super(left, right);
    }
    // this changes evaluate to subtract instead of add!
    // note the override keyword
    override int evaluate() { return a - b; }
}
```

6. Finally, you'll construct some instances and use them as follows:

```
auto add = new AddExpression(1, 2);
printResult(add);
auto subtract = new SubtractExpression(2, 1);
printResult(subtract); // same function as above!
```

The usage will print 3 and 1, showing the different operations. You can also create a `BrokenAddExpression` function and assign it to add as follows:

```
add = new BrokenAddExpression(1, 2);
printResult(add); // prints -1
```

How it works...

Classes in D are similar to classes in Java. They are always reference types, have a single inheritance model with a root object, and may implement any number of interfaces.

Class constructors are defined with the `this` keyword. Any time you create a new class, it calls one of the constructors. You may define as many as you want, as long as each has a unique set of parameters.

> Classes may have destructors, but you typically should not use them. When a class object is collected by the garbage collector, its child members may have already been collected, which means that they cannot be accessed by the destructor. Any attempt to do so will likely lead to a program crash. Moreover, since the garbage collector may not run at a predictable time (from the class' point of view), it is hard to know when, if ever, the destructor will actually be run. If you need a deterministic destruction, you should use a struct instead, or wrap your class in a struct and call the destructor yourself with the `destroy()` function.

Object instances are upcasted implicitly. This is why you could assign `BrokenAddException` to the `add` variable, which is statically typed as `AddExpression`. This is also the reason why you can pass any of these classes to the `printResult` function, since they will all be implicitly cast to the interface when needed. However, going the other way, when casting from interface or a base class to a derived class, you must use an explicit `cast`. It returns null if the `cast` fails. Use the following code to better understand this:

```
if(auto bae = cast(BrokenAddExpression) expression) {
    /* we were passed an instance of BrokenAddExpression
        and can now use the bae variable to access its specific
        members */
} else { /* we were passed some other class */ }
```

In classes, all methods are virtual by default. You can create non-virtual methods with the `final` keyword, which prevents a subclass from overriding a method. Abstract functions, created with the `abstract` keyword, need not to have an implementation, and they must be implemented in a child class if the object is to be instantiated. All methods in an interface that are not marked as final or static are abstract and must be implemented by a non-abstract class.

When you override a `virtual` or `abstract` function from a parent class, you must use the `override` keyword. If a matching function with any method marked override cannot be found, the compiler will issue an error. This ensures that the child class's method is actually compatible with the parent definition, ensuring that it is substitutable for the parent class. (Of course, ensuring the behavior is substitutable too is your responsibility as the programmer!)

The mixin template is a feature of D that neither C++ nor Java have. A mixin template is a list of declarations, variables, methods, and/or constructors. At the usage point, use the following code:

```
mixin BinaryExpression!();
```

This will essentially copy and paste the code inside the template to the point of the `mixin` statement. The template can take arguments as well, given in the parenthesis. Here, you didn't need any parameterization, so the parentheses are empty. Templates in D, including mixin templates, can take a variety of arguments including values, types, and symbols. You'll discuss templates in more depth later in the book.

There's more...

Using interfaces and mixin templates, like you did here, can also be extended to achieve a result similar to multiple inheritance in C++, without the inheritance of state and avoiding the diamond inheritance problem that C++ has.

See also...

▸ The *Simulating inheritance with structs* recipe in *Chapter 6*, *Wrapped Types*, shows how you can also achieve something subtyping and data extension, similar to inheritance with data, using structs.

▸ The official documentation can be found at `http://dlang.org/class.html` and it goes into additional details about the capabilities of classes.

2
Phobos – The Standard Library

In this chapter, we will learn how to use the D standard library and explore the language concepts used in the implementation. You will learn the following recipes:

- Performing type conversions
- Finding the largest files in a directory
- Creating a network client and server
- Using Base64 to create a data URI
- Generating random numbers
- Normalizing a string and performing Unicode comparisons
- Searching with regular expressions
- Writing a digest utility
- Using the `std.zlib` compression
- Using the `std.json` module

Introduction

The D standard library, Phobos, provides a variety of modules that do a variety of tasks. This chapter will only cover a portion of its ever-growing capabilities.

Performing type conversions

D is a strongly typed language, which means converting between types often has to be done explicitly. The language's built-in `cast` operator only works when the types are already mostly compatible, for example `int` to `short`, or in cases where the user has defined an `opCast` function. This doesn't cover the very common need of converting strings to integers and vice versa. That's where Phobos' `std.conv` module is helpful.

How to do it...

Now it's time to perform type conversions by executing the following steps:

1. Import `std.conv`.

2. Use the `to` function as follows:

```
import std.conv;
auto converted = to!desired_type(variable_to_convert);
```

   This is pretty simple, and it works for a lot of types.

3. To convert a string to an integer, use the following line of code:

```
auto a = to!int("123"); // a == 123
```

That's all you have to do!

How it works...

The `std.conv.to` function strives to be a one-stop shop for type conversions. The `to` function isn't just one function. It is actually a family of functions from a template, one body that is parameterized on a list of compile-time arguments. That's why it has the `!` operator in the name. In D, you pass two sets of arguments to a function template: a compile-time argument list and a normal runtime argument list. The syntax is as follows:

```
function_name!(compile, time, arguments)(run, time, arguments);
```

If you're familiar with C++, this is similar to the `function_name<type, list, here>(arguments, here);` function of that language. D chose `!()` over `<>` because it has less lexing ambiguity. Compile-time arguments are similar to runtime arguments, so they look similar too.

If there is only one compile-time argument and it is syntactically simple (made up of only one token, for example, `int`, `string`, or `object`, but not `const (int)` or `mymodule.Something`), the parentheses around the compile-time argument are not necessary. The `to!int` function is equivalent to `to! (int)`.

The compiler can often figure out compile-time arguments automatically if a runtime list is provided. This is called **implicit function template instantiation** (**IFTI**). In fact, this is how `std.stdio.writeln` works; you can pass it any arguments you want, and it automatically converts them to strings and prints them out. Try the following line of code:

```
writeln! (int) (10); // works!
```

The reason `writeln` converts variables to string is that like `to`, it is a template function. D's templates let you write functions that generically handle a variety of types at once with convenient syntax. Phobos uses them extensively.

 There's also a function called `std.conv.text ()` that works in the same way as `writeln`, but returns the string instead of printing it out. You can use this to convert several variables to string at once, for example, `string s = text(10, " is ten!");`.

There's more...

To enable `to` on custom types, either implement a constructor that takes the target type or implement `T opCast (T:Target) ()`. Converting a type to string can also be done with a member function: `string toString() const { return "string representation"; }.`

Finding the largest files in a directory

Suppose you're out of disk space. A solution may be to delete old, large files from a directory. Let's write a D program to perform this task.

How to do it...

Execute the following steps to find the largest files in a directory:

1. Use the `std.file.dirEntries` function to get a listing of all files.
2. Define the `DirEntry` variable as an array.
3. Sort the array by size in descending order by using `std.algorithm` and a lambda function.

4. Filter out the newer files with `std.algorithm.filter`.

5. Delete the top 10 files with the `std.file.remove` function.

The code is as follows:

```
void main() {
    import std.file, std.algorithm, std.datetime, std.range;
    DirEntry[] allFiles;
    foreach(DirEntry entry; dirEntries("target_directory",
      SpanMode.depth))
        allFiles ~= entry;
    auto sorted = sort!((a, b) => a.size > b.size)(allFiles);
    auto filtered = filter!((a) =>
      Clock.currTime() - a.timeLastModified >> 14.days)(sorted);
    foreach(file; filtered.take!(10))
        remove(file.name);
}
```

How it works...

Phobos provides the `std.file` module for high-level operations on files and directories. With it, we can read and write files, list files in a directory, get file information, and perform common operations such as deleting and copying files.

The `dirEntries` function returns an object that works with `foreach`. Depending on the type you request in the loop, it will provide different information. The `foreach(string name; dirEntries())` function gives you just the filenames. The `foreach(DirEntry entry; dirEntries())` function gives details.

This is implemented with a function called `opApply`. D's `foreach` loop understands four kinds of items: a numeric interval, arrays (or slices), input ranges, and objects with a member function called `opApply`. These are explained in detail in the following paragraphs.

Numeric intervals are a simple start-to-finish progression of integers, as shown in the following line of code:

```
foreach(num; 0 .. 10) { /* loops from num = 0 up to, but not
    including, num = 10 */ }
```

Input ranges are iterable objects that are used throughout much of Phobos. Indeed, the `sort`, `filter`, and `take` functions we use here from `std.algorithm` both consume and return input ranges. Ranges will be covered in greater depth later in this book.

While input ranges are useful for a variety of tasks, they aren't ideal for everything. The `opApply` function is used for these cases. It is a special member function on a struct or a class that takes a delegate. The arguments to the delegate are the `foreach` iteration variable types, and the body of the delegate is automatically set to be the inner code of the loop. The delegate's return value gives flow control, similar to blocks in Ruby.

After gathering the data, we use `std.algorithm` to sort, filter, and limit the size of the results. These functions show the power of input ranges and lambda functions. The syntax `(a) => a;` is a lambda function. First, there is a parameter list in parentheses. Types are optional here; if excluded, the lambda function is implemented as a template with implicit types from context. Then, the symbol `=>` is the key indicator of a lambda function, and finally you have the return value. The short lambda syntax is only usable for a single expression and cannot return void.

The `(a) => a` function is actually a function template. The compile-time parameters it needs for its parameter list are determined from context by the compiler.

The `(a) => a` function, in this context, could alternatively be written as `a => a`. If it has only one argument, the parentheses are optional. It could also be written as `int delegate(int a) { return a; }`, `function(int a) { return a; }`, or even `(int a) { return a; }`. The `delegate` and `function` options make two separate but related types. The difference between a delegate and a function is that a delegate has a context pointer whereas a function does not. The context pointer gives the delegate access to variables from the surrounding scope. A function can only access global variables, data through its arguments, and static data. If you do not specify one of the two keywords, delegate is usually the default; the compiler will give you what you require.

With that background information, let's look at the following line of code in more detail:

```
sort!((a, b) => a.size > b.size)(allFiles);
```

The `std.algorithm.sort` function takes two arguments: an optional comparison function, given as a compile-time argument for maximum efficiency, and a random access range to sort. A random access range is any iterable object from where you can jump around to different indexes. The most common random access range is an array or a slice. This is why we built an array of `DirEntry`. Firstly, because the `dirEntries` function uses the `opApply` iteration, so it isn't a range, and secondly, to sort, we need the whole list ready at once.

The next line is very similar. Again, we use a function from `std.algorithm` that takes a range and a function (called a predicate in the `std.algorithm` documentation). The filter returns a new range with all the properties of the sorted list except items that don't match the filter requirement. For example, the file that was last modified more than 14 days before the current time is removed.

Let's also look at the syntax of `14.days`. The `days` function is a function in the module `core.time` with the `@property Duration days(int a);` signature. This uses a D feature called **Uniform Function Call Syntax** (**UFCS**). With UFCS, a call to `foo.bar` may be rewritten as `bar(foo)`. This lets us extend any type, including built-in types such as integers and arrays in our code, adding new pseudomembers and properties. When used properly, this gives extensibility, readability, and can even help encapsulation, allowing you to write extension methods outside the original module, thus limiting access to private data.

Finally, we complete our task by using `take(10)` (via a UFCS call), which takes the first 10 items off the filtered list, and calling `remove` from `std.file` to remove (delete) the file.

Creating a network client and server

Networking is a common requirement in modern applications. Phobos offers a module, `std.socket`, which provides a foundation for networked applications. We'll write a client and server pair to demonstrate how to use it. The client will send lines from standard input to the server. The server will accept any number of connections, say hello to new clients, and then echo back whatever it received.

How to do it...

We'll be building two separate applications: the client and the server.

Client

Let's create a client by executing the following steps:

1. Create a `Socket` object.
2. Connect to the server.
3. Declare a buffer to hold the received data. The buffer must be preallocated to the maximum amount of data you want to handle in a single call to receive the data. Here, we'll use a static array of length 1024; it will have plenty of room to hold our message.
4. Receive the hello message we sent in the server.
5. Then, send each line of the message to the server, wait for the response, and print it out.

The code is as follows:

```
void main() {
    import std.socket, std.stdio;
    auto socket = new Socket(AddressFamily.INET,
      SocketType.STREAM);
```

```
char[1024] buffer;
socket.connect(new InternetAddress("localhost", 2525));
auto received = socket.receive(buffer);
// wait for the server to say hello
writeln("Server said: ", buffer[0 .. received]);
foreach(line; stdin.byLine) {
  socket.send(line);
  writeln("Server said: ",
    buffer[0 .. socket.receive(buffer)]);
}
}
```

Server

Let's create a server by executing the following steps:

1. Create a Socket object.

2. Bind it to the listening address.

3. Call the listen() method to start listening.

4. Create a list of connectedClients objects and a SocketSet object for multiplexing.

5. Enter a main loop.

6. Reset the SocketSets object.

7. Add your listener and all connected clients to the readSet function.

8. Call Socket.select() and pass your SocketSet objects to it.

9. If any client is ready to read, receive its data with the socket's receive method and reply to the client with the socket's send method.

10. If your listener was set in the readSet function, call accept to accept a new connection and send our welcome message.

The code is as follows:

```
void main() {
    import std.socket;
    auto listener = new Socket(AddressFamily.INET,
      SocketType.STREAM);
    listener.bind(new InternetAddress("localhost", 2525));
    listener.listen(10);
    auto readSet = new SocketSet();
    Socket[] connectedClients;
    char[1024] buffer;
    bool isRunning = true;
    while(isRunning) {
```

```
                readSet.reset();
                readSet.add(listener);
                foreach(client; connectedClients) readSet.add(client);
                if(Socket.select(readSet, null, null)) {
                    foreach(client; connectedClients)
                      if(readSet.isSet(client)) {
                          // read from it and echo it back
                          auto got = client.receive(buffer);
                          client.send(buffer[0 .. got]);
                      }
                    if(readSet.isSet(listener)) {
                        // the listener is ready to read, that means
                        // a new client wants to connect. We accept it here.
                        auto newSocket = listener.accept();
                        newSocket.send("Hello!\n"); // say hello
                        connectedClients ~= newSocket; // add to our list
                    }
                }
            }
        }
    }
```

How it works...

Phobos' `std.socket` module is a wrapper of the BSD socket API available on all major operating systems. The `std.socket` module is a thin wrapper. If you've used sockets in other languages, you'll feel at home with Phobos.

Clients simply connect and then send and receive data. The `send` and `receive` functions both take a buffer as their argument instead of returning a newly allocated array. This provides maximum performance by allowing you to reuse memory. Note that they may not use the whole buffer. These methods will wait until they can do *something* (unless you set the `blocking` property to `false`), and then they will do as much as they can immediately before returning. If only one byte is available on the network connection, `receive` will write that byte to the buffer and return the value; it won't wait to fill the buffer entirely. This lets you handle partial and variable size messages as soon as possible. Similarly, `send` may not send your whole message at once. A robust socket code should check the return value to ensure that all the data actually made it out.

On the server side, instead of connecting, you bind the `Socket` object to an address and then listen for connections. The argument to `listen` is the maximum number of clients to queue. This is typically a relatively small number, for example, 10.

There are several techniques to handle multiple connections. You can use threads, processes, or various event-based checks. Each technique has pros and cons in simplicity and speed. In the example, we used `std.socket`, an easy-to-use and portable function to multiplex several connections in an application. The `select` function doesn't scale well to large numbers of connections because it must loop through each one to check `isSet`, but for small numbers of connections, it performs adequately and is fairly simple to use.

The `SocketSet` class in `std.socket` is used to pass collections of sockets to `select`. You can create it outside your loop and then add your connections to it. Don't forget to add the listening socket too when it is ready to read. This means that a new client is trying to connect.

When `select` indicates that a socket is set in the `SocketSet` object, it is ready to be used immediately. You should handle the data as quickly as possible to minimize the wait time for other clients. The server simply continues these same steps in a loop until it is terminated.

There's more...

Here, we created a socket that uses TCP, the Internet protocol upon which many common application protocols are built, including HTTP for the Web, SMTP for e-mail, and more. You can also create UDP and Unix sockets with `std.socket`. To create a Unix socket (not available on Windows operating systems), pass `AddressFamily.UNIX` to the `Socket` constructor instead of `AddressFamily.INET`. Then, when connecting or binding, use the new `UnixAddress` instead of `InternetAddress`. Other than that, the API is the same as the TCP socket. Unix sockets only work with clients on the same computer, so they provide more security and speed than a TCP socket. However, they are only useful for specialized purposes. To use UDP—a connectionless protocol that is faster but less reliable than TCP—you can create the socket with `SocketType.DGRAM` and then use the `sendTo` and `receiveFrom` methods instead of `send`, `receive`, and `connect`.

See also

▸   `http://vibed.org/` is a server framework that is inspired by Node.js and written in D

Using Base64 to create a data URI

Given a CSS file, we want to replace all instances of a particular image URL with a data URI to reduce the number of requests. Let's write a small D program to do this replacement.

How to do it...

Let's create a data URI by executing the following steps:

1. Load the image file with `std.file.read()`.
2. Create the data URI with `std.base64` as shown in the following code:

    ```
    pure char[] makeDataUri(string contentType, in void[] data) {
        import std.base64;
        return "data:" ~ contentType ~ ";base64," ~ Base64.
    encode(cast(const(ubyte[]))) data;
    }
    ```

3. Load the CSS file with `std.file.readText`.
4. Use `std.array.replace` to replace the URL with the data URI.
5. Save the CSS file with `std.file.write`.

Putting it all together in `main`, you will have the following code:

```
void main() {
    import std.file, std.array;
    auto imageData = std.file.read("image.png"); // step 1
    string dataUri = makeDataUri("image/png", imageData);
    // step 2
    auto cssFile = std.file.readText("style.css"); // step 3
    cssFile = cssFile.replace("image.png", dataUri); // step 4
    std.file.write("style-combined.css", cssFile); // step 5
}
```

How it works...

Phobos' `std.file` module, in addition to directory listing functions, also includes high-level file functions. The functions `read`, `readText`, and `write` give one-step access to file contents. The `read(filename)` function reads the entire file in one go, returning `void[]`, which must be cast to another type (for example, `char[]` or `ubyte[]`) to be used. The `readText(filename)` function validates that the file is UTF-8 and returns a string. The `write(filename, contents)` function writes the contents directly to the file, overwriting it if it already exists.

Phobos' `std.array` module includes several generic functions to operate on arrays that are callable with member-style syntax thanks to UFCS. Since a string in D is simply an array of characters, all these functions also work on strings. The `replace` function searches the haystack for all occurrences of the needle and replaces them with the replacement argument, returning the new data without modifying the original.

Our `makeDataUri` function uses `std.base64` to create a data URI that is usable in CSS files. The `std.base64` module uses a template with value parameters to customize the behavior from the following source:

```
alias Base64Impl!('+', '/') Base64;
alias Base64Impl!('-', '_') Base64URL;
template Base64Impl(char Map62th, char Map63th, char Padding = '=')
```

D's templates can take values as compile-time parameters, which can be used the same way as regular runtime parameters in the code. Here, the implementation can have three characters swapped out so the code can be easily used by other Base64 variants. The alias lines give a convenient name to different parameterizations. The aliases are different types, similar to subclasses of Base64, which parameterize it with virtual functions or in the constructor. However, unlike classes, there's no runtime cost here. The compile-time values are exactly equivalent to character literals in the generated code.

As `Base64.encode` takes `ubyte[]` and our `makeDataUrl` function takes the generic array type `void[]`, we had to cast the data to use it. We take the parameter of type `in void[]` because we inspect the data but don't store or modify it, and it can be any type. All arrays implicitly cast to `const(void)[]`, making it (or `in void[]`) ideal for functions that just generically need data. The data argument of `std.file.write` is also `const(void)[]`.

Finally, you might have noticed that `makeDataUrl` returns a mutable reference yet was assigned to a string, which is an immutable character array. Normally, that wouldn't compile, so why does it work here? The key is because `makeDataUri` is marked pure. Pure functions are not allowed to modify anything outside their own arguments. This means the return value can be assumed to be unique. A related function is `assumeUnique` from `std.exception`, which is used in a Phobos idiom to convert mutable data to immutable data. It should only be used when you are sure that the reference is indeed unique and that no other pointers exist into the data. After calling it, you should stop using the original reference. Pure functions use this same principle implicitly: as long as the reference was not passed in through its argument list (the function would be called **strongly pure** in D), there can be no other references. So, it is safe to assume that it is unique. This means if you stop using the old reference, it is guaranteed to be immutable! We'll learn more about pure functions later in this book.

Generating random numbers

Random numbers are commonly necessary in computer programs. Phobos' `std.random` module offers a variety of random number generators and other functions related to randomization. Here, we'll create a little number guessing game with a replay function. The user guesses the generated number, and then the program tells them if they were high or low.

How to do it...

Let's generate random numbers by executing the following steps:

1. Create a random number generator, seeding it with the replay value, if given, or `unpredictableSeed` for a new game.

2. Generate a random number between 0 and 100.

3. Ask the user for their guess. Tell them if they were low or high and let them continue trying until they get it. Save each line of user input to the replay file.

4. When the user is done playing, let them know how many tries they took to get the correct number.

The code is as follows:

```d
import std.random, std.conv, std.string, std.stdio;

int playRound(ref Random generator, File userInput, File saveFile) {
    int tries = 0;
    auto value = uniform(0, 100, generator);

    writeln("Guess the number between 0 and 100:");
    while(true) {
        tries++;
        auto guess = userInput.readln().strip().to!int;;;
        if(saveFile.isOpen) saveFile.writeln(guess);
        // save in the replay file
        if(guess == value) break; // correct!
        writefln("Your guess of %s was too %s, please try again,",
            guess, guess > value ? "high" : "low");
    }
    writefln("Correct! You guessed %d in %d tries.", value,
        tries);
    return tries;
}
void main(string[] args) {
    Random gen;
```

```
    File userInput, saveFile;
    // prepare input and seed the generator
     if(args.length > 1) {
         // use the given replay file
         userInput = File(args[1], "rt");
         gen.seed(to!uint(userInput.readln().strip()));
         // using the saved seed = same game
    } else {
         // new game, use an unpredictable seed and
         //create a replay file
         userInput = stdin; // take input from the keyboard
         auto seed = unpredictableSeed;; // a random game
         gen.seed(seed);
         saveFile = File("replay.txt", "wt");
        saveFile.writeln(seed);
         // save the seed so we can reproduce the game later
     }
    int totalTries = 0;
    foreach(round; 0 .. 3)
         totalTries += playRound(gen, userInput, saveFile);
    writefln("You guessed three numbers in %s tries!", totalTries);
 }
```

How it works...

The overall idea of the game is to create numbers that look random, but can actually be reproduced for the replay. To achieve this goal, we used Phobos' `std.random` module and created our own random number generator, logging the seed we use for each game. The user's input is also logged. Given the random seed and user input, we can reliably recreate a game.

 If you don't need precise control over the random number generator, you can use the default settings by calling the functions without the final argument. For example, `auto randomNumber = uniform(0, 100);` gives a number from a preselected and automatically seeded default random number generator.

Let's look at the code, starting from `main`. The first thing you'll notice is that this `main` function took arguments. These are passed to the program on the command line. The `args[0]` variable will be set to the name of the program, then `args[1 .. $]` are the other arguments the user passed, if any. For example, if the program is executed with the following command line:

game replay.txt arg2

Then, the `args` variable passed to `main` would have the following content: `["game", "replay.txt", "arg2"]`. That's why we use `if(args.length > 1)` instead of `args.length > 0`. There's always at least one command-line argument: the name of the program in `args[0]`.

There are two `File` variables. File is the file I/O of `std.stdio`. It wraps C's I/O which is based upon `FILE*` to provide maximum C compatibility while presenting a more D-like interface. Our two files are `userInput` and `saveFile`. The `userInput` file is used to feed the user input to the program. The `saveFile` file is used to save the user input for later use in the replay.

If the replay file is provided on the command line, we use it as user input. The first line of this is the random seed, so we immediately load that. If no replay file is provided, we use `stdin`, the keyboard, for user input and open a new file called `replay.txt`, which is opened as a **writable text** (**wt**) file, for `saveFile`. We also make an `unpredictableSeed`, use it to initialize the random number generator, and save it to the file for future use.

The `stdin` file is readable and the `stdout` file is writable. All the methods that you can use on these files can also be used on any other file and vice versa. In fact, the global `writeln` function simply forwards to `stdout.writeln`.

Once we're set up, we used `foreach` over a numeric interval to run `playRound` three times and then write out the results. The `writefln` function, unlike `writeln`, uses a format string instead of printing out each argument in order. The format string, which comes from C's `printf` function, can get very complex. Here, we only used a simple one. The text in the string is printed, with `%s` instances being replaced with the value of the next argument to `writefln`. Unlike in C, in D you can always use the `%s` specifier for any argument and it will be automatically converted to string for you. Other specifiers, such as `%d`, can be used to give more control over formatting, such as leading zeroes, field length, precision, and more. Look up the options for `printf`, including Posix positional parameters, to see more options.

Next, let's look at the `playRound` function. The first thing to note is that it takes the random number generator by `ref`. This is important; since `Random` is a struct, passing it to a function means the function would work on a copy. When we called `playRound` the second time, since the variable in `main` would not be updated, it would always create the same random number! Passing the random number generator by reference ensures that it gets updated and won't repeat the same values. You will almost always want to pass random number generators to functions by reference.

Let's also look at the following line of code in more detail:

```
userInput.readln().strip().to!int;
```

The `readln` method is a method of the `File` object that reads the next line, including the new line character at the end. To get rid of the new line character, we call `strip`, a function from `std.string`. The `strip` function removes whitespace from both the beginning and the end of a string. Finally, we convert the string to an integer by using `std.conv.to`. Thanks to UFCS, we can write this using left-to-right dot syntax. There's no parentheses at the end of `to!int` because empty parentheses on a function call are optional. This is part of D's property syntax, which we'll discuss in more depth later.

The final piece of syntax that may be new to you is `guess > value ? "high" : "low"`. This is called the ternary operator, inherited from C. The syntax is `condition ? ifTrue : ifFalse`. It is essentially a miniature `if` statement.

There's more...

The best way to win this game is to use a binary search algorithm. First, guess 50. If you are too high, try 25. If too low, try 75. For each guess, you can cut the possibilities in half until you land at the solution. You should be able to consistently guess each number in about six tries. In Phobos' `std.algorithm` module, there are specializations on the search algorithms for sorted ranges that use this same technique to very rapidly search even large sets of data.

Phobos' `std.random` function is not cryptographically secure. While it is useful for games and other insensitive tasks, if you need to protect your data, a better source of randomness is required. Third-party cryptographic libraries such as `OpenSSL` provide functions for these tasks. Bindings can be found in the Deimos collection at `http://github.com/d-programming-deimos`.

Normalizing a string and performing Unicode comparisons

We want to make a filename or URL based on an article title. To do this, we'll have to limit the size to an appropriate number of characters, strip out improper characters, and format the string in a consistent way. We also want it to remain in the valid UTF-8 format.

How to do it...

Let's normalize a string by executing the following steps:

1. Use `std.uni.normalize` to get Unicode characters into a consistent format.
2. Use `std.string.toLower` to convert everything to lowercase for consistency.
3. Use `std.regex` to strip out all but a small set of characters.

4. Use `std.string.squeeze` to collapse consecutive whitespace.

5. Use `std.array.replace` to change spaces into dashes.

6. Use `std.range.take` to get the right number of characters, then convert the result back to string.

The code is as follows:

```
void main(){
    string title = "The D Programming Language: Easy Speed!";
    import std.uni, std.string, std.conv, std.range,std.regex;
    title = normalize(title);
    title = title.toLower();
    title = std.regex.replaceAll(title, regex(`[^a-z0-9 \-]`), "");
    title = title.squeeze(" ")
     .replace(" ", "-")
     .take(32).to!string;
    import std.stdio;
    writeln("The title is: ", title);
}
```

How it works...

D has excellent facilities to work with strings. Functions from all over Phobos are useful while performing string operations. The `std.string` function contains functions such as `toLower`, `indexOf`, `strip`, and other functions that are specific to string processing.

D's strings are essentially arrays of immutable characters. This means array functions work too. The `replace`, `repeat`, `join`, and other functions from `std.array` work, as well as the built-in concatenation and append operators (a `~` b and a `~=` b).

Where things might be surprising is if you use strings as ranges with `std.algorithm`. As strings are arrays, you might expect them to be a full random access range, and thus be usable in all the algorithms, including sort. However, this is not the case, but why? D and Phobos try to reach a happy compromise on Unicode strings that work correctly in all cases and have top performance.

The D language itself works on a low level. A string is simply an array of immutable UTF-8 code units (bytes). It also offers `wstring` for UTF-16 and 2 bytes per code unit, which allows one index to cover most written language's characters. The `wstring` type is the default Unicode string type in the Windows operating system. Finally, there is `dstring`, an array of `dchars`, which are UTF-32 code units. In the current Unicode specification, a single `dchar` can hold any code point, which, after calling `normalize` on the string, brings us as close as we can get to one index being one character. This is at the cost of about four times the memory consumption of a UTF-8 string. D gives you the choice of using the string type appropriate for your own use case.

However, if a string is an array of characters, why doesn't `take` return a string? First, `std.algorithm` returns new types that do their calculations lazily. However, there is a function, `std.range.array`, that eagerly evaluates a range result, converting it from a lazy type back to the underlying array type. If we try this here, we would find the result is `dchar[]` instead of `string`.

This is because the Phobos library builds on top of the D language's flexibility to choose a generally correct trade-off of speed for correctness. It avoids expensive full normalization, translating various compatible forms into a single representation, for example, combining characters (though this is available upon request through the `std.uni.normalize` function). However, it does perform UTF decoding, yielding `dchars`. This insulates user code from the complexity of explicit multibyte code point decoding—each code point as a single item, instead of one to six, as is the case with raw `chars`.

The downside of this choice is that computation needs to be done. When decoding the string, it is impossible to perform random access because each UTF-8 point has variable length. You can't jump ahead because you don't know how far to jump!

The `std.algorithm.sort` function doesn't work on strings without an additional step, either converting to `dstring` or casting to an array of bytes (`std.string.representation` is the idiomatic function for performing this cast). This is a good thing because sorting an array of characters probably doesn't do what you want anyway. It would break apart multibyte characters, yielding an invalid string!

However, since many algorithms do not require random access, this is mostly a net win. Things that work efficiently also work correctly, and things that don't work correctly can be made to work. It's your choice whether you want to work on the bytes or convert to `dstring`.

Getting back to the example, once we perform the algorithm, we can simply convert the final result back to string with `std.conv.to`.

Searching with regular expressions

Regular expressions are a common tool to perform advanced operations on text, including complex searches, replacements, splitting, and more. Unlike JavaScript or Perl, D does not have regular expressions built into the language, but it has all the same power—and more—as those languages through the `std.regex` Phobos module. To explore regular expressions in D, we'll write a small program that searches `stdin` for a particular regex that is given on the command line and prints out the matching lines.

How to do it...

Let's use the search operation with regular expressions by executing the following steps:

1. Create a `Regex` object. If you are using string literals, D's `r" "` or `` ` ` `` syntax makes it much more readable.

2. Loop over the matches and print them out.

Pretty simple! The code is as follows:

```
void main(string[] args) {
    import std.regex, std.stdio;
    auto re = regex(args[1], "g");
    foreach(line; stdin.byLine)
        if(line.match(re)) writeln(line, " was a match!");
}
```

How it works...

Regular expressions in D are a library type instead of a built-in type, but this doesn't affect their usability, their speed, or their simplicity. Declare a regular expression with the `regex(pattern, flags)` helper function. If you are using a string literal for the pattern, it will look nicer if you use one of D's raw string syntaxes, either `r"pattern here"` or `` `pattern here` ``. In those strings, the backslash doesn't have to be escaped, allowing the regular expression to look natural. The pattern syntax in D is almost similar to the syntax used in JavaScript.

After the regex is declared, you can use methods from `std.regex` to do all the basic tasks. The `string.matchAll(pattern)` function returns a list of matches in the string. You can check it in an `if` statement to see if it matches at all, or you can perform a `foreach` loop over it to get the details of the match.

The `std.regex` function also provides methods to replace instances, including a callback function, or to split a string. These functions work in the same way as `replace` and `split` from `std.string`.

There's more...

D's regular expressions are able to outperform most other regex engines by being processed at compile time. Instead of writing `regex`, write `ctRegex!` and make sure that the variable is `static`. The regular expression and the usage code do not have to be changed, as shown in the following code:

```
static ex = ctRegex!`[0-9]{3}-[0-9]{4}`;
foreach(match; "My phone number is 123-4567!".match(ex))
    writeln(match);
```

The output is as follows:

```
["123-4567"]
```

With `ctRegex`, `std.regex` will then create D code to implement your specific regular expression and compile it, generating a fully optimized function to implement it. We'll learn how to create this kind of code later in the book.

See also

> ▸   `http://dlang.org/phobos/std_regex.html` is the official documentation of the module. It explains the regex syntax used, the flags, and the full API.

Writing a digest utility

Phobos provides a package called `std.digest` that offers checksum and message digest algorithms through a unified API. Here, we'll create a small MD5 utility that calculates and prints the resulting digest of a file.

How to do it...

Let's print an MD5 digest by executing the following steps:

1. Create a digest object with the algorithm you need. Here, we'll use MD5 from `std.digest.md`.
2. Call the `start` method.
3. Use the `put` method, or the `put` function from `std.range`, to feed data to the digest object.
4. Call the `finish` method.
5. Convert hexadecimal data to string if you want.

The code is as follows:

```
void main(string[] args) {
    import std.digest.md;
    import std.stdio;
    import std.range;

    File file;
```

```
            if(args.length > 1)
                file = File(args[1], "rb");
            else
                file = stdin;
            MD5 digest;
            digest.start();
            put(digest, file.byChunk(1024));
            writeln(toHexString(digest.finish()));
        }
```

How it works...

The `std.digest` package in Phobos defines modules that all follow a common API. The digest structures are output ranges, which means you feed data to them by calling their `put` method. Each digest algorithm is in a separate module, but they all follow the same pattern: you create the object, call `start()`, put your data into it, and then call `finish()` to get the result. If you want it as a printable string, call `toHexString` on the result.

 If you pass a digest structure to a function, be sure to pass it as a reference, because they are value types. So, without a reference, data added to it inside a function won't be visible outside the function!

The `put` method on the structure itself offers only one form, accepting one array of data at a time. However, the `std.range` module includes additional helper functions to expand the capabilities of any output range. The `std.range.put` function can also accept input ranges. The end result is we build something very similar to a Unix pipeline; `put(digest, file. byChunk(1024))` will read a file, one kilobyte chunk at a time, and feed that data into the digest algorithm. The `std.range.put` method looks like the following:

```
    foreach(chunk; input) output.put(chunk);
```

It is a generic function that works to connect any kind of output range to any kind of input range with a matching element type.

There's more...

Phobos' digest API also provides two other ways to get digests: a convenience function if all the data is available at once, `md5Of`, and the OOP API (an interface and classes) if you need to swap out implementations at runtime.

```
    writeln("The MD5 hash of 'test' is ", toHexString(md5Of("test")));
```

There are also other algorithms available in `std.digest` with the same API, including SHA1 and CRC.

See also

▸ *Chapter 3, Ranges,* will show you how to create your own input and output ranges that can be connected to the digest structures

▸ `http://dlang.org/phobos/std_digest.html` is the documentation of the package

Using the std.zlib compression

Phobos provides a wrapper for the common `zlib/gzip/DEFLATE` compression algorithm. This algorithm is used in the `.zip` files, the `.png` images, the HTTP protocol, the common `gzip` utility, and more. With `std.zlib`, we can both compress and decompress data easily.

How to do it...

Let's compress and decompress data by executing the following steps:

1. Import `std.zlib`.
2. Create an instance of `Compress` or `UnCompress`, depending on what direction you want to go.
3. Call the `compress` or `uncompress` methods for each block of data, concatenating the pieces together as they are made.
4. Call `flush` to get the last block of data.

The code is as follows:

```
void main() {
   import std.zlib, std.file;
   auto compressor = new Compress(HeaderFormat.gzip);
   void[] compressedData;
   compressedData ~= compressor.compress("Hello, ");
   compressedData ~= compressor.compress("world!");
   compressedData ~= compressor.flush();
   std.file.write("compressed.gz", compressedData);
}
```

Running the program will create a file, `compressed.gz`, which can be unzipped to become a text file with `Hello, world!`.

How it works...

The `std.zlib` module doesn't follow exactly the same pattern as `std.digest` (the implementation of `std.zlib` was written before ranges were incorporated into Phobos), but it is a very simple API. It works with one block of data at a time, returning the compressed or uncompressed block. When finished, the `flush` method clears any partial blocks, returning the final piece of data.

There are also convenience functions, `compress` and `uncompress`, that can perform the operation in a single function call if you have all the data available as a single array at once.

Using the std.json module

JSON is a common data interchange format used on the Web. Phobos has a `std.json` module that can be used to read and write JSON data. The `std.json` module is an old module that doesn't take advantage of many of D's advanced features, making it somewhat difficult to use. While newer JSON libraries exist for D, including ones that can be used with syntax and convenience, which is extremely similar to JavaScript itself, Phobos has not yet adopted any of them. Here, we'll read a JSON string, print the current contents, add a new field, and then print out the new JSON.

How to do it...

Suppose we're consuming a web API that returns an array of person objects with a `name` and `ID` field. We get the following JSON string from the API:

```
[{"name":"Alice","id":1},{"name":"Bob","id":2}]
```

Let's execute the following steps to use the `std.json` module:

1. Parse the JSON string.
2. Loop over the array, getting objects out.
3. Print the information we need, getting the types out of the web API's specification.
4. Create the new object.
5. Append the new object to the list.
6. Print out the JSON representation.

The code is as follows:

```
void main() {
    import std.json, std.algorithm, std.stdio;
    auto list = parseJSON(`[{
      "name":"Alice","id":1},{"name":"Bob","id":2}]`);
    foreach(person; list.array.map!(a => a.object)) {
        writeln("ID #", person["id"].integer, " is ",
          person["name"].str);
    }
    JSONValue newPerson;
    JSONValue[string] obj;
    obj["name"].str = "Charlie";
    obj["id"].integer = 3;
    newPerson.object = obj;
    list.array = list.array ~ newPerson;; // append it to the list
    writeln(toJSON(&list)); // print out the new json
}
```

It will print the following output:

```
[{"name":"Alice","id":1},{"name":"Bob","id":2},{
  "name":"Charlie","id":3}]
```

How it works...

Phobos' `std.json` module provides a tagged union to represent a dynamic `JSONValue`. To use it, you can explicitly check the type with the `type` property, or simply access the type you need through its `str`, `object`, `array`, `integer`, and other properties. It will throw an exception if you try to access a property of the wrong type. You can query the current type with the `type` property.

Array elements in `std.json` are also `JSONValues`, which means they need to be accessed through the `type` properties. That is why we called `map` on the array. We can't work directly with `JSONValue`, so mapping it to an object gives something we can immediately use. The `map` function is a function from `std.algorithm` that calls the given predicate on each element in the array.

`JSONValue` properties are either read or write. We cannot modify them in-place. Instead, we read the data or create a temporary file to do our edits then set the finished data back to it.

Finally, `toJSON` takes a pointer to a root element and returns the JSON string it represents.

See also

▸ `http://dlang.org/phobos/std_json.html` is the documentation of the `std.json` module.

▸ `http://dlang.org/phobos/std_variant.html` is the documentation of Phobos' other dynamic type: `Variant`. Unlike `JSONValue`, `Variant` can store any type, but it does not do serialization to and from string.

▸ `http://wiki.dlang.org/Jsvar` describes a module that provides a `var` struct with convenient syntax and a similar type model to JavaScript. We'll also learn some of the techniques that are used in that module later in this book.

3
Ranges

In this chapter, we will investigate the concept of ranges, which is used throughout the D code. We'll look at the following recipes:

- Using ranges when implementing an algorithm
- Creating an input range
- Creating an output range
- Creating a higher-order range
- Putting a range interface on a collection
- Creating an input range over a tree structure
- Using runtime polymorphic (class) ranges
- Storing a range as a data member
- Sorting ranges efficiently
- Searching ranges
- Using functional tools to query data

Introduction

This chapter goes into the details of an artefact central to the Phobos standard library with a little core language support: ranges. Ranges are user-defined objects used to build iterators over a collection of items. The collection may be pre-existing, such as an array, or it may be generated on the fly by the range object.

Ranges are defined in a way that they can be plugged together like building blocks with generic algorithms and other transformations. Command-line pipelines and range code can be very similar.

The Unix command-line command `cat file.txt | sort | uniq` can be expressed similarly in D, using ranges from `std.stdio` and `std.algorithm` and a helper function from `std.range`, as shown in the following code:

```
foreach(line; File("file.txt").byLine.map!(a=>a.idup).array.sort.uniq)
    writeln("Unique line: ", line);
```

Each range feeds into the next, building a system of generic building blocks that can be combined to perform a variety of tasks. In this chapter, we'll look at how to use ranges and how to create our own.

Using ranges when implementing an algorithm

D code favors the use of ranges when implementing algorithms because ranges are a natural abstraction for operating on sequences of elements. We'll implement a function that takes a range and calculates the average of the values.

Getting ready

First, we need to sketch out our algorithm and determine what functions and types we'll need from the range. The algorithm should accept a range as generic as possible for element types that make sense for us, without sacrificing efficiency. Since our algorithm is taking an average value, the elements should be numeric. We'll also need to be able to iterate over each individual item. However, we don't need to know the length ahead of time (we can keep a count while calculating the sum); we don't need random access and we don't need to save our position. All we need to know is whether it is empty, the current item, and be able to advance the iteration. The result is we need an **input range**, nothing more. Other types of ranges are as follows:

> ▸ **Forward ranges**: These are input ranges where a particular point can be saved and used later. You'll want a forward range when you need to look ahead and return the part of the range already passed for review.

> ▸ **Bidirectional ranges**: These offer backward iteration as well as forward iteration.

> ▸ **Random access ranges**: These are input ranges that also offer fast access to any index. You'll want a random access range when your algorithm needs to jump around rapidly.

> ▸ **Output ranges**: These are ranges that receive data instead of iterating over data.

> You can go to `http://dlang.org/phobos/std_range.html` for the official documentation on ranges and detailed definitions of each type.

There are also additional features you may offer on top of the core range primitives. These include infiniteness, slicing, length, and there may be more in the future. They are checked independently of the range type and are used, if available, for added efficiency in algorithms.

It is also important to look at what kind of ranges our algorithm cannot handle. Our simple average algorithm will loop over all the values, which is impossible if we have passed an infinite range—an input range that is never empty. Thus, we will reject infinite ranges in our function signature when implementing the average algorithm.

It is possible to use additional facilities if and only if they are actually available. For example, `std.range.walkLength` has two constraints; it needs to be iterable, so it needs to be an input range, and it must not be infinite. However, the function body of `std.range.walkLength` starts with the following code:

```
static if(hasLength!Range) return range.length;
```

The `hasLength` function is a function from `std.range` that checks for the presence of a `length` member. If a `length` member is available from this range, it returns that value instead of looping over the values and calculating a count, increasing the efficiency of the algorithm.

How to do it...

The following steps show how to use ranges when implementing an algorithm:

1. Import the `std.range` and `std.traits` modules. They have functions to help perform compile-time checks on range capabilities.

2. Create a function that takes the range we need, with a constraint for both the range type and the range's element type.

3. Determine a good type for the return value. For our average, we want a type that can hold a large sum of the range's elements. So, if the range we received has an element type of floating point, we'll use `double`. Otherwise, we'll use `long`.

4. Implement your algorithm in terms of the range primitives you required in the constraint. For our `average` function, we'll loop through the values and add them to a running total and count, and then we'll calculate the arithmetic average by dividing the sum by the count.

5. Return the result. The result should be as useful as possible. The code is as follows:

```
import std.range, std.traits;
auto average(Range)(Range range)
```

```
if(isInputRange!Range && !isInfinite!Range &&
isNumeric!(ElementType!Range))
{
    static if(isFloatingPoint!(ElementType!Range))
        double sum = 0;
    else
        long sum = 0;
    int count = 0;
    foreach(item; range) {
        count++;
        sum += item;
    }
    return sum / count;
}
```

6. Test it by passing it an array (or any other numeric range object!), as shown in the following line of code:

```
writeln(average([1, 2, 3])); // prints 2
```

How it works...

Ranges are generally used by constrained function templates. That's what the first few lines of code are: a function template declaration and the constraint. The syntax is as follows:

```
return_type name(compile, time, args)(run, time, args)
if(constraint_condition)
```

The compile-time arguments are all available in the constraint condition. If the constraint fails, the template is not considered a match for the arguments. This allows you to be specific about what you will and won't accept, and also to overload your templates on different conditions. For example, we could write a separate function with the same name and same arguments, but leave out the `!isInfinite!Range` condition. Then, if we try to call the function with an infinite range, it would use the second function instead of the first.

The constraint condition's contents are just like any other `if` statement. You can call functions; combine conditions with `&&`, `||`, or parenthesis; and you can reference the compile-time arguments along with any literals or manifest constants (`enum` values defined elsewhere in the module). Here, we used three functions from `std.range` and tone from `std.traits` to describe exactly what we need. These functions perform type checks to ensure that the passed object conforms to the range interface we need. When accepting a generic input range, this does not mean to accept anything. It simply means to accept the most generic input that makes sense for you. If data transformation is required to get it into the form you need, don't accept that data—let the user do the transformation if they choose to. This keeps the cost of your algorithm predictable.

It is also possible to write unconstrained templates that match types with pure duck typing. Duck typing is named from the saying "if it quacks like a duck, it's a duck". In code, it means if `duck.quack()` compiles, it will be used as a duck, regardless of whether it explicitly implements the duck interface or not. In fact, this is exactly how `isInputRange` and friends are implemented. However, it is generally considered bad practice to write an unconstrained template in D. This is because figuring out what their requirements are can be difficult and it is easy to miss bugs in the implementation, since it may be passed objects that it has no idea how to handle.

Once the compile-time arguments are validated by the constraint, they can also be used in the runtime arguments or inside the function as types or values, depending on the compile-time argument. That's what (`Range range`) is. The compile-time argument `Range` is used as a wildcard type for the runtime argument `range`.

The other notable aspect of this function's signature is the return type. Here, we returned `auto`. This means, like with auto local variables, that the compiler will automatically determine the return type by looking at the first `return` statement in the function body. An `auto` template function must return one specific type—it is illegal to try to return both a string and an integer, for example—but you don't have to specify the type yourself. This is useful for more than just convenience. Here, we used the `auto` return type because the specific type returned depends on the result of the `static if` statement in the function body. Automatic type deduction lets us have more complex logic inside the function to return the best possible type for any particular input type. Functions returning `auto` are also useful to return nested `struct` types whose name may not be accessible outside the function's scope. Phobos uses this pattern when implementing some higher order ranges.

Our function's body is pretty straightforward, with one exception: the use of `static if`. The `static if` function works like `regular if`, but with two key differences that are given as follows:

- It runs at compile time, meaning only compile-time information, such as variable types or compile-time template arguments, is available to it.

- It does not introduce a new scope. Variables declared inside the `static if` function are still available outside the `static if` function. This is why we were able to use `sum` in the rest of the function.

The `static if` function is very useful when specializing functions and looking at information received by compile-time reflection. As you can customize just part of a template, it helps with code reuse. There is no need to write a whole new function when the only difference in sum is a `float` value instead of an `int` value. The branch of `static if` that is not true does not get compiled into the program at all. It must have valid syntax, but the code isn't actually compiled. So, you can safely use `static if` for conditional compilation or to filter out code that does not work with a given set of arguments.

Finally, we can look at how the function is called. Note how simple it is. The caller doesn't have to worry about the specifics of compile-time arguments, as they are 100 percent automatically deduced, nor does the caller need to worry about passing it a specific type, since the function is very generic! It *just works*.

> There are times when the user may have to care about the specifics. The most frequent case is when they pass the function types it doesn't support. The D compiler's error messages may be difficult to read and may falsely place the error in a library function instead of the user's code. If this happens to you, the key information to watch for is the constraint the compiler says does not match. If your call says `no matching template [...] candidates are: foo(T) if (isInputRange!T)`, look at where you called `foo` and be sure it is actually being passed an input range. Note that static arrays are not input ranges; they need to be sliced with the `[]` operator.

Creating an input range

Input ranges are D's improvement to the iterators of C++ that are safer, potentially more efficient, and can also generate their own data. Here, we'll create an input range that generates numbers in a Fibonacci sequence to see how it can be done and briefly explore how well it integrates with `std.algorithm` automatically.

How to do it...

Let's execute the following steps to create an input range that generates numbers in a Fibonacci sequence:

1. Create a struct with, minimally, the three core input range members: the properties `front`, the properties of `empty`, and the function `popFront`. It should also hold whatever state is necessary for iteration with successive calls to `popFront`.

2. Add all other functionality as possible without breaking the complexity guarantee. Our Fibonacci generator can also implement a simple `save` property, so we will add it, upgrading it to a forward range.

3. Test it with `static assert` for the interface you need and perform unit tests.

4. Write a helper method to create it.

5. Use it! We'll print out the first several entries with `std.range.take` and `writeln`.

The code is as follows:

```
import std.range;
struct FibonacciRange {
```

```
    // input range required methods
    // Fibonacci is an infinite sequence, so it is never empty
    enum bool empty = false;
    @property int front() { return current; }
    void popFront() {
        previous = current;
        current = next;
        next = current + previous;
    }
    // data members for state between calls
    private {
        int previous = 0;
        int current = 0;
        int next = 1;
    }
    // other range functions we can implement cheaply
    @property FibonacciRange save() { return this; }
}
// explicit check that it fulfils the interface we want
static assert(isForwardRange!FibonacciRange);

// helper function to create the range
FibonacciRange fibonacci() {
    return FibonacciRange();
}

void main() {
    import std.stdio;
    auto numbers = fibonacci();
    writeln(numbers.take(15));
}
```

Running it will print the first 15 Fibonacci numbers as follows:

```
[0, 1, 1, 2, 3, 5, 8, 13, 21, 34, 55, 89, 144, 233, 377]
```

How it works...

Input ranges are defined in terms of two required properties and one required function, and they can be extended with a number of optional functions and properties. Any object that implements the functions and properties is considered an input range.

The three required members are `front`, `empty`, and `popFront`. The `front` property is the current item at the front at the list. The `empty` property is true when there are no more items left. The `popFront` member advances to the next item.

The `front` property should always be valid unless the range is empty, including immediately after construction. For some ranges, this means you should prime it by calling `popFront` in the constructor, or you can do what we did here and set up valid data with the variable's initializers.

As they can be called multiple times in a single loop, `front` and `empty` should always be very fast properties or, when appropriate, direct data members. The `popFront` property should execute as fast as possible, but it is also permitted to perform expensive computations to prepare the next value if necessary.

The optional range primitives, such as `save`, which returns a new range that is a copy of the current range and can be advanced independently, or `opIndex`, which offers random access to the range's contents, should only be implemented if you can do so quickly (*O(1)* algorithmic complexity). As a general rule, if your design for `save` has to perform a large memory copy or allocation, don't implement it. The typical `save` property does exactly what we did here: return this inside a struct. Assigning a struct automatically performs a shallow copy—a fast operation. A struct copy will be usable independently as long as there are no mutable references. Here, our only members are integers, so the copy works.

Generally, if you are writing a loop inside a range primitive, you should rethink if your range really supports that function. Range primitives are typically used in loops, so a loop inside these functions risks higher algorithmic complexity than the consumer expects, and that will make the function slow. We'll experiment with this later in this chapter.

While implementing the range properties, you may implement them as a data member, an `enum`, or a `@property` function. The `@property` functions are the most common. The `@ property` function is a function that can be replaced with a data member, ideally without breaking any code. They aren't quite interchangeable as the `@property` function can restrict access to the variable (for example, a getter function without a corresponding setter results in a read-only variable to which references cannot exist—something impossible with regular data members). However, for the most part, the goal of a `@property` function is to look like a variable to the outside world.

The `enum` storage class in D is also similar to a data member, but is different in one important way; an `enum` variable, at the usage point, is identical to a data literal and not a variable. If you write `enum a = 10; int b = a;`, the compiler will translate that into `int b = 10;`. It is impossible to get a reference or pointer to an `enum` type, just like it is impossible to get a pointer to an integer literal; neither have an address in memory.

The enum variables are interesting because their value is always accessible at compile time and the fact that they are enum variables is also apparent at compile time. This means an enum variable can be tested in a `static if` statement, in a template constraint or any other compile-time context. It also means their initializer is always evaluated at compile time, giving a key gateway into the world of **compile-time function evaluation** (**CTFE**). Here, however, we didn't need to evaluate any function. Our Fibonacci range is simply never empty, since the Fibonacci sequence is infinite. The `enum bool empty = false;` statement (or simply `enum empty = false;` as the type could be automatically deduced) advertises this fact, and unlike `bool empty = false`, the enum version can always be tested at compile time. Thus, our range would pass the `std.range.isInfinite` test; a fact our average function in the previous recipe tested. It is impossible to get the average of all Fibonacci numbers.

The enum keyword is also used to create enumerations; this is a new type that has members associated with a literal, similar to enum variables in other languages. The implementation of these two features is mostly the same, which is why they share a keyword, though the two usages are generally separate.

If you were writing a range that wasn't infinite, the `empty` or `@property` function should be a data member, just like `front`.

The Fibonacci struct is our range. It is customary, however, to write at least two other pieces of code: the static assert(s) to ensure the range actually fulfils the required interface and a helper instantiator function to help create the range. You will often also wish to write unit tests for your range, testing it with a variety of input and ensuring it generates correct outputs.

A static assert is given a condition and, optionally, a message that is tested at compile time. If the test fails, the compiler prints the location of the failed assertion, the message (if provided), and the call stack of any template instantiation. A failing static assert will result in a failed build with a compile error. Static asserts are flexible tools used to test code, compile flags, and the supported platforms by generating user-defined compile errors. Here, we use it to ensure our code does what it needs to do to implement the interface. It isn't strictly necessary, but helps us to ensure that we didn't make any mistakes that otherwise wouldn't appear until a user tried to actually create our range.

Finally, the helper function, `fibonacci`, serves as a convenience constructor. Here, we didn't really need it, since our range is fairly simple. However, with more complex ranges, the helper function gives us a chance to enforce our invariants (for example, ensure the constructor that primes the range—ensuring `front` is always valid unless empty—is called) and can significantly simplify the creation due to implicit function template instantiation. Recall how compile-time arguments are often automatically deduced when calling a function. Let's start with the following code:

```
to!string(10) == to!(string, int)(10)
```

Deductions don't happen with the `struct` constructors, but do happen with helper functions, as shown in the following code:

```
struct Test(T) { T t; }
auto test = Test(10); // compile error!
auto test = Test!int(10); // this is needed instead
```

When you use the `auto helper` function, you can save the user from having to list out the exact types by doing it for them just once, as shown in the following code:

```
auto helper(T)(T t) { return Test!T(t); }
auto test = helper(10); // works!
auto test2 = helper("foo"); // also works!
```

Helper functions' ability to deduce types simplifies the use of complex ranges considerably. This, combined with the ability to call the constructor on your terms, makes ranges and helper functions often go hand-in-hand.

There's more...

Many algorithms from `std.algorithm` work with our Fibonacci range. Experiment with them to see the possibilities! It is interesting to note that even complex functions such as `std.algorithm.map` and `std.algorithm.filter` will work with our range, despite the fact that it is infinite. This is accomplished because they use lazy evaluation. They only evaluate a result upon request, so passing them an infinite amount of data does not mean they must do an infinite amount of work.

If you need to pass it to a function that cannot work with infinite data, such as `writeln` or our `average` function, `std.range.take` can be used to limit the size to something more manageable.

Creating an output range

As input ranges serve as generators or iterators over data, output ranges serve as sinks for data. Output ranges may print data, perform one-way algorithms (such as message digests or hashes), collect data, or whatever else you can achieve with its required `put` method.

Here, we'll write an output range that prints the arrays it receives out in hexadecimal format. We'll write sixteen bytes per line, always ending with a new line.

How to do it...

Let's create an output range by executing the following steps:

1. Create a struct with a `put` method that takes the data we want to consume. As our hex dumper takes any kind of array and doesn't store it, we want in `void[]`. The `put` method will perform the printing we need.

2. Add any data we need to preserve between calls to `put`. To format our lines, we'll need to keep a count of how many items we've outputted so far.

3. Add other functions we need, such as destructors, constructors, or other methods. We want to ensure there's always a new line at the end, so we'll add a `writeln` function in the destructor.

4. Test the function with a static assert for `isOutputRange` for the types it must accept.

The code is as follows:

```d
import std.range;
import std.stdio;
struct HexDumper {
    int outputted;
    void put(in void[] data) {
        foreach(b; cast(const ubyte[]) data) {
            writef("%02x ", b);
            outputted++;
            if(outputted == 16) {
                writeln();
                outputted = 0;
            }
        }
    }
    ~this() {
        if(outputted)
            writeln();
    }
}
static assert(isOutputRange!(HexDumper, ubyte));
static assert(isOutputRange!(HexDumper, char));
void main() {
    HexDumper output;
    output.put("Hello, world! In hex.");
}
```

Run it and you'll see the following output:

```
48 65 6c 6c 6f 2c 20 77 6f 72 6c 64 21 20 49 6e
20 68 65 78 2c
```

How it works...

An output range is much simpler than an input range. It only has one required method: `put`. An output range has no required invariant; you are not required to set anything up in the constructor.

The `put` method doesn't have to do anything in particular. Its only requirement is to accept a single argument of the type the range can handle. Typically, the `put` method does one of the following three things:

- Consume the received data with an algorithm. The `std.digest` provides output ranges of this style.
- Collect the data, for example, by building an array. The `std.array.Appender` is an output range of this style.
- Display the received data. This is what our example does.

Using an output range at the core consists only of creating the object and calling the `put` method to feed the object with data. Some ranges, such as the `std.digest` ranges, also require calls to methods such as `start` and `finish` to inform the object that you have finished the process so that it can perform finalization. In our case, we used the destructor to finalize.

A destructor is declared in a struct with the syntax `~this() { /* code */ }`. The destructor runs immediately when the struct object goes out of scope.

 Destructors are not run when a pointer to a struct goes out of scope, which means a dynamic array of structs will not necessarily do a clean up as soon as possible, since a dynamic array uses a pointer.

Destructors are used for clean up—freeing memory, releasing resources, or finalizing an operation, with the limitation that the object is no longer available.

The `std.digest` cannot use a destructor as its `finish` method changes the data and returns the final result. A destructor cannot return a value; by the time the destructor runs, the object is no longer available, so it would be impossible to get the results. Our `HexDumper` method can output a new line in the destructor, as that does not need to return data.

The implementation of our `put` method loops over the data and writes it in hexadecimal using `std.stdio.writef`. The loop includes a cast to `const ubyte[]` because the function accepts generic data in the form of `in void[]`. Any array will implicitly cast to `void[]`, allowing us to pass anything to the `put` method, including strings and other arrays. However, a `void[]` array is only usable if it is explicitly casted to something else first. We want to print out the individual bytes, so we casted to `const ubyte[]`. Then, the `foreach` loop will go one byte at a time.

Finally, the `writef` function works like `writefln`, but does not print an automatic new line at the end. The `writef` function is D's version of the classic C `printf` function. The first argument is a format string. Our format string, `"%02x"`, means pad with zeroes to at least two digits wide, and then put out the argument in hexadecimal, followed by a space.

There's more...

The `std.range.put` function is a generic function that extends the ability of your output range to accept data. You only need to implement the core data type your function needs. Let other transformations such as accepting generic input ranges be handled by the standard library. An example of this can be seen in the *Creating a digest* recipe in *Chapter 2, Phobos – The Standard Library*.

See also

▶ `http://dlang.org/phobos/std_format.html` has the documentation on the `writef` function's format string

Creating a higher-order range

Analogous to a higher-order function that is a function that returns a function, a higher-order range is a range that returns another range. This technique allows the lazy evaluation of results and maximum propagation of range features (for example, random access or bidirectionality) for best efficiency and type safety as you compose algorithms. Phobos' `std.algorithm` module has several higher-order ranges. Here, we'll create a simplified version of `std.algorithm.map` to explore the implementation and usage of this flexible concept.

How to do it...

Let's create a higher-order range by executing the following steps:

1. Make a `struct` template that stores another struct.
2. Do your transformation in relevant places.
3. Forward all possible methods of the input range via `static if`.

4. Create a helper method to create it conveniently.

5. Use a static assert to ensure it properly fulfils the interfaces.

6. Try using the interfaces!

The code is as follows:

```
import std.range;
import std.traits;
struct OurMap(alias transformation, T)
    if(isInputRange!T)
{
    this(T range) {
        this.range = range;
    }

    T range;

    // forward infiniteness
    static if(isInfinite!T)
        enum bool empty = false;
    else
        @property bool empty() { return range.empty; }

    // forward the basic functions
    void popFront() { range.popFront(); }
    @property auto front() { return transformation(range.front); }

    // forward advanced functions, if available...
    static if(isForwardRange!T)
        @property auto save() {
            return OurMap!(transformation, T)(range.save);
        }

    static if(isBidirectionalRange!T) {
        @property auto back() {
            return transformation(range.back);
        }
        void popBack() {
            range.popBack();
        }
    }

    static if(isRandomAccessRange!T)
```

```
            auto opIndex(size_t idx) {
                return transformation(range[idx]);
            }

        static if(hasLength!T)
            @property auto length() { return range.length; }
    }

    // check the basics with InputRange from std.range
    static assert(isInputRange!(OurMap!((a) => a, InputRange!int)));
    // check the forwarding with an array - a fully functional range
    static assert(isRandomAccessRange!(OurMap!((a) => a, int[])));

    // the helper function
    auto map(alias transformation, T)(T t) {
        return OurMap!(transformation, T)(t);
    }

    void main() {
        import std.stdio;
        // try using it!
        foreach(item; map!((a) => a*2)([1,2,3]))
            writeln(item);
    }
```

This will print the following output:

```
    2  4  6
```

Here, we created a `struct` template. It works just like a function template. We write a struct, add a list of compile-time parameters, we add a constraint (if desired), and then use the compile-time parameters at any point inside the definition.

One of our compile-time parameters, `transformation`, is listed as an `alias` parameter. The `alias` parameters in D take some other compile-time entity as argument. It might be a variable, a function, a template, or any other D symbol. Inside the template, when the `alias` parameter is used, it refers directly to the passed-in entity. Unlike a `value` parameter, which receives a copy of or reference to a variable's contents, an `alias` parameter refers to the variable itself.

> If you used reflection capabilities on an `alias` parameter, it would tell you about the original item. We use it here to provide maximum speed access to the function passed by the user. It isn't a function pointer, which would need to be dereferenced at run time; it is the function and is called directly by the generated code.

A higher-order range, in the same way as a range-consuming function, takes a range as input to its constructor and is constrained by the most general type you can handle. A higher-order range also is a range, so it has the same methods and properties as any other range.

The `OurMap` struct is a higher-order range that takes a transformation function and an input range and applies the transformation function to all the data within, upon request (lazily). Using `static if`, it presents the same interface as the inner range, ensuring that no capabilities are lost. The helper functions used in the `static if`, `hasLength`, `isInfinite`, and other functions are found in the `std.range` module. If we did a transformation that could no longer present part of an interface efficiently (filter, for example) we would leave the slower parts out because efficiency guarantees are an important part of the conceptual range interface. With filter, random access would be impossible at full speed, since it wouldn't know how many elements were filtered without looking at all of them. So, even if the input range offered random access, we couldn't present it in our range. `OurMap`, however, has all functions that could be forwarded without a loss of efficiency.

After the `struct` definition, we used two static asserts to test. When given an input range, we need to ensure our range is also an input range. As we can forward random access efficiently, we also ensured that our range correctly implemented a random access range when given an array (arrays provide random access).

Finally, the helper function is important here to make our range usable without hassle and thus has the presentable name of `map`. As functions allow implicit type deduction, the helper function saves the user the lengthy, repetitive boilerplate of listing the type of each range they pass to the function when calling the constructor. With the helper function, they can simply pass it a transformation and some data and it just works.

Putting a range interface on a collection

A range is a view into a collection. Ranges are typically mutable (though the individual elements may be immutable), so you can advance their position with `popFront`, but collections may be immutable. Here, we'll implement a stack data structure that exposes ranges to inspect it.

Getting ready

First, let's implement our stack type. A stack is a data type that fundamentally only needs two operations: `push` and `pop`. You push data on to the stack, and then pop data off in reverse order to which it was pushed. Popped data is removed from the stack. If we push 1 and then 2, we should pop 2 then 1. Popping from an empty stack is an error.

It is possible to use a built-in array directly as a stack, using slicing and the append operator (a ~ b), but this is woefully inefficient. Instead, we'll use a static buffer that can grow, if necessary, with a companion position variable. We can slice into a statically sized buffer to get started, and if this proves to be too small, we can simply grow the length. This allows the runtime to be reallocated as required on the garbage collected memory heap—a somewhat slow but infrequent step. Otherwise, the code is pretty straightforward as shown:

```
struct Stack(T, size_t expectedMaxSize = 32) {
    T[expectedMaxSize] initialBuffer;
    T[] buffer;
    size_t currentPosition;
    bool isEmpty() { return currentPosition == 0; }
    void push(T item) {
        // initialization
        if(buffer is null) buffer = initialBuffer[];
        // growth if needed
        if(currentPosition == buffer.length) buffer.length += 64;
        // the actual push operation
        buffer[currentPosition++] = item;
    }
    T pop() {
        if(currentPosition == 0)
            throw new Exception("Empty stack cannot pop.");
        return buffer[--currentPosition];
    }
}
```

Our stack can be used as shown:

```
Stack!int stack;
stack.push(1);
stack.push(2);
writeln(stack.pop()); // prints 2
writeln(stack.pop()); // prints 1
assert(stack.isEmpty()); // passes, we've used all the data
```

Now, let's look at how to put a range interface on it.

How to do it...

Let's put a range interface on a collection by executing the following steps:

1. Write a range by using the data members of your collection to implement the range primitives you can write efficiently. The range can use private members, but since it is part of the public interface, be careful not to break encapsulation and expose something you don't want to commit to.

2. Try to avoid modifying the original data. A data member that keeps the current position will be useful. For our stack, we'll take a slice into the stack buffer and keep this private so that our implementation details don't leak out.

3. Make the range's constructor private. The code for the viewing range is as follows:

```
struct StackView(T) {
    // we'll start with the data members and constructors that
peek into the collection
    private const(T)[] data; // our read-only view into the data
    private this(const(T)[] data) {
        this.data = data;
    }
    // and our range primitives
    @property bool empty() const {
        return data.length == 0;
    }
    @property const(T) front() const {
        return data[$ - 1]; // the stack pops backwards in the
array
    }
    void popFront() {
        data = data[0 .. $ - 1];
    }
}
```

4. Add a method to the collection that returns the range. The method should have a relevant name for the kind of range it returns. Inside our `Stack` struct, add the following code:

```
@property auto view() const {
    return StackView!T(buffer[0 .. currentPosition]);
}
```

How it works...

Whenever possible, a range should operate independently of a collection. Ranges provide their own interface and keep track of their own position. Thus, typically, ranges and collections are two separate types, but they are located in the same module so that the range can take advantage of the collection's private implementation for maximum efficiency.

The name of the method the collection provides to return a range can be anything. Here, we're using `view` because the range lets us look into the data, nothing more. The analogous range methods on `std.stdio.File` are called `byLine` and `byChunk`, as they iterate over the file by lines and chunks, respectively. A collection may have multiple ranges that work with it in different ways.

Many containers use `opSlice` as the function to get a range, including built-in arrays, for example, `auto viewer = container[]; // calls opSlice`. You may use this too if there's one range that works best for your entire container.

If it is impossible to advance a range without modifying the underlying collection or stream, you may still provide a range interface. For example, the ranges on a file must read more data from the file to get the next lines. This is a necessary cost in that situation. Additional stream-based functions, such as seeking, are not exposed in the range. While, in theory, using file seeking and buffering, `File.byLine` could provide primitives such as `save` or bidirectionality, in practice, these would break the efficiency guarantees of the range interface and thus are not exposed. Stream or collection-specific functions are implemented on their native type.

With a different implementation of `Stack`, we may have been forced to use the primitive `pop` instead of `view` into its internal buffer. This would have been acceptable, but not ideal since `pop` modifies the underlying data as you look through it.

Creating an input range over a tree structure

Using ranges in cases where you would typically use a recursive function can be a bit tricky. As the function flow when using ranges is controlled externally, you can't use recursion. Instead, you must maintain a stack of state inside your range structure. Here, we'll implement an input range that iterates over a tree structure of arbitrary depth.

Getting ready

First, let's look at the most straightforward way to implement this loop, which is with a recursive function. This is shown in the following code:

```
struct TreePart {
    string payload;
    TreePart[] children;
}
void walkTree(void delegate(string) visitor, TreePart root) {
    visitor(root.payload);
    foreach(child; root.children)
        walkTree(visitor, child);
}
```

This function lends itself easily to the `opApply` iteration, which is great for `foreach` loops, but internal iteration doesn't interact well with the other algorithms and ranges in Phobos and other libraries. How can we make a range that does this same iteration?

The first thing to observe is that a recursive function makes use of stack space to store local variables, including function arguments. We'll need a stack too. Phobos doesn't yet have a stack container, so let's reuse the `Stack` struct we wrote in the previous recipe.

How to do it...

Let's create an input range over a structure tree by executing the following steps:

1. Write an input range skeleton with the three required members.

2. Look at the recursive implementation; which variables do we need? There are two variables: the root `TreePart` and the iteration position on children. The `visitor` function isn't explicitly needed, since our range will be usable in a `foreach` loop instead.

3. Create an inner struct with the required variables.

4. Add two members to our range: a stack of the inner struct and a current variable. These represent the local variables and call the stack of the recursive implementation.

5. Write our constructor. Take the argument the recursive function needed to get started and also set up local variables.

6. Implement `front` by looking at where the visitor was called in the recursive implementation. As `visitor` was only called on the current root's payload, we'll return `current.root.payload` as `front` here too.

7. Implement `empty` by determining the position where the recursive implementation would return. It returns when the loop is completed, which happens when the current index is equal to the length of the children. We also aren't complete until all the child calls have completed, which happens when the stack is empty.

8. Implement `popFront`. What happens after each call to the visitor in the recursive implementation? It increments the child position to continue the `foreach` loop. If the loop is empty, the function returns, and if the next step is also empty, it continues to return. If not, we proceed into the child's subtree. Calling a function means pushing the current state onto the stack and resetting the variables. Let's do exactly this.

9. Finally, put in the usual tests and try using it.

The code is as follows:

```
struct TreeVisitor { // step one, the skeleton
    // steps two and three, struct with our variables
    struct Position {
        TreePart root;
        int childPosition;
    }
```

```
    // step four, create the required locals and stack
    Stack!(Position) stack;
    Position current;

    // step five, constructor
    this(TreePart root) {
        current.root = root;
        // we use childPosition == -1 to indicate that
        // we haven't entered the child loop yet
        current.childPosition = -1;
    }

    // step six
    @property string front() {
        return current.root.payload;
    }

    // step seven
    @property bool empty() {
        return
          // if we're at the end of the children…
          current.childPosition + 1 == current.root.children.length
          // …and the stack is empty, we're done
          && stack.isEmpty;
    }

    // step eight
    void popFront() {
        current.childPosition++; // advance position
        if(current.childPosition == current.root.children.length) {
            // the foreach loop would have just returned, so we
            // start walking back up the tree…
            current = stack.pop();
            // picking up where we left off, if possible
            if(!empty)
                popFront();
        } else {
            // we're still inside the loop,
            // proceed deeper into the tree
            stack.push(current);
            // and reset our variables for the next part
            current.root = current.root.children[current.
childPosition];
```

```
                    current.childPosition = -1;
            }
        }
    }
    // step nine
    static assert(isInputRange!TreeVisitor);

    void main() {
        import std.stdio;

        void visitor(string part) {
            writeln(part);
        }

        // initialize our test tree
        TreePart root;
        root.payload= "one";
        root.children = [TreePart("two", [TreePart("three", null)]),
    TreePart("three", null)];

        // first, walk it recursively
        walkTree(&visitor, root);

        writeln("****"); // separator for easy viewing

        // then use our range to do the same thing
        foreach(part; TreeVisitor(root))
            visitor(part);
    }
```

The output will be as follows:

```
one
two
three
****
one
two
three
```

Both the methods matched and showed the entire structure. The range works!

How it works...

The code is fairly straightforward once you have an approach. The local variables and internal call stack of the recursive function translated directly into the struct variables and stack member of our range. All we did is change the internal iteration to external iteration. This same process could be used for almost any function.

There's more...

D also supports internal iteration with the `foreach` syntax. This is done by providing a method called `opApply` in your object. It works in the same way as the `visitor` function we wrote. If we add this function to `TreePart`, you will have the following code:

```
int opApply(int delegate(string) visitor) {
    if(auto result = visitor(this)) return result;
    foreach(child; this.children)
        if(auto result = child.opApply(visitor))
            return result;
    return 0;
}
```

Then, we'd be able to run `foreach(part; root) writeln(part);` and once again repeat our result from the preceding code.

The way `opApply` works is the code the user puts in the `foreach` body is passed to you as a delegate, with the arguments being the loop variables. The `opApply` object's job is to loop what it needs to and call the delegate for each item.

The compiler-provided delegate returns `int` to signify if and how the user code tried to break out of the loop. Your `opApply` function must always test this value, and immediately return it unmodified if it is nonzero. When you finish iterating, it always return zero. Otherwise, this code is the same as the recursive implementation. Use this in place of an explicitly passed starting parameter.

The downside of the `opApply` iteration is that it doesn't interact well with external tools such as ranges and algorithms in Phobos and other libraries.

Using runtime polymorphic (class) ranges

The `std.range` module also provides interfaces for many of the range types. These are slower than using ranges with structs and templates directly, but have the advantage of using a single type for any object that matches the interface, This means that you can swap out the range implementation at runtime. It also has the advantage of providing a common application binary interface for cases such as class interfaces and building DLLs.

How to do it...

Let's make use of runtime polymorphic ranges by executing the following steps:

1. Use the `inputRangeObject` or `outputRangeObject` functions, passing an instance of any range to them.

2. Store and use the returned object by using the `InputRange!type` or `OutputRange!type` interfaces. The type there is the type returned by `front`.

3. You can pass it to a function by using the element type and the interface, or `cast` it to a more specific range type (for example, `cast(RandomAccessRange)`) if more capabilities are needed.

4. Remember to check for null whenever casting class objects.

The code is as follows:

```
import std.range;
InputRange!int myRange = inputRangeObject([1, 2, 3]);
foreach(int item; myRange) /* use item */
```

How it works...

The range interfaces are parameterized on the type of `front`, but otherwise work like any other class hierarchy. The implementation of the interface is automatically generated by `inputRangeObject` or `outputRangeObject` using reflection and code generation to build the most specific object possible from the given type.

As interfaces use virtual functions, including for all the (usually cheap) range properties, there's a performance penalty to polymorphic ranges. Typically, runtime polymorphic ranges run at about half the speed as their compile-time counterparts, and thus they should be avoided unless your use case requires them.

Storing a range as a data member

Storing a range instance in a non-template class or struct can be difficult because the type isn't always obvious and is sometimes completely unavailable. Ranges are typically for temporary use, and thus they don't need to be stored for long and are usually eligible for `auto` type deduction, but if you do need to store it, there are two options.

How to do it...

We can store a range as a data member by executing the following steps:

1. The first option is to use one of the object-oriented wrappers as follows:
   ```
   import std.range;
   InputRange!int rangeObj;
   rangeObj = inputRangeObject(your_range);
   ```

   Remember, there is a performance penalty for this method, but it does have the advantage of being reassignable by different types of ranges as needed.

2. Alternatively, we can use the `typeof` operator to get the range type out of the function, as shown in the following code:

```
typeof(function_that_returns_a_range) rangeObj;
```

The code is as follows:

```
import std.algorithm;
typeof(filter!((a) > 0)([1,2,3])) filteredRange; // declare it
this() {
    filteredRange = filter!((a) > 0)([1, 2, 3]); // initialize it
}
```

How it works...

The `typeof` operator can be used anywhere in D where you need a type. When passed a variable or expression, it returns the static (compile-time) type of that variable or expression. When passed a function call, it returns the return type of the function. This can be used as a tool in compile-time reflection, for convenience with complex types, or generic code.

The `typeof` operator works even when the type is not otherwise available, such as a struct in a module you haven't imported, or if the type has no name. In Phobos, many range functions return nested structs, as shown in the following code:

```
auto hiddenType() {
    struct Foo { }
    return Foo();
}
auto test = hiddenType(); /* test has a type whose definition is
not available outside the hiddenType function. Calling it Foo or
hiddenType.Foo will not work because types declared inside
functions are not available outside. */
```

This is sometimes called a *Voldemort type*, referencing a fictional character whose name is not allowed to be spoken.

When using `auto` type deduction, everything just works; however, if you need to declare a variable of that type before it is used, this presents a problem. The `typeof` operator is a solution, as shown:

```
typeof(hiddenType()) test = hiddenType(); // works!
```

As ranges often have complex or hidden type names, `typeof` may be the only way to refer to them without an `auto` type deduced variable.

Sorting ranges efficiently

Phobos' `std.algorthm` includes sorting algorithms. Let's look at how they are used, what requirements they have, and the dangers of trying to implement range primitives without minding their efficiency requirements.

Getting ready

Let's make a linked list container that exposes an appropriate view, a forward range, and an inappropriate view, a random access range that doesn't meet its efficiency requirements. A singly-linked list can only efficiently implement forward iteration due to its nature; the only tool it has is a pointer to the next element. Implementing any other range primitives will require loops, which is not recommended. Here, however, we'll implement a fully functional range, with assignable elements, length, bidirectional iteration, random access, and even slicing on top of a linked list to see the negative effects this has when we try to use it. The code for this can be found at `Chapter03\Code\03` of your code bundle.

We'll also create a skeleton main program that initializes the list. You can find the code for this at `Chapter03\Code\03` of your code bundle.

How to do it...

We're going to both sort and benchmark this program.

To sort

Let's sort ranges by executing the following steps:

1. Import `std.algorithm`.
2. Determine the predicate you need. The default is `(a, b) => a < b`, which results in an ascending order when the sorting is complete (for example, `[1,2,3]`). If you want ascending order, you don't have to specify a predicate at all. If you need descending order, you can pass a greater-than predicate instead, as shown in the following line of code:

    ```
    auto sorted = sort!((a, b) => a > b)([1,2,3]); // results: [3,2,1]
    ```

3. When doing string comparisons, the functions `std.string.cmp` (case-sensitive) or `std.string.icmp` (case-insensitive) may be used, as is done in the following code:

    ```
    auto sorted = sort!((a, b) => cmp(a, b) < 0)(["b", "c", "a"]); //
    results: a, b, c
    ```

4. Your predicate may also be used to sort based on a `struct` member, as shown in the following code:

```
auto sorted = sort!((a, b) => a.value < b.value)(structArray);
```

5. Pass the predicate as the first compile-time argument. The range you want to sort is passed as the runtime argument.

6. If your range is not already sortable (if it doesn't provide the necessary capabilities), you can convert it to an array using the array function from `std.range`, as shown in the following code:

```
auto sorted = sort(fibanocci().take(10)); // won't compile, not
enough capabilities
auto sorted = sort(fibanocci().take(10).array); // ok, good
```

7. Use the sorted range. It has a unique type from the input to signify that it has been successfully sorted. Other algorithms may use this knowledge to increase their efficiency.

To benchmark

Let's sort objects using benchmark by executing the following steps:

1. Put our range and skeleton main function from the *Getting ready* section of this recipe into a file.

2. Use `std.datetime.benchmark` to test the sorting of an array from the appropriate walker against the slow walker and print the results at the end of `main`. The code is as follows:

```
auto result = benchmark!(
    {    auto sorted = sort(list.walker.array);    },
    {    auto sorted = sort(list.slowWalker);      }
)(100);
writefln("Emulation resulted in a sort
that was %d times slower.",
    result[1].hnsecs / result[0].hnsecs);
```

3. Run it. Your results may vary slightly, but you'll see that the emulated, inappropriate range functions are consistently slower. The following is the output:

```
Emulation resulted in a sort that was 16 times slower.
```

4. Tweak the size of the list by changing the initialization loop. Instead of 1000 entries, try 2000 entries. Also, try to compile the program with inlining and optimization turned on (dmd -inline -O yourfile.d) and see the difference. The emulated version will be consistently slower, and as the list becomes longer, the gap will widen.

On my computer, a growing list size led to a growing slowdown factor, as shown in the following table:

List size	Slowdown factor
500	13
1000	16
2000	29
4000	73

How it works...

The interface to Phobos' main `sort` function hides much of the complexity of the implementation. As long as we follow the efficiency rules when writing our ranges, things either just work or fail, telling us we must call an array in the range before we can sort it. Building an array has a cost in both time and memory, which is why it isn't performed automatically (`std.algorithm` prefers lazy evaluation whenever possible for best speed and minimum memory use). However, as you can see in our benchmark, building an array is much cheaper than emulating unsupported functions.

The `sort` algorithms require a full-featured range and will modify the range you pass to it instead of allocating memory for a copy. Thus, the range you pass to it must support random access, slicing, and either assignable or swappable elements. The prime example of such a range is a mutable array. This is why it is often necessary to use the array function when passing data to `sort`.

Our linked list code used `static if` with a compile-time parameter as a configuration tool. The implemented functions include `opSlice` and properties that return `ref`. The ref value can only be used on function return values or parameters. Assignments to a `ref` value are forwarded to the original item. The `opSlice` function is called when the user tries to use the slice syntax: `obj[start .. end]`.

Inside the `beSlow` condition, we broke the main rule of implementing range functions: avoid loops. Here, we see the consequences of breaking that rule; it ruined algorithm restrictions and optimizations, resulting in code that performs very poorly. If we follow the rules, we at least know where a performance problem will arise and can handle it gracefully.

For ranges that do not implement the fast `length` property, `std.algorithm` includes a function called `walkLength` that determines the length by looping through all items (like we did in the slow `length` property). The `walkLength` function has a longer name than length precisely to warn you that it is a slower function, running in *O(n)* (linear with length) time instead of *O(1)* (constant) time. Slower functions are OK, they just need to be explicit so that the user isn't surprised.

See also

▸ The `std.algorithm` module also includes other sorting algorithms that may fit a specific use case better than the generic (automatically specialized) function. See the documentation at `http://dlang.org/phobos/std_algorithm.html` for more information.

Searching ranges

Phobos' `std.algorithm` module includes search functions that can work on any ranges. It automatically specializes based on type information. Searching a sorted range is faster than an unsorted range.

How to do it...

Searching has a number of different scenarios, each with different methods:

▸ If you want to know if something is present, use `canFind`.

▸ Finding an item generically can be done with the `find` function. It returns the remainder of the range, with the located item at the front.

▸ When searching for a substring in a string, you can use `haystack.find(boyerMooreFinder(needle))`. This uses the Boyer-Moore algorithm which may give better performance.

▸ If you want to know the index where the item is located, use `countUntil`. It returns a numeric index into the range, just like the `indexOf` function for strings.

▸ Each `find` function can take a predicate to customize the search operation.

▸ When you know your range is sorted but the type doesn't already prove it, you may call `assumeSorted` on it before passing it to the search functions. The `assumeSorted` function has no runtime cost; it only adds information to the type that is used for compile-time specialization.

How it works...

The search functions in Phobos make use of the ranges' available features to choose good-fit algorithms. Pass them efficiently implemented ranges with accurate capabilities to get best performance.

The `find` function returns the remainder of the data because this is the most general behavior; it doesn't need random access, like returning an index, and doesn't require an additional function if you are implementing a function to split a range on a given condition. The `find` function can work with a basic input range, serving as a foundation to implement whatever you need on top of it, and it will transparently optimize to use more range features if available.

Using functional tools to query data

The `std.algorithm` module includes a variety of higher-order ranges that provide tools similar to functional tools. We've already used many of them in this chapter. Here, we'll put it all together to see how D code can be similar to a SQL query.

A SQL query is as follows:

```
SELECT id, name, strcat("Title: ", title)
    FROM users
    WHERE name LIKE 'A%'
    ORDER BY id DESC
    LIMIT 5;
```

How would we express something similar in D?

Getting ready

Let's create a struct to mimic the data table and make an array with the some demo information. The code is as follows:

```
struct User {
    int id;
    string name;
    string title;
}
User[] users;
users ~= User(1, "Alice", "President");
users ~= User(2, "Bob", "Manager");
users ~= User(3, "Claire", "Programmer");
```

How to do it...

Let's use functional tools to query data by executing the following steps:

1. Import `std.algorithm`.

2. Use `sort` to translate the `ORDER BY` clause. If your dataset is large, you may wish to sort it at the end. This will likely require a call to an array, but it will only sort the result set instead of everything. With a small dataset, sorting early saves an array allocation.

3. Use `filter` to implement the `WHERE` clause.

4. Use `map` to implement the field selection and functions. The `std.typecons.tuple` module can also be used to return specific fields.

5. Use `std.range.take` to implement the `LIMIT` clause.

6. Put it all together and print the result.

The code is as follows:

```
import std.algorithm;
import std.range;
import std.typecons : tuple; // we use this below
auto resultSet = users.
    sort!((a, b) => a.id > b.id). // the ORDER BY clause
    filter!((item) => item.name.startsWith("A")).
    // the WHERE clause
    take(5).
    map!((item) => tuple(item.id, item.name,
  "Title: " ~ item.title)); // the field list and transformations
import std.stdio;
foreach(line; resultSet)
    writeln(line[0], " ", line[1], " ", line[2]);
```

It will print the following output:

```
1 Alice Title: President
```

How it works...

Many SQL operations or list comprehensions can be expressed in D using some building blocks from `std.algorithm`. They all work generally the same way; they take a predicate as a compile-time argument. The predicate is passed one or two items at a time and you perform a check or transformation on it. Chaining together functions with the dot syntax, like we did here, is possible thanks to uniform function call syntax. It could also be rewritten as `take(5, filter!pred(map!pred(users)))`. It depends on author's preference, as both styles work exactly the same way.

It is important to remember that all `std.algorithm` higher-order ranges are evaluated lazily. This means no computations, such as looping over or printing, are actually performed until they are required. Writing code using `filter`, `take`, `map`, and many other functions is akin to preparing a query. To execute it, you may print or loop the result, or if you want to save it to an array for use later, simply call `.array` at the end.

There's more...

The `std.algorithm` module also includes other classic functions, such as `reduce`. It works the same way as the others.

D has a feature called pure functions, which we'll look at in more depth later in the book. The functions in `std.algorithm` are conditionally pure, which means they can be used in pure functions if and only if the predicates you pass are also pure. With lambda functions, like we've been using here, the compiler will often automatically deduce this for you. If you use other functions you define as predicates and want to use it in a pure function, be sure to mark them `pure` as well.

See also

- Visit `http://dconf.org/2013/talks/wilson.html` where Adam Wilson's DConf 2013 talk on porting C# to D showed how to translate some real-world LINQ code to D

4
Integration

In this chapter, we will look at how to integrate D with other environments and programming languages. We'll learn about the following:

- ▸ Calling the Windows API functions
- ▸ Removing the Windows console
- ▸ Making Linux system calls
- ▸ Writing part of a C program in D
- ▸ Interfacing with C++
- ▸ Using structs to mimic the C++ object structure
- ▸ Communicating with external processes
- ▸ Communicating with a dynamic scripting language
- ▸ Using Windows' COM

Introduction

D has direct access to functions that use the C, Windows, or C++ conventions as well as the C++ interfaces and low-level control over memory layouts. D also has syntax sugar that can make accessing dynamic interfaces easy and beautiful. This allows a high degree of interoperability with almost any environment. Generally, if you can integrate something with a C program, you can also integrate it with D.

Calling the Windows API functions

The Windows API provides a rich set of functionalities for applications. The entire Windows API is directly accessible from D. Here, we'll demonstrate this by popping up an information message box and a file chooser dialog box using the standard Win32 API functions.

Getting ready

First, make sure you have correctly installed the DMD compiler for Windows. If you want to build 64-bit applications, you must download and install Visual Studio (any version that supports C++ development, including Express) first because dmd on 64-bit Windows uses the Microsoft linker and libraries for better cross-language compatibility.

You'll also want to create or download the Windows API bindings since the Windows bindings that come with dmd are quite incomplete. You can create your own, as required, by copying and pasting the function and struct prototypes from MSDN.

If you are on 32 bit, you might also want to get the newer .lib files from Microsoft and convert them to the OMF format that the 32-bit dmd uses. This often isn't necessary, but if you want to use features from Windows Vista and newer versions, it likely will be. To do this, first download the Windows SDK from http://www.microsoft.com/en-us/download/details.aspx?id=8279, and then get the **Basic Utilities Package** (**BUP**) from http://digitalmars.com/ (you can purchase it for $15). Use coffimplib from the BUP on the .lib files from the SDK to generate the OMF-format libraries for dmd.

How to do it...

Let's call the Windows API functions by executing the following steps:

1. Import core.sys.windows.windows.
2. Create an OPENFILENAME structure and fill in the required fields.
3. Call GetOpenFileName to pop up the file dialog.
4. Use the MessageBox function to give feedback to the user.
5. Link the file with comdlg32.lib by adding it to the dmd command line.

The code is as follows:

```
import core.sys.windows.window;
void main() {
        wchar[256] filenameBuffer;
        filenameBuffer[0] = 0;
        OPENFILENAMEW info;
```

```
info.lStructSize = OPENFILENAMEW.sizeof;
info.lpstrFilter =
"Text Files\0*.txt\0ImageFiles\0*.png;*.jpg\0\0"w.ptr;
info.lpstrFile = filenameBuffer.ptr;
info.nMaxFile = filenameBuffer.length;
if(GetOpenFileNameW(&info)) {
    MessageBoxW(null, info.lpstrFile,
    "You picked"w.ptr, 0);
}
}
```

How it works...

D understands the Windows calling convention. Calling any Windows function is possible by simply declaring the function prototype with `extern(Windows)`.

> You may see `extern(System)` in the preceding code. The `extern(System)` function signifies the calling convention of system libraries on the current platform. In practice, this means `extern(Windows)` will be used on 32-bit Windows and `extern(C)` will be used everywhere else.

Windows functions that deal with strings come in two variants: ASCII and Unicode. These are denoted by the suffix `A` or `W` on the function names. In C and some D bindings, a `UNICODE` macro aliases the names to the appropriate suffix as needed. Here, we called the `W` functions explicitly for maximum compatibility and demonstration purposes.

MSDN often references `TCHAR`, `TSTR`, and so on. Like with the function prototypes, the meaning of `TCHAR` is different if you are using Unicode or ASCII macros. With ASCII, it should be `char` in D, whereas with Unicode, it should be `wchar`.

As D strings are Unicode, it is best to use the `W` versions of functions (it will let you pass strings to the `A` function, and it will work if the strings are all ASCII; however, if they include any non-ASCII characters, the string will be corrupted.) D has built-in support for wide-character strings (UTF-16) that can be used on Windows. The UTF-16 character type is `wchar`. An immutable array of `wchar` types is also called `wstring`, analogously to how arrays of UTF-8 characters are called `string` literals. The `wstring` literals are denoted with the `w` suffix, for example, this is a `wstring` literal, w. The `wstring` literals, like the string literals, are zero terminated. However, unlike `string` literals, they do not automatically convert to pointers; so, to pass a `wstring` literal to a Windows function, use the `.ptr` property. To pass a non-literal string to a Windows function, use `std.utf.toUTFz!(wchar*)(your_string)`. This works both for `wstring` literals and UTF-8 strings—it appends the zero, converting the format only if necessary.

The `GetOpenFileName` uses a common pattern in Windows programming; it takes a struct, which knows its own size, as an argument. In C or C++, declaring these structs would typically be followed with a call to `memset` or `ZeroMemory`. This is not normally necessary in D because D, unlike C, initializes variables automatically. However, it is still important to initialize any static `char`/`wchar` array or `float` members since D initializes them by default to invalid values instead of zero (it does this in such a way that the use of an uninitialized value triggers an error as soon as possible). This is why we set `filenameBuffer[0] = 0` to ensure it is properly terminated as an empty string. Pointers to strings and floats are by default initialized to `null` and may not have to be explicitly set.

See also

▸ Several Windows programming samples translated to D at `https://github.com/AndrejMitrovic/DWinProgramming`

▸ Bindings to the Windows API to replace and expand the minimal set found in `core.sys.windows.windows` can be found at `http://dsource.org/projects/bindings/wiki/WindowsApi`

Removing the Windows console

When you write a GUI program on Windows, you'll often want to suppress the automatic allocation of a console window while building the release executable.

How to do it...

Let's remove the Windows console by executing the following steps:

1. Write your program normally.
2. While compiling, pass `-L/subsystem:windows` to dmd.

How it works...

A D program compiles the program to an `.exe` file, which means it can use all the same linker capabilities as a program in C, including subsystems, 16-bit stubs (though D itself cannot be compiled to 16 bits), resources, and manifests.

The `-L` option of `dmd` forwards the given option to the linker. This can be used to pass any command to the linker, including the platform-specific ones, such as `/subsystem`, seen here. By choosing the Windows subsystem, the operating system will not allocate a console.

There's more...

It is also possible to write a `WinMain` function in D. If you write `WinMain` instead of `main`, the linker will automatically mark it as using the Windows subsystem, without having to use the / `subsystem` switch. If you do, be sure to call `Runtime.initalize()` before doing anything. However, it is generally better to write programs with a normal `main` function and use the linker switch since this ensures the runtime functions are always called correctly without the boilerplate. If you need the module handle or command line in a `main` function, use `GetModuleHandle(null)` and `GetCommandLineW`, respectively.

See also

▸   The `dmd` ZIP file that contains `dmd2/samples/d/winsamp.d` has a sample of how to write a `WinMain` function

Making Linux system calls

Linux system calls are typically performed via a C interface. D can call these just like any other C library functions (see the *Using external libraries* recipe in *Chapter 1, Core Tasks*). Here, we'll write a "Hello World" program using the standard C function for the system call, and say "hello" using inline assembly to demonstrate how that can be done as well.

How to do it...

Making Linux system calls with inline assembly is quite different than making them with the C interface. First, we will look at how it is done with the function, then we'll translate it to the assembly.

With the C interface

Let's make Linux system calls by executing the following steps:

1.   Import the appropriate header from the `core.sys.posix` package, or if it is not present, write the prototype with `extern(C)`.

2.   Call the function like you would call any other function.

The code is as follows:

```
import core.sys.posix.unistd; // analogous to #include <unistd.h>
string hello = "Hello, world!";
write(1 /* stdout file descriptor */, hello.ptr, hello.length);
```

With inline assembly

1. Decompose the arrays you need into separate variables for their pointer and lengths.

2. Use version blocks for each supported architecture and OS.

3. Write the code using the Linux reference documentation for the appropriate registers and numerical arguments.

4. End each group of versions with `static assert(0)` to trigger a compile error on unsupported systems.

The code is follows:

```
string hello = "Hello, world!";
auto hptr = hello.ptr;
auto hlength = hello.length;
version(linux) {
version(D_InlineAsm_X86)
asm {
    mov ECX, hptr;
    mov EDX, hlength;
    mov EBX, 1; // stdout
    mov EAX, 4; // sys_write
    int 0x80; // perform the operation
} else version(D_InlineAsm_X86_64)
asm {
    mov RSI, hptr;
    mov RDX, hlength;
    mov RDI, 1; // stdout
    mov RAX, 1; // sys_write
    syscall; // perform the operation
} else static assert(0, "Unsupported Processor for inline asm");
} else static assert(0, "Unsupported OS for this function");
```

When you run the program, it will print `Hello, world!`.

Inline assembly with the syntax given here only works with the DMD and 1DC compilers on x86 processors (32 or 64 bit). The GDC compiler has different and changing support for the assembly language.

How it works...

Standardized C headers are available in `druntime` under the core package. The `core.stdc.*` package has the standard C library headers. The `core.sys` module has standard headers for the operating system.

The following table has some illustrative examples of a header file and its corresponding D module names:

C header	D module
`#include <stdio.h>`	`import core.stdc.stdio;`
`#include <stdlib.h>`	`import core.stdc.stdlib;`
`#include <unistd.h> /* Unix header */`	`import core.sys.posix.` `unistd;`
`#include <sys/socket.h>`	`import core.sys.posix.` `sys.socket;`
`#include <epoll.h> /* Linux specific */`	`import core.sys.linux.` `epoll;`

If you are unsure whether a header is standardized in Posix or is specific to a particular system such as Linux, you can check the man page for a *Conforming to* section, or simply try to import the module from `core.sys.posix` first, and if that doesn't work, try again with `core.sys.linux`.

If you need a function that is not provided in any core module, you can still call it by copying the function and struct prototypes into your D program, marking them `extern(C)`, as shown in the following code:

```
/* import the basic type definitions */
import core.sys.posix.sys.types;
/* Copy the function prototype from the system documentation */
extern(C) ssize_t write(int fd, const void* buf, size_t count);
// we can now call write!
```

D also has built-in support for the inline assembly code. While the main compilers currently have differing support for inline assembly, here, we're using the syntax for the DMD compiler, which is based on the Intel assembly syntax.

A block of assembly code is denoted by the `asm { }` structure. Inside, the syntax remains similar to D—comments remain in the same D forms, instructions must be separated by semicolons, and D identifiers are still usable. Unlike most assemblers, D's inline `asm` syntax is case sensitive. Instruction names must be in lowercase and register names must be in uppercase.

The assembly language code is rarely portable, so it is also advisable to always put `asm` blocks inside `version` blocks, and be as specific as you can be, at least based on the processor family. Here, we broke it down by the operating system, then by 32-bit and 64-bit `asm` on the x86 processor because the code needs to be different in each case. The `else static assert` function at the end of each group of versions ensures that an unimplemented configuration results in a compilation error rather than the silently buggy or incomplete code. Any time you use version statements, consider terminating the group with `else static assert(0, "message")` for future maintenance.

See also

▶ Go to `http://dlang.org/iasm.html` to read the inline assembly documentation for DMD

▶ Additional documentation for using inline assembly with the LDC compiler at `http://wiki.dlang.org/LDC_inline_assembly_expressions`

▶ Search the Web for a Linux system call reference to learn more about the numbers and arguments of the available functions

Writing part of a C program in D

C and D can link together. This lets us use C functions in D and also lets us use D functions from C. Here, we'll integrate some of the code in D into a C project. This knowledge is also useful for writing callback functions in D while using a C library from the D code, and can be used for the JNI or P/Invoke code in Java and .NET as well. Thanks to `extern(C)`, anything that can interface with C can also interface with D.

Getting ready

If you are using DMD on 32-bit Windows, you'll also want to get DMC for Windows—the Digital Mars C compiler. DMC is automatically installed by the D installer. If you are using DMD from the ZIP file distribution, you can get DMC as a ZIP file from `http://digitalmars.com/`.

How to do it...

Let's execute the following steps to write a part of a C program in D:

1. Before calling any D function from C, be sure to call `rt_init()`. You can declare this to be `extern int rt_init();`. Don't forget to check the return value—it returns `0` if initialization fails.

2. In your D file, write the functions you want as `extern(C)`, taking and returning only the types known to C (for example, integers, structs, pointers, and so on) and not throwing exceptions back to C. The D program can also call functions from the C program by declaring the function prototypes with `extern(C)`.

3. In the C file, copy the function prototype of the D functions and call them.

4. Call `rt_term()` before terminating so that you can terminate the D runtime.

5. Compile and link the programs. Don't forget to link the Phobos library as well.

The following is our C program, `program.c`:

```c
#include <stdio.h>

int rt_init(); // prototypes of standard D runtime functions
void rt_term();

void helloD(); // the prototype of own our D function

void helloC() { // an existing C function we'll call from D
    printf("Hello from C!\n");
}

int main() {
    if(!rt_init()) { // init the D runtime
        fprintf(stderr, "D rt init failed.\n");
        return 1;
    }

    helloD(); // call the D function

    rt_term(); // end the D runtime
    return 0;
}
```

The following is our D file, `test.d`:

```d
import std.stdio, core.stdc.stdio : stderr;

extern(C) void helloC() nothrow; // a function from C

extern(C)
void helloD() nothrow {
    helloC();
    try {
        writeln("hello from D!");
    } catch(Throwable t) {
        fprintf(stderr, "writeln threw an exception.\n");
    }
}
```

Compile the program on 32-bit Windows system using the following commands:

dmc -c program.c
dmd test.d program.obj phobos.lib

Compile the program on Linux using the following commands:

```
gcc -c program.c
dmd test.d program.o
```

You may also choose to compile the D file separately with `dmd -c test.d`, then link both object files together in a separate step. This method may be easier to integrate into a more complex C program build process. Add the D object files in the same way you add any other C object file, and don't forget to link them in the Phobos library as well. You may have to add the location of the Phobos library to your linker command line; for example, adding the `-Lpath/to/dmd2/linux/bin32/lib` argument to `ld` on Linux.

How it works...

D functions with the `extern(C)` linkage follow the C calling convention, and D compilers produce standard object files—just like C compilers. This works both ways; D can access C functions and C can access D functions. While integrating D into a C program, it is important to initialize the D runtime before calling most D functions. The `druntime` library provides the C interface functions, `rt_init` and `rt_term`, to do this for you—just be sure to call them and check for failure, and the D runtime library will handle the other details of its initialization.

D and C cannot read each other's source code directly. This makes it necessary to reproduce the data structure and function prototype declarations in both languages. Often, this isn't much work, but care is required to ensure they remain in sync. If the definitions get out of sync, the code may still compile, but then crash at runtime due to an inconsistency between over what data goes where. This process can often be automated in both directions; `dstep` is a utility that reads C header files and generates a matching D interface module, and `dtoh` reads a D file and generates a corresponding C header file.

The D language will allow `extern(C)` functions to do everything any other function can do, and in many cases, you can make them work in C as well. However, it is recommended to follow the following rules while interfacing with C:

- ▶ Don't pass immutable data to or from a C program because C cannot guarantee that it will not be changed. If immutable data is changed, the result is undefined behavior in D.

- ▶ Don't throw exceptions of any type that pass through the C program. The C compiler knows nothing about exceptions and may not generate the correct code to continue stack unwinding—the exception may be silently lost and the C code almost certainly is not exception-safe, putting it at risk for resource leaks even if the code does work. Note that D's `nothrow` annotation does not apply to unrecoverable errors that, nevertheless, use the exception mechanism. So, it is important to wrap the outermost interface functions in a `try/catch` block, catching the generic `Throwable` superclass to cover both errors and exceptions.

▶ Don't pass the **garbage collector** (**GC**) allocated data that may be stored by the C code. If no reference exists on the D heap—even though C might still hold a reference to the object—the garbage collector will consider it unused and may free it. If your C program stores any pointers, be sure the resource is managed in a way that is compatible with C; for example, passing pointers to buffers created with `malloc` to receive data instead of storing the dynamic array pointers in D).

Once, I was writing an event loop program using the self-pipe technique. The pipe pair was created with an operating system function. The event loop wrote pointers to event structures of the pipe and read them back out on the other side. Under heavier use, it started to crash at random. The reason was that for the split second between writing an event and reading it back out, the garbage collector ran and found no reference to the event object (since the only existing reference was the pointer sitting in the operating system's pipe buffer), thus freeing it. I fixed the problem by allocating the event objects with `malloc` and freeing them with `free` when they were consumed, instead of relying on the garbage collector.

To help with the passing data, it is useful to pass `pointer+length` pairs instead of arrays and pointers to structs instead of classes, similar to how you'd write the functions in C. Internally, your D program may use any features, just mind the interface.

See also

▶ For the source of the `dstep` program, refer to `http://github.com/Jacob-carlborg/dstep`

▶ For the source of the `dtoh` program, refer to `http://github.com/adamdruppe/dtoh`

Interfacing with C++

If you have an existing C++ program and want to start using D, it probably isn't practical to rewrite the entire application. However, it may be possible to start writing new components of the application in D. Let's look at how this can be done.

Getting ready

Review how D interfaces with C. Any `extern` functions of C work exactly the same way in C++. You'll also need to get the appropriate C++ compiler. On 32-bit Windows, you'll need the Digital Mars C compiler to pair with DMD. On 64-bit Windows, the Microsoft Visual C++ compiler will work. On Linux, use g++.

Let's interface D with C++ by executing the following steps:

1. Use C++ functions by marking them `extern(C++)`; otherwise, use them in the same way as you use C functions. You can also write a D function with the `extern(C++)` linkage and use it from C++ by writing the prototype.

2. Use interfaces marked `extern(C++)` to access objects or to implement objects. Any virtual function in the C++ class should have a corresponding method in the D interface, appearing in exactly the same order. If possible, use pure virtual functions in an abstract class in C++; this will exactly match the D interface. If not, you can make it work with a careful listing of all virtual functions.

3. If you implement a C++ object in D, inherit it from the interface and mark each method `extern(C++)`. If you had to define unusable entries to make the virtual table match (for example, a virtual destructor), implement these as do-nothing methods.

4. Pass object references between the languages and access the methods. In addition, create factory and destruction functions that deal with the interface. Manage all memory that is stored across language boundaries manually. Failure to do this may cause an object to get accidentally garbage collected while being used by the C++ code.

The following is some example code. First, we'll look at the C++ code. We won't use header files for brevity:

```cpp
#include<stdio.h>
#include<stdlib.h>

// our C++ class
class Animal {
public:
  // ideally, we would prefer to use classes
  // with no member variables and no additional
  // functions. D and C++ don't understand each
  // other's constructors and destructors and will
  // have different ideas as to where members will be found.

  // But, perfection may not be realistic with
  // existing code, so we'll see how to possibly work with it.
  int member; // we must not use this on a D object *at all*

  virtual ~Animal() {}

  // this is what we really want: abstract virtual
```

```
    // functions we can implement with an interface.
    virtual void speak() = 0;
};

// A concrete C++ class we'll use in D via the interface
class Dog : public Animal {
  void speak() {
    printf("Woof\n");
  }
};

// Our D functions
extern "C++" void useAnimal(Animal* t);
extern "C++" Animal* getCat();
extern "C++" void freeCat(Animal* cat);

// D Runtime functions from the library
extern "C" int rt_init();
extern "C" void rt_term();

// RAII struct for D runtime initialization and termination
struct DRuntime {
  DRuntime() {
    if(!rt_init()) {
      // you could also use an exception
      fprintf(stderr, "D Initialization failed");
      exit(1);
    }
  }
  ~DRuntime() {
    rt_term();
  }
};

void main() {
  // be sure to initialize the D runtime before using it
  DRuntime druntime;

  Dog dog;
  // use a C++ class in a D function
  useAnimal(&dog);
```

```
    // use a D class from C++
    // you may use a smart pointer or RAII struct here too
    // so the resource is managed automatically.
    Animal* cat = getCat(); // use a factory function
    cat->speak(); // call the function!
    // it was created in D, so it needs to be destroyed by D too
    freeCat(cat);
}
```

Now, let's have a look at the code at the D side, which is as follows:

```
import std.stdio;
import core.stdc.stdlib; // for malloc

extern(C++)
interface Animal {
   // since the C++ class had a virtual destructor
   // we must define an entry, but we don't want to use it
   void _destructorDoNotUse();
   void speak();
}

class Cat : Animal {
   // Note that we did *not* copy the C++ member variable.
   // Doing so would be futile; the layouts will not match.
   // Creating D child classes of a C++ class with member
   // variables should be avoided if at all possible.

   extern(C++)
   void _destructorDoNotUse() {}

   extern(C++)
   void speak() { try {writeln("Meow!");}catch(Throwable) {} }
}

// We'll implement a factory function for getting Cats
extern(C++)
Animal getCat() {
   // Manage the memory with malloc and free for full control
   import std.conv;
   enum size = __traits(classInstanceSize, Cat);
   auto memory = malloc(size)[0 .. size];
   return emplace!Cat(memory);
}
```

```
extern(C++)
void freeCat(Animal animal) {
  auto cat = cast(Cat) animal;
  if(cat !is null) {
    destroy(cat);
    free(cast(void*) cat);
  }
}

// This can also use an object from C++
extern(C++)
void useAnimal(Animal t) {
  t.speak();
}
```

Compile and run the program separately, just like with C, remembering to link it in Phobos. It will print the result of the Dog and Cat objects speaking to each other.

How to do it...

Always create and destroy objects using methods from the same language where it was created, and always use them through pointers (in C++) or interfaces (in D). Remember to keep a reference to D objects somewhere in D, or manage the memory manually so that the garbage collector doesn't reap it prematurely.

To create and destroy the D class instances with malloc, we must not use the built-in new operator. Instead, we will allocate memory and initialize the object separately. We learn the number of bytes needed by using __traits(classInstanceSize, ClassName). Then, we allocate the memory to the block using malloc and immediately slice it to the appropriate size. This lets D functions know the size of the block (which they would not know with a pointer).

Finally, the std.conv.emplace function constructs the given argument in the specified memory buffer, returning the reference to it. After the memory block argument, emplace will also take constructor arguments for the class, if any.

Complementing destruction is the free function. Similar to construction, this is done in two steps: first destroying the object, then freeing the memory.

Memory management can be improved by also using other C++ techniques such as a smart pointer, and/or the D functions could provide reference counting. Use C++ practices consistent with the rest of your project for best integration.

The preceding example neglected a C++ member variable. If it's possible, do not implement child classes of a C++ class with members in D. You may use a C++ class with members, but inheriting from it is potentially risky because if the member is used by any C++ function on the D object, it may corrupt your memory. It is strongly recommended to refactor the C++ code to use abstract interface-style classes and inherit from them in D, instead of trying to match it.

All the rules that apply to the writing part of a C program in D also apply here, with the biggest difference being that you can use some C++ or D classes. In particular, despite C++ supporting exceptions, you should not throw exceptions across language boundaries, since the two language's exception models may not be compatible. This is why our `speak` method swallows any exception thrown by `writeln`.

Keeping two sets of definitions in sync is bug-prone work. The `dtoh` and `dstep` tools that work with the C code also work with C++; try to use them when you can.

See also

▶ You can view Manu Evans' talk from *DConf 2013*, where he discussed integrating D with a C++ game engine, at `http://dconf.org/2013/talks/evans_1.html`

Using structs to mimic the C++ object structure

With D's low-level control, we can access any kind of data structure and paint nice types over it. To demonstrate this, we'll access a C++ object from D. The same technique can also be used for memory-mapped hardware.

You need to take caution that this is not portable. It may not work even across different versions of the same C++ compiler. If you use this trick, make sure it is in an environment where you know the binary layout.

How to do it...

Let's mimic the C++ object structure by executing the following steps:

1. Investigate the C++ ABI on your system. Typically, but not necessarily, a C++ object consists of a pointer to the virtual function table, the members of the parent class (recursively), and the members of the child class. If the C++ object has no virtual functions, it does not have a virtual table; the layout is then compatible with a C struct with the same data members.

2. Create an `extern(C++)` interface for the virtual table, like we did for the regular interaction between D and C++. The interface should inherit from the parent class' virtual function table interface.

3. Make a struct to represent the C++ object. First, put a `void*` member that represents the virtual table.

4. Write a property that returns the `this` pointer casted to the virtual interface type.

5. Use `alias this` with the property we wrote in step 4.

6. List the data members in the same order in which they appear with compatible types as the C++ object.

7. Write a function prototype, which is a placeholder for the C++ object's constructors, and use `pragma(mangle)` to assign it a matching name. You may have to figure out the C++ mangles experimentally; compile the C++ application and inspect its object file.

8. Write D constructors that forward to the C++ constructors.

9. Rewrite C++ destructors—calling it directly tends to attempt deallocating the object, which will result in a crash.

10. List non-virtual functions normally.

11. Use the object and hope it doesn't crash! Here, I used dmd 2.065 and g++ 4.4.4 on 32-bit Linux.

The following is the C++ code to define the object:

```cpp
class Class {
    public:
        Class(int n);
        virtual void add(int a);
        void print();
      int number;
};
void Class::print() { printf("Number = %d\n", number); }
Class::Class(int n) { printf("constructed\n"); number = number; }
void Class::add(int a) { number += a; }
```

The following is the D code to access the C++ object:

```d
struct Class {
    extern(C++) interface Vtable {
        void add(int a);
    }
     void* vtbl;
     @property Vtable getVirtuals() {  return cast(Vtable) &this; }
     alias getVirtuals this;
```

```
        extern(C++) void print();
        int number;
    pragma(mangle, "_ZN5ClassC2Ei")
    extern(C++) void ctor(int a);
    this(int a) { ctor(a); }
}
void main() {
    Class c = Class(0);
    c.num = 10;
    c.add(10);
    c.print();
}
```

It will print the following output:

```
constructed
Number = 20
```

How it works...

Data is data as far as the computer hardware is concerned. If we can map a type to the same bits in memory and use it in the appropriate places, it will work, irrespective of whether that type declaration is written in C++, D, or any other language.

In addition to D's built-in C++ support and other similar features, such as constructors and destructors, we can use a few other features to make this smoother to use.

The first one is `alias this`. When a member that is is requested is not in the object itself, or when an implicit conversion is requested, it attempts substituting the `alias this` value instead. This allows method forwarding and controlled implicit conversion, which implements a kind of subtyping—this is very similar to class inheritance.

The second is `pragma(mangle)`. This changes the name of the function in the object file. If we match calling convention, arguments, return value, and name, we can call the code. The computer doesn't care about anything beyond that! It would also be possible to write code that automatically mangles D functions with C++ names and passes the return value of that function to `pragma(mangle)`. The function would be evaluated at compile time to build the name string. We'll look at these techniques later in the book. Here, we got the mangled name experimentally (in this case, it is correct for my version of g++ on Linux; your results may vary).

We also used a nested interface for the virtual function table. This simply keeps the outer namespace clean; it has no functionality difference.

Communicating with external processes

If you are performing a task and encounter a stage where another program does an excellent job, is it possible to call that program and use the results in your D program? The answer is yes. Here, we'll look at using `std.process` to run another program and send it input and read its output.

How to do it...

Let's communicate with external processes by executing the following steps:

1. Import `std.process`.
2. Call `pipeProcess` to start the program you want, storing the return value. You may want to put the external process name in a version block, as the same program might not be available on other operating systems.
3. Use the returned handles to communicate with the process as though it was a file.
4. Close the handles when you are finished.
5. Wait for the process to exit.

The code is as follows:

```
import std.process, std.stdio;
auto info = pipeProcess("child_program");
scope(exit) wait(info.pid);
info.stdin.writeln("data to send to the process");
info.stdin.close();
foreach(line; stdout.byLine)
    writeln("Received ", line, " from child.");
```

The child program may be anything that writes to its `stdout` handle. For example, have a look at the following code:

```
import std.stdio;
void main() {
    writeln("Hello!");
    writeln("Second line.");
}
```

Calling the function from the preceding program will print the following:

```
Received Hello! from child.
Received Second line. from child.
```

How it works...

Phobos' `std.process` module includes several cross-platform functions to communicate with other processes. It can run programs, spawn shells, and create pipes on standard handles. Once created, the resultant pipes are presented as `std.stdio.File` objects and can be written to (in the case of the `stdin` handle, you write to the child program's input) the input and read from (for `stdout` and `stderr`, reading the child process' output) the output like any other file.

You can also access the operating system or C functions yourself, bypassing the Phobos functions. This is necessary if you need asynchronous I/O with the process.

You may also wish to define an RPC protocol to use over your pipes, to call functions as well as pass data. Any network application protocol can be adapted to work with local processes and pipes. For example, there are D bindings to Apache Thrift that may be of use.

See also

▶ The D bindings to Apache Thrift can be accessed at `http://code.dlang.org/packages/thrift`

Communicating with a dynamic scripting language

D's features also lead to easy integration with dynamic languages. It can host a dynamic type as well as dynamic objects.

Getting ready

To begin, download bindings to a scripting language. Here, we'll use the one I wrote whose syntax is inspired by both D and JavaScript. It was written with the goal to blur the line between the D code and the script code—the scripting language's dynamic type can also be used in D itself. Download `jsvar.d` and `script.d` from the following website:

▶ `http://github.com/adamdruppe/script`

Build your program with all three files on the command line, as follows:

```
dmd yourfile.d jsvar.d script.d
```

How to do it...

Let's execute the following steps to communicate with JavaScript:

1. Create an object to wrap the script engine with a friendlier API.

2. Prepare the script engine by passing data and function references to it. It may be necessary to wrap D functions in transforming functions to match the script engine's layout.

3. Use `opDispatch` and `variadic` arguments to forward the D function call syntax to the script to use user functions.

4. Evaluate the user script.

5. Call a user-defined script function.

The code is as follows:

```
struct ScriptEngine { // step 1
    import arsd.script;

    this(string scriptSource) { // step 2
        scriptGlobals = var.emptyObject;

        // add a function, transforming functions and returns
        import std.stdio;
        scriptGlobals.write = delegate var(var _this, var[] args) {
            writeln(args[0]);
            return var(null);
        };

        // run the user's script code (step 4)
        interpret(scriptSource, scriptGlobals);
    }

    var scriptGlobals;

    auto opDispatch(string func, T...)(T t) { // step 3
        if(func !in scriptGlobals)
            throw new Exception("method \"" ~ func ~ "\" not found in
script");
        var[] args;
        foreach(arg; t)
            args ~= var(arg);
        return scriptGlobals[func].apply(scriptGlobals, args);
    }

}
```

```
void main() {
    // step 5
    auto scriptContext = ScriptEngine(q{
        // this is script source code!
        function hello(a) {
            // call the D function with the argument
            write("Hello, " ~ a ~ "!");

            // and return a value too
            return "We successfully said hello.";
        }
    });

    // call a script function and print out the result
    import std.stdio;
    writeln("The script returned: ", scriptContext.hello("user"));
}
```

How it works...

If a method isn't found in an object, and the object implements a member called `opDispatch`, D will rewrite the missing method as follows:

```
obj.name(args...); // if obj doesn't have a method called
nameobj.opDispatch!"name"(args...); // it is rewritten into this
```

The method name is passed as a compile-time argument. The `opDispatch` implementation may thus be able to handle this without a runtime cost. If the lookup must happen at runtime, as is the case here, we can use the compile-time argument in the same way that we'd use a runtime argument, including forwarding it to a runtime lookup function.

The `opDispatch` function, like any other function, can also take both additional compile-time and runtime arguments. Here, we defined it as a variadic template with T..., which is an arbitrary length list of types. The exact list is determined automatically when you call the function. In short, this function can accept any number of arguments of any types. This is perfect for forwarding to a dynamic function, like a user-defined script method.

 The `writeln` function of `std.stdio` is also a variadic template in this form. That is why you can pass it a mixed list of strings, integers, or any other types and it knows how to handle them all, even with a generic format string.

In a `(T...)` `(T t)` template argument list, T is the list of types and t is the list of values. Both T and t can be looped over with `foreach`, similar to an array.

Inside the loop, we will build an array of dynamic variables to pass to the script engine. The constructor of `var` automatically handles conversions from arbitrary types by using `std.traits` to categorize them into basic categories, and keeps a flag internally that says which category it is currently holding. The following code is an excerpt:

```
this(T)(T t) {
    static if(isIntegral!T) {
        this._type = Type.Integral;
        this._payload._integral = to!long(t);
    } else static if(isSomeString!T) {
        this._type = Type.String;
        this._payload._string = to!string(t);
    } else static assert(0, "Unsupported type: " ~ T.stringof);
}
```

The constructor takes an argument of any type T. Using `static if`, it checks whether the type is a type of integer or a type of string. For these types, the code stores the internal flag and the value, which is converted to one uniform type that can represent the whole category. This lets us automatically handle as many D types as possible with the least amount of script glue code. The full implementation in `jsvar` checks every supported category it can handle, including objects, floating point values, functions, and arrays. They all follow a pattern similar to this.

> The script engine has already provided an implementation of various operators, including calling functions. You can simply write `scriptGlobals["hello"]("user")` using either the `opIndex` function written in `jsvar` or `scriptGlobals[name](t)` written in our `opDispatch`—forwarding the variadic argument list—and it would build the `args` array for us. The `var` type—a user-defined dynamic type from the `jsvar` module you downloaded—also implements `opDispatch`, though calling functions with it currently requires a second set of parenthesis to disambiguate function calling from property assignment.

We also return a value from this function. In some cases, you'd have to write a converter for the script engine's return value, checking its type flag type and offering an `opCast`, `to`, or `get` function, which works in the reverse of the preceding constructor example, or perhaps convert it to a string with `toString`. The `var` type used here implements a `get` function using the type family check like the constructor as well as a `toString` function, which makes it just work in `writeln`.

We also made the `writeln` function available to the script by wrapping it in a helper function that accepts script variables, calls the D function, and then returns an appropriate variable back to the script. Like with calling functions, this can be (and is, in `jsvar`) automated so that nothing is necessary beyond writing `scriptGlobals.write = &writeln!var;`, but we did it the long way here to show how it is done. The automatic generator implementation works in the same way using a bit of compile-time reflection to get the details right for each function. We'll cover the reflection features later in the book.

Why would we have to write &writeln!var instead of just &writeln? As writeln has compile-time arguments—though they are typically deduced automatically while calling writeln (they are always there)—we have to specify which ones we want at compile time before it is possible to get a runtime function pointer. Different compile-time arguments may mean a different function pointer. If the function didn't have compile-time arguments, then &func would work.

Lastly, we used a peculiar type of a string literal for the source, that is, a q{ string literal }. This works the same as any other string literal, with one difference; the q{} literal needs to superficially look like the valid D code (technically, it must pass the D tokenizer). It must not have unterminated quotes and unmatched braces. As far as the consuming function is concerned though, it is just a string, like any other. We could have also loaded the script from a file. We used q{} here because the script source looks like D source. Most syntax-highlighting editors continue to highlight q{} strings like regular code, giving us colorization for the script as well. However, which kind of string literal you use comes down to the circumstances and personal preference.

Using Windows' COM

Component Object Model (**COM**) is a Microsoft technology used for interoperability between Windows programs. D has built-in support for basic COM, and using its features, we can also automate the implementation of advanced COM features.

Here, we'll write a COM server and client with the help of a library and look at the implementation.

Getting ready

Download the Win32 bindings from http://dsource.org/projects/bindings and the comhelpers.d file from http://github.com/adamdruppe/com.

How to do it...

COM, like shared libaries, uses a client-server model. First, we'll write a COM server and then write its corresponding COM client.

COM server

Let's write a COM server by executing the following steps:

1. Generate GUIDs for your interface and class using a GUID generation tool.
2. Import win32.unknwn and comhelpers.

3. Write your interface definition, inheriting from `IUnknown` and marking all methods `extern(Windows)`. Attach the IID (interface's GUID) to the interface with the `ComGuid` attribute. Each method should return `HRESULT`.

4. Add the CLSID to the interface file as a constant.

   The code for the preceding steps is as follows:

```
import win32.basetyps;
import win32.unknwn;

import comhelpers;

@ComGuid(GUID(0x00421140, 0, 0,
[0xC0, 0, 0, 0, 0, 0, 0, 0x46]))
interface IHello : IUnknown {
    extern (Windows) :
    int Print();
}


// this is the class id that we can use to instantiate in the
client and attach to the
// class in the implementation
enum GUID CLSID_Hello = GUID(0x30421140, 0, 0,
[0xC0, 0, 0, 0, 0, 0, 0, 0x46]);
```

5. Create a separate file with the class definition. Inherit this class from the interface you defined and attach the CLSID to the class using the `ComGuid` attribute.

6. Use the `mixin ComObject!()` method in your class and implement your interface.

7. To enable COM automation on your object, for example, to make it usable from VBScript or JScript, also inherit from `IDispatch` when defining your class and add `mixin IDispatchImpl!()` to the class body.

8. At the bottom of the file, add `mixin ComServerMain!(YourClass, "ProgId", "1.0")` class, where `"ProgId"` is your desired Program ID (for example, `"MSXML2. XmlHttp"`) and `1.0` is your version number. The program ID and version number are used by clients to locate your object.

9. You may have to compile with `dmd -d` to enable deprecated features because the Win32 bindings are infrequently updated. The code for this is as follows:

```
import win32.winuser;

import comhelpers;
import ihello;

@ComGuid(CLSID_Hello)
class CHello : IHello, IDispatch {
```

```
            mixin ComObject!();
            mixin IDispatchImpl!();

            extern(Windows)
            public override HRESULT Print() {
                    import std.stdio; writeln("cool?");
                    MessageBoxA(null, "CHello.Print()", null, MB_OK);
                    return NOERROR;
            }
    }

    mixin ComServerMain!(CHello, "Hello", "1.0");
```

10. Create a module definition file (`yourname.def`) with the following contents:

```
LIBRARY          yourname
EXETYPE          NT
SUBSYSTEM        WINDOWS
EXPORTS
        DllGetClassObject     = _DllGetClassObject@12
        DllCanUnloadNow       = _DllCanUnloadNow@0
        DllRegisterServer     = _DllRegisterServer@0
        DllUnregisterServer   = _DllUnregisterServer@0
```

11. Compile your interface file, class file, module definition file, and the downloaded `comhelpers.d` file together to generate your DLL.

12. Register your server with `regsvr32 yourdll.dll` (this will require administrator access on the computer), or use a manifest file to enable registration-free COM in your client application.

COM client

Let's write a COM client by executing the following steps:

1. Import `comhelpers.d` and the interface file you created for the server.

2. Create the object with `createObject!interface(CLSID)`. If you are using an object without the `ComGuid` attribute, you can specify it manually in the compile-time argument list after the interface. Alternatively, you may call `CoCreateInstance` from the Windows API directly.

3. Use it. The `createObject` object of `comhelper` returns a wrapper object that automatically handles calling `AddRef` and `Release`.

The code is as follows:

```
import comhelpers;
import ihello;
```

```
void main() {
        auto obj = createObject!(IHello)(CLSID_Hello);
        obj.Print();
}
```

How it works...

D has some built-in understanding of COM—it recognizes the `IUnknown` interface. Anything derived from it is known to be a COM object. This is a bit rudimentary and D can do better with the help of a library—that's where `comhelpers.d` comes in. It is not necessary, nor part of the standard library; you can always call the Windows functions yourself. It handles some boilerplate code (with `mixin` templates) and binds GUIDs to interfaces and classes with a D feature called user-defined attributes to make the code easier to write.

There's more...

If you are on a 64-bit Windows system and building a 32-bit DLL, you'll have to register the COM server using the 32-bit version of `regsrv32`.

5
Resource Management

In this chapter, we will look at the resource management techniques of D. We'll learn the following:

- ▸ Avoiding the garbage collector
- ▸ Making a reference-counted object
- ▸ Manually managing class memory
- ▸ Using scope guards to manage transactions
- ▸ Creating an array replacement
- ▸ Managing lent resources
- ▸ Creating a `NotNull` struct
- ▸ Using unique pointers
- ▸ Using RAII and handling the limitations of class destructors

Introduction

Resource management is an important aspect of most programs. D's rich abstraction support makes it possible to use a variety of techniques, from script-like quick coding with the garbage collector to low-level manual control.

Avoiding the garbage collector

D programs typically use a garbage collector that can make memory management both easier and more efficient. With the garbage collector, you don't have to keep track of object ownership and can defer free memory to a later point, which can boost performance.

However, while the garbage collector is useful, it doesn't absolve you of all thought in the area of memory management, especially when performance is important. In tight loops, you'll want to avoid the garbage collector. The way to do this is to avoid garbage collection allocations. No garbage collection allocation means no garbage collection cycle.

How to do it...

In order to avoid the garbage collector, perform the following steps:

1. Find the hotspots in your application. Typically, this means focusing on your innermost loops.

2. Remove functions and operations that call into the GC:
   - Array literals, except the ones initializing a variable marked static
   - Array append or concatenation
   - Array length assignment
   - Any associative array operation or literal
   - The `new` expression
   - Closures, except the ones marked `scope` in the function's parameter list
   - Nested structs that use local variables that are returned from a function
   - Any function that does one of these things

3. Move the allocations outside the hotspot or replace them with alternatives:
   - Make `static` and `immutable` array literal initializers
   - Use static array buffers when possible instead of dynamically allocated arrays
   - Use stack-allocated classes
   - Mark delegate arguments `scope` in the function definition

> If you load your program in a debugger and set a break point at the beginning of your hotspot, you can then break on the gc_alloc and gc_qalloc functions to find allocations at runtime. Also, if you use the ldc compiler, try the -nogc command-line switch when compiling a module.

How it works...

The D garbage collector only runs at program termination and when a garbage collector allocation is attempted. It doesn't have enough available memory to fulfil the request. Garbage collector allocations are not necessarily easy to find. The syntax may not stand out or they may be hidden behind library functions; however, if you successfully avoid these language constructs, you will successfully avoid the garbage collector.

You'll still have to manage your resources. We'll look at various techniques to help with this throughout the rest of this chapter.

 Can we write a program without a garbage collector at all? Yes, in fact, we can write D programs that use the majority of the language, yet don't use the full D runtime or standard library at all and will even work on bare metal without an operating system. However, since this severely limits your library choices, it isn't always a practical option.

Making a reference-counted object

A common technique to manage resources is reference counting. D's structs provide the necessary infrastructure to automate reference counting.

How to do it...

In order to make a reference-counted object, perform the following steps:

1. Write a struct with its only data member being a pointer to the object. You may write a nested `struct` to hold the data, or it may be a pointer to a library.

2. Add `alias this` to the pointer so that operations will be automatically forwarded to it.

3. Make a **constructor**, if possible, or a static factory method that acquires the object and increases the reference count.

4. Write a **postblit** that increases the reference count.

5. Write a **destructor** that decreases the reference count and frees the object if necessary.

6. Keep in mind that the data pointer may be null, and check for that in each function. Consider the following code:

```
struct RefCountedObject {
  private struct Implementation {
    /* other contents here */

    int refcount;
  }

  Implementation* data;

  alias data this;

  static RefCountedObject create() {
```

```
        RefCountedObject o = void;
        o.data = new Implementation();
        o.data.refcount = 1;
        writeln("Created."); // so we can see it in action
        return o;
    }

    this(this) {
        if(data is null) return;
        data.refcount++;
        writeln("Copied.    Refcount = ", data.refcount);
    }

    ~this() {
        if(data is null) return;
        data.refcount--;
        writeln("Released. Refcount = ", data.refcount);
        if(data.refcount == 0)
        writeln("Destroyed.");
    }
}
```

How it works...

The general idea of reference counting is to increment the count every time the reference is copied and decrement it every time a reference ceases to exist. D's structs provide two functions that can do exactly this: postblits and destructors.

When a `struct` object is copied, the data is first blitted (bit-block transfer; a straightforward copy of the object's memory) to the new location (a shallow copy operation). Then the postblit function, if present, is called on the recipient object. The postblit is defined with the syntax `this(this) { /* code */ }`.

Whenever `struct` provably ceases to exist—goes out of scope after being left behind by a thrown exception, being written over, or being collected by the garbage collector—its destructor is called, if present. The destructor is defined with the syntax `~this() { /* code */ }`.

It is important that the reference count is stored separately from `struct`. If the count were a regular member variable, it would be copied along with the reference, making it useless. A static member variable would be shared across all instances of the struct, which makes it unsuitable to manage distinct objects as well. Instead, we use a pointer to the object with the reference count.

 If we were using a C object with functions to add and remove references, we could hold the pointer to the C object and simply call those functions in the postblit and destructor, respectively.

Since our key member is a pointer, we need to remember that it may be null and offer a way to initialize it. Since D's structs cannot have default constructors, we instead use a factory function. The factory function acquires the function and initializes the reference count to one.

Afterward, we can use the object normally, thanks to `alias this`. All method calls will be forwarded to the inner object. The `alias this` declaration also allows implicit conversion to the inner object's type, which could break the reference counting encapsulation. This is why we made `Implementation` private. If it is not possible to make the inner object private, avoid this situation by either writing forwarding functions yourself (this can be automated with code generation, which we'll cover later in the book) or implement a code review policy, prohibiting the direct declaration of the inner object's type.

See also

▶ `http://dlang.org/phobos/std_typecons.html#RefCounted` is a standard library wrapper that adds reference counting to an existing object. It will not (at the time of writing this book) work with class objects, nor will it give you the same level of control as doing it yourself.

Manually managing class memory

The new operator in D uses the garbage collector, but it isn't the only option. When interfacing with other languages' code or working in a constrained-resource environment (possibly including tight loops on fast PCs!), it is useful to avoid the new operator. Let's see how.

How to do it...

In order to manage class memory manually, perform the following steps:

1. Get the size of the memory block you need to use:
   `__traits(classInstanceSize, ClassName)`.
2. Allocate the memory, slicing it to get a sized array.
3. Use `std.conv.emplace` to construct the class in place and cast the memory to the new type.
4. Stop using the untyped memory block. Instead, use only the class reference.
5. When you are finished, use `destroy()` to call the object's destructor, then free the memory.
6. Be careful not to store the reference where it might be used after the memory is freed. You may want to create a reference counting `struct` to help manage the memory.

How it works...

The __traits function retrieves information about a type that uses compile-time reflection. The first argument is the data you want and the subsequent arguments are specific to each query. Typically, the second argument is an identifier or a type and the third argument, if necessary, is a member name string to drill down to more details. The __traits function returns data in the same way as a function call.

Here, we use __traits(classInstanceSize), which takes a class type as an argument and returns the number of bytes needed by the instantiated object. We cannot use ClassName.sizeof directly because objects are always reference types in D; ClassName.sizeof returns the size of a pointer to the data (a constant), not the size of the data itself.

Once we get the size of the object, we can allocate the memory. This can be done by any method. We could use the C standard libraries: import core.stdc.stdlib; and void* buffer = malloc(size). We could also define a static array ubyte[size] buffer;. Here, size would need to be available at compile time for the static array method. To achieve that, use enum: enum size = __traits(classInstanceSize, ClassName); or we could use any other method.

After getting the memory block, we need to slice it to the right size. Slicing it ties a length to the pointer, which used by the emplace function to ensure the buffer is large enough. Consider the following code snippet:

```
auto bufferSlice = buffer[0 .. size];
```

Finally, we pass the slice to std.conv.emplace. Consider the following code snippet:

```
import std.conv;
auto classReference = emplace!ClassName(bufferSlice,
  args_to_constructor...);
```

This casts the memory block to the correct type (that is why it is in std.conv—it converts untyped memory into typed memory via in-place construction), copies the initial memory image to the block, and calls the appropriate constructor to initialize the object.

The implementation of std.conv.emplace performs two of the three steps of the new operator. The new operator allocates memory of the class size, copies the initial contents (typeid(Class).init) to the newly allocated memory, and calls the requested class constructor on the new object. The emplace function does the latter two steps, but not the first, thereby giving you control over the memory allocation strategy.

Once the object is created, accessing its memory directly is undefined behavior. Thus, you shouldn't use the buffer variables again, except to free them (if necessary) once you are sure no more references will be used. You can use it normally through the reference to call methods, perform dynamic casts, or do anything else that you could do through any other reference.

The `destroy` function, which is located in the automatically imported `object.d` module, calls the class' destructor but does not attempt to free the memory. After destroying the object and making sure that no more references to it exist, you may free the memory using the `pair` function with your allocator (for example, free if you allocated with `malloc`). If necessary, you may cast the reference back to `void*`:

```
MyClass c = myMallocAllocator!MyClass(); // allocate with malloc
free(cast(void*) c); // cast the reference back to a pointer
```

See also

▶ Check out `http://dlang.org/traits.html` for a complete list of all trait arguments

▶ Also, have a look at `http://dlang.org/phobos/std_traits.html` for library wrappers and enhancements for the compile-time reflection built into the language

Using scope guards to manage transactions

D doesn't require you to make wrapper types or write try/catch statements all the time. You can also use scope guards. They can be triggered by three conditions: `exit`, `success`, or `failure`. Here, we'll perform a multistep transaction with scope guards to ensure exception safety.

How to do it...

In order to use scope guards to manage transactions, perform the following steps:

1. Begin your transaction.
2. Write a `scope(success)` guard to commit the transaction immediately after starting it (if committing isn't implicit).
3. Write a `scope(failure)` guard to roll back the transaction immediately after starting it. You may use multiple blocks to rollback multiple steps.
4. Write a `scope(exit)` guard to free any resources. Write the free code immediately after the acquisition code. You may use multiple blocks to free multiple resources.

5. Write the following code for your transaction:

```
{
    // performing a SQL transaction
    database.query("START TRANSACTION");
    scope(success) database.query("COMMIT");
    scope(failure) database.query("ROLLBACK");
    database.query(step_one); // these should throw on failure
    database.query(step_two);
}
{
    // performing a multi-part file download
    auto connection = Connection.acquire();
    scope(exit) connection.close(); // release code immediately
    after acquisition
    connection.download("file1");
    scope(failure) std.file.remove("file1"); // undo code
        immediately after perform code
    connection.download("file2");
    scope(failure) std.file.remove("file2");
}
```

How it works...

D's scope guards are very useful to manage resources in an exception-safe way at the point of use. Each scope statement registers the code to be run on the given condition; `success` if the function returns without throwing an exception, `failure` if it exits by exception, or `exit`, which is unconditional. The code is executed in the reverse order of registration and registration happens with regular flow control, as shown in the following code snippet:

```
scope(exit) writeln("Running scope exit");
scope(success) writeln("Running scope success");
return;
scope(exit) writeln("This is never run since the function returned
before it was registered.")
```

Running this code will print `Running scope success` and then `Running scope exit`.

 Implementation wise, `scope(exit)` is rewritten into a `finally{}` block, `scope(success)` is rewritten into code appended to the end of a `try {}` block, and `scope(failure)` is implemented at the end of a `try catch {}` block, which rethrows the original exception after running the handler.

The advantage of `scope(success)` over putting the `commit` code at the end of the function is that `scope(success)` is written once, but always run, even if you have multiple exit points (return statements) from the function.

Creating an array replacement

Many operations on D's built-in array slices use the garbage collector. If you want to use alternate resource management strategies, you'll want a replacement type, which implements operators that can be used with the other strategy and disables those that cannot be used. It is possible to avoid all allocations using a static stack buffer, which can give a considerable performance improvement. We'll create an array replacement, which uses a static buffer for a predicted size and grows into a dynamically allocated buffer, if required.

How to do it...

To create an array replacement, perform the following steps:

1. Define a struct that takes an element type and expected size.

2. Define variables with the key components: a static buffer with the expected size, a slice to the current buffer, and the current length.

3. Write a destructor to free the memory, if you are managing it manually.

4. Overload the convenience operators you want on the array: length, capacity, reserve, append, and slice.

5. Disable the operators you do not want to use. For example, concatenation or copying may be disabled because those operations are inconvenient and error prone without the garbage collector's help.

6. Use `alias this` if you want implicit slicing. Consider the following code:

```
struct MyArray(T, size_t expectedSize = 0) {
  private T[expectedSize] staticBuffer;
  private T[] activeBuffer;
  private size_t currentLength;

  /+
  // if you want to use malloc instead of gc

  // don't copy this; we own our own memory
  // note that if you slice this, that is a borrowed
    reference;
  // don't store it.
  @disable this(this); // disable copying

  ~this() {
    // frees the memory if it was malloced
    if(activeBuffer.ptr !is staticBuffer.ptr)
    free(activeBuffer.ptr);
  }
  +/
```

```
public void reserve(size_t s) {
  if(s > activeBuffer.length)
  activeBuffer.reserve(s); // GC operation.
    alternatively, you could use realloc
}

public @property size_t length() {
  return currentLength;
}

public @property void length(size_t newLength) {
  // make sure we're using the static buffer first
  if(activeBuffer is null)
  activeBuffer = staticBuffer[];

  // then if we don't have enough room, we'll reallocate
    with
  // the GC (its own capacity should optimize this)
  if(newLength > activeBuffer.length) {
    activeBuffer.length = newLength; // GC operation
    // alternatively, you could use realloc
  }

  if(newLength < currentLength)
  activeBuffer[newLength .. currentLength] = T.init;

  currentLength = newLength;
}

public void clear() { length = 0; }

// disable concatenation
@disable void opBinary(string op : "~")(T t){}
@disable void opBinary(string op : "~")(T[] t){}

// but customize appending
public T opOpAssign(string op : "~")(T t) {
  length = currentLength + 1;
  return activeBuffer[currentLength - 1] = t;
}

public T[] opOpAssign(string op: "~")(T[] t) {
  auto start = currentLength;
  length = start + t.length;
```

```
        return activeBuffer[start .. start + t.length] = t[];
    }

    public T[] opSlice() {
        return activeBuffer[0 .. currentLength];
    }
    alias opSlice this;
}
// test usage
void main() {
    // declare your array of ints with an optimized size of
        ten
    MyArray!(int, 10) intArray;
    myArray ~= 1; // populate it
    myArray.length = 3; // change the length
    import std.stdio;
    writeln(myArray[]); // print the current contents
}
```

How it works...

This array replacement serves two purposes; it optimizes the number of allocations and gives us control over the allocation method. To understand why this is valuable, we need to compare it against similar operations with built-in dynamic (garbage collection allocated) arrays.

Garbage collection arrays do contain appending and preallocation optimizations, including a reserve method that, like our reserve method, preallocates space up to at least the given capacity so that the subsequent append operations perform faster.

However, slice semantics are very conservative. To avoid the possibility of stomping over another slice's memory, reducing the length of a slice always zeroes out its capacity:

```
int[] a = [1, 2, 3]; // a.capacity == 3; appending will not
    realloc
int[] b = a[0 .. 2]; // b.capacity == 0
```

If you were to write b ~= 4, you can expect b == [1,2,4], but you can also still expect a == [1,2,3]. To ensure this is the case, appending to a partial slice will always reallocate—it will copy the array to a new location and append it there, leaving the original memory alone.

While this gives predictable and generally useful slice semantics, it isn't always best for performance. Consider the following code snippet:

```
a ~= 4; // append a 4
a.length = 0; // reset the array…. but this also clears the
    capacity
a ~= 1; // this reallocates a brand new array
```

Capacity is not stored with the slice. It is stored with the memory block returned by the garbage collector. Querying capacity thus is more than a simple member lookup—it must walk a garbage collector structure. The garbage collector implementation contains a cache of most recently used capacities to accelerate this process, allowing multiple appends on one array to perform well.

If you are adding and removing elements often, this becomes a serious bottleneck. (Refer to the recipe in *Chapter 3, Ranges*, where we used these same techniques in the stack collection.)

By keeping a separate `length` variable, `MyArray` is a bit more heavyweight than a basic slice, but the benefit is that our array gives precision control. It owns its own memory, so it doesn't have to worry about stomping on another function's data. As a result, changing the length, appending or clearing, only reallocates when strictly necessary.

A further optimization—again at the expense of additional variables in the structure—is the static array. Using a compile-time parameter, we let the user tweak this to their specific use case. If you know you are working with a small data set, using stack memory (a static array) to hold it avoids all allocations. This gives the best possible speed.

The rest of the implementation of `MyArray` is aimed towards making it convenient to use while minimizing the likelihood of writing buggy code with it. We implement the `~=` operator:

```
public T opOpAssign(string op : "~")(T t);
public T[] opOpAssign(string op: "~")(T[] t);
```

Operator overloading in D is done by implementing functions with a particular name: `opBinary` for a `op` b operators, `opAssign` for a = b, `opOpAssign` for a `op=` b, and others. Visit `http://dlang.org/operatoroverloading.html` for a complete list.

The compile-time parameter is the operator that is passed as a string. Here, we used template specialization syntax to only implement `op == "~"`. In a compile-time parameter list, any parameter may be followed by a colon, then a specific value for that argument. If the template is instantiated with that argument, this function is used instead of any other overloads. This lets us write special implementations for particular arguments or to only implement the function for those particular arguments.

We implement the operator twice, once for a single element so that `array ~= 1` works, and then again for an array so that we can efficiently implement `array ~= [1,2,3]` as well.

We also used operator overloading syntax to disable the binary ~ operator:

```
@disable void opBinary(string op : "~")(T t){}
```

The @disable annotation can be attached to any function to statically disallow its use. Any attempt to write our_array ~ value will cause a compilation failure. The reason we disabled this is that the concatenation operator makes it very easy to hide allocations and lose references. Consider a = b ~ c; here, we would allocate a new array, copy b into it, append c into it, and assign it to a. It may not append into the existing memory block of b due to the conservative nature of the concatenation operator. It does not modify its arguments; instead it returns a new array. Since this custom array is meant to control memory allocations, this is undesirable.

Another worry with binary concatenation is b ~ c ~ d. Here, b~c is evaluated first, which returns a new array (we'll call it tmp). Then, tmp ~ d is evaluated, returning another new array, which is the value of the expression. The problem is that the tmp array reference is completely lost! When using garbage collector arrays, this is OK (convenient, though somewhat inefficient); the garbage collector will clean it up. However, with manual memory management, a lost array reference results in a memory leak. The safest thing to do here is to disable the operator entirely and force the user to explicitly manage their arrays.

Why do we have to explicitly disable the operator instead of simply leaving it unimplemented? Since we wrote alias opSlice this, any operator that isn't found on the object itself will be attempted on the return value of opSlice, which returns a built-in slice. Since ~ is implemented on built-in slices, in terms of the garbage collector, this would succeed; however, this isn't what we wanted.

Lastly, we implemented opSlice without arguments—the [] operator—and used that with alias this. The alias this declaration allows the transparent forwarding of unimplemented operations as well as implicit conversion to the child type. This is known as **subtyping**. This lets our array conveniently interact with other D functions that aren't familiar with our implementation. However, it does have a downside; the other D functions may escape references to our data, which would become invalid when we free the memory.

If you pass a slice to a function, whether explicitly with the [] operator or via implicit conversion with alias this, be sure the function manages it as a lent resource and does not keep the reference.

Managing lent resources

A lent resource is conceptually any reference to memory that you do not own and is not garbage collected. D does not have ownership or borrowed concepts in its type system, but there are techniques that we can use to make our job a little easier.

How to do it...

In order to manage lent resources, perform the following steps:

1. Use the garbage collector whenever possible. Avoid garbage collector allocations in your application's hotspots, but take advantage of its convenience and general correctness throughout the rest of your application.

2. When writing functions, mark references you intend not to store with the `scope` storage class.

3. If you do intend to store a reference, accept immutable data, if possible.

4. Make private copies of mutable data you intend to store.

5. It may be useful to write reference-counted objects.

6. Implement a code review policy to ensure other resources are managed correctly.

How it works...

The `scope` storage class is not fully implemented at the time of writing this; however, there are places where it helps. The `scope` delegate arguments will not allocate a heap closure and as the compiler improves, it will help to statically catch escaping references.

In the D type system, `immutable` is another feature that helps with resource management. A reference to immutable data can be used just like value types—they are cheap to pass around and can be stored with confidence.

Otherwise, unless you rely on the garbage collector, D is essentially in the same boat as C++ with regard to managing lent resources. Code reviews, private copies, and wrapper structs will form the tools you use to keep track of your manually managed resources.

Creating a NotNull struct

By disabling default construction, we can force initialization of a type. Using this feature, we'll make an object reference that will force the user to check for null before using it.

How to do it...

To create a NotNull struct, perform the following steps:

1. Create `struct NotNull(T)` with a private member of type `T`.

2. Disable default construction with `@disable this();`.

3. Write a private constructor that takes `T` and `assert(t !is null);`.

4. Write a property function that returns the payload and use it with `alias this`.

5. Write a helper `struct CheckNull(T)`, with a member `T`. The member `T` is a property that returns `NotNull!T` and has `opCast(T : bool)`, which checks the payload for null and returns `true` if it is not null.

6. Write a helper function, `checkNull`, which takes a `T` member and returns `CheckNull!T`.

7. Write your functions to accept and return `NotNull!T` whenever possible.

8. Optionally, write a generic factory function that returns `NotNull!T`.

9. Use the function with `if(auto nn = test.checkNull) {}`.

The following is the code:

```
struct NotNull(T) {
  private T notNullPayload;
  @disable this();
  private this(T t) {
    assert(t !is null);
    notNullPayload = t;
  }
  inout(T) getNotNullPayload() inout {
    return notNullPayload;
  }
  alias getNotNullPayload this;
}

struct CheckNull(T) {
  private T payload;
  bool opCast(T : bool)() { return payload !is null; }
  inout(NotNull!T) getNotNullPayload() inout {
    return NotNull!T(cast(T) payload);
  }
  alias getNotNullPayload this;
}
```

```
CheckNull!T checkNull(T)(T t) {
  return CheckNull!T(t);
}

// test usage in a function
void test(NotNull!(int*) nn) {
  import std.stdio;
  writeln(*nn, " was not null");
}

void main() {
  import std.stdio;
  int item;
  int* ptr = &item;

  // how to do the test, also try if ptr is null
  if(auto nn = ptr.checkNull) {
    test(nn);
  } else {
    writeln("Null");
  }
}
```

How it works...

There are three key points in this implementation: `alias this`, which allows us to control implicit conversions; the disabled default constructor, which forces initialization of any `NotNull` member or local variable; and the helper type with `opCast(T:bool)`, which enables the type transformation inside the `if` statement.

We use a getter property with `alias this` instead of going directly to the member, because the getter property prohibits assignment. If we used `alias this` directly with the property, it would allow the assigning of `null`:

```
NotNull!Object o = ...;
o = null; // this would be allowed because alias this would
   rewrite it to o.payload = null, bypassing our check!
```

The getter property uses `inout` to provide a start to const-correctness.

We use `@disable this();` to force initialization of the object. The syntax for a default constructor is `this()`. While D's structs cannot have default constructors, the language nevertheless lets you write a prototype specifically to disable it. All variables in D are initialized to default values upon declaration (unless you specifically skip initialization with `=void` at the declaration point). The default value of a reference is `null`. Thus, to ensure that a `NotNull` structure is never `null`, we must force explicit initialization. The language will require an initializer at any local variable declaration and an initializer in the constructor if `NotNull` is used as an object member.

Moreover, we made the constructor private, forcing the initialization process to go through our helper functions and type. This gives us control similar to languages with special nullable types built into the language. It forces a check and gives us an opportunity to limit the scope of the not null type to the correct `if` branch.

Next, the `CheckNull` type and the helper constructor serves as an intermediate between normal, nullable types and the `NotNull` type, with its guarantees. On using `alias this`, it allows implicit conversion to `NotNull` upon request (which then performs an additional check for `null` at assignment time via `assert` in non-release mode). However, first, the `opCast` allows it to be checked inside an `if` statement.

The compiler converts `if (a)` to `if (cast (bool) a)`. The `opCast` method gives us control over explicit casting to any type, which is given as a compile-time parameter. Here, we specialize on the argument of `bool` since that is the only operation we care about with this type. It returns `true` if the object is not null. Then, using a variable declaration inside the `if` statement, we assign the new type to a local variable and can then use it or pass it to functions as `NotNull!T`. This, in turn, implicitly converts back to the original type `T`, allowing easy access to all the original type's methods and operations. A not null reference is always substitutable for a possibly `null` reference.

> The `CheckNull` type is necessary in addition to the `NotNull` type because `CheckNull` might be null, whereas `NotNull` is guaranteed not to be. Adding `opCast` to `NotNull` is tempting to simplify the code, but then we'd have to remove the assertions for the `if` branching to work, thereby breaking the not-null invariant. It would let you write `NotNull!T test = checkNull(a_null_reference)` without compile-time and runtime null checking.

It is possible to write `Object o = null; NotNull!Object obj = checkNull(o);`. This will compile despite the lack of an `if` statement to test null, triggering a runtime assertion failure. This is the best we can do with a library type, but note that this is easy to catch upon code review and it is still an improvement over not using `NotNull` at all, since it will trigger the error immediately at assignment time instead of some indeterminate point later in the code when the reference is finally used. The difficult part of debugging null dereference errors is often figuring out why the value was `null` in the first place. The assertion failure at assignment time will significantly narrow down the possibilities.

There's more...

A const-correctness implementation of `NotNull` is in Phobos' `std.typecons` module. The FIXME comment is not true right now, but should be by the time this is published. Confirm that is the case.

Using unique pointers

Unique pointers are a restrained type that are used when clear ownership of a resource needs to be established. Here, we'll create a `UniqueArray(T)` object, which enforces that only one reference to its payload can exist at any time.

How to do it...

In order to use unique pointers, perform the following steps:

1. Create a struct `UniqueArray(T)` with a member of type `T`.
2. Disable the postblit by using `@disable this(this);`.
3. Write a private constructor that takes `T`.
4. Write a `release` method that nullifies the current object and returns `UniqueArray` with the payload.
5. Write a destructor to perform cleanup, if necessary.
6. Offer a method to create a new unique resource.
7. Implement other methods to use the object. Do not use `alias this` or any other method that may escape your reference.
8. To use the method any time, you need to pass the reference somewhere. This can be done by calling `release`, as shown in the following code snippet:

```
import core.stdc.stdlib;
struct UniqueArray(T) {
  private T[] payload;
  @disable this(this);

  private this(T[] t) {
    payload = t;
  }

  this(size_t count) {
    payload = (cast(T*) malloc(count * T.sizeof))[0 ..
      count];
  }

  UniqueArray!T release() {
    auto p = this.payload;
    this.payload = null;
    return UniqueArray!T(p);
  }

  ~this() {
```

```
        if(payload !is null)
        free(payload.ptr);
    }

    auto opDispatch(string method)() {
        return mixin("payload." ~ method);
    }
    T opIndex(size_t idx) { return payload[idx]; }
    T opIndexAssign(T t, size_t idx) { return payload[idx] =
        t; }
    // You may also choose to implement other operators
}
// testing use
void main() {
    auto ptr = UniqueArray!int(5);
    // use release since plain assign will fail to compile
    auto ptr2 = ptr.release;
    import std.stdio;
    // ensure the first reference is indeed null
    writeln(ptr.ptr is null);
    // and that the second reference is correct
    writeln(ptr2.length);
}
```

Running the program will print **true** and **5**, confirming the correct operation.

Try writing `auto ptr2 = ptr;` as well to get the error message **Error: struct unique. UniqueArray!int.UniqueArray is not copyable because it is annotated with @disable**. This error will force you to think about where the reference lives and explicitly release it, if required.

How it works...

Postblits are only run on the recipient objects, making them useless to implement unique move semantics. However, the ability to disable them opens a new possibility; a disabled postblit will force the users toward another method of your choosing if they want to reassign it. We forced them to use `release`, which nullifies the sending object, maintaining the reference's uniqueness.

Apart from that, we used all the same techniques we've seen before, with one major difference; we did not rely upon `alias this` here to forward operations to the payload. Since `alias this` allows implicit conversion, it would let the user bypass the disabled postblit, escaping a reference to the data:

```
int[] arr = ptr;
// this would work with alias this
```

Instead, we do all forwarding internally. For brevity, in this example we didn't implement all possible operators, opting to implement only basic indexing and partial method forwarding. String mixins and `opDispatch` are incredibly flexible tools in D, which we'll explore in greater detail in a later chapter. Here, we just scratched the surface of what they can do by building a code string, `"payload." ~ member` and then compiling it as the function body with the `mixin` expression. This gives us easy access to most of the payload members, letting us inspect that the code worked as expected.

Using RAII and handling the limitations of class destructors

D can use the **Resource Acquisition Is Initialization** (**RAII**) idiom from C++. This is when resources are acquired when the variable is initialized and automatically released when the variable goes out of scope.

How to do it...

Perform the following steps:

1. Write a struct that performs cleanup operations in the destructor.
2. If you use a class destructor, be certain that you don't access any memory external to the object or manually manage the class memory.

How it works...

Structs with destructors are called deterministically, just like in C++. Class destructors are less reliable. D's garbage collector may be implemented with a variety of strategies, so the language semantics are flexible. The garbage collector is free to release memory referenced by the object's pending finalization. This means accessing child objects or arrays in a class destructor risks a crash. Accessing manually managed objects or shallow class references (value types embedded in the instance) is safe. You may use a class destructor to free C resources when the garbage collector runs, for example.

You may manually call `destroy(obj)` to destroy any object immediately. Together with a `scope(exit)` guard, you can deterministically call a class destructor. The `destroy` function does not free memory, it merely finalizes the object.

In modern D, there is no `delete` operator. D used to have a `delete` operator, like C++; however, it was deprecated because it limits the garbage collector implementation and is not memory safe. If you want to manually release memory, you should also manually allocate it.

Given these limitations of class destructors, implementing the RAII idiom in D is typically done with structs. Struct destructors always run immediately when the struct ceases to exist and have full access to all child memory.

6

Wrapped Types

In this chapter, we will explore D's rich abstraction capabilities to wrap, extend, or constrain other types. We'll learn about:

- ▶ Creating a struct with reference semantics
- ▶ Simulating inheritance with structs
- ▶ Creating a ranged integer
- ▶ Creating an opaque handle type
- ▶ Creating a subtyped string for i18n
- ▶ Forwarding methods with `opDispatch`
- ▶ Creating a tagged dynamic type
- ▶ Creating a structure with two views into the same data
- ▶ Simulating multiple inheritance with mixin templates

Introduction

D's struct has a wealth of possibilities. It is defined by the D spec as a way to "paint a data structure over hardware or an external type", and thus gives us various modeling tools that come without runtime or memory cost. We've already used or seen some of the techniques from this chapter earlier in the book.

Creating a struct with reference semantics

D structs are typically a value type (different variables are always different objects), as opposed to D's classes, which are always a reference type (different variables may refer to the same object). Sometimes, we want the struct that has reference semantics to ensure that assignment is cheap, for example.

How to do it...

To create a struct with reference semantics, we will execute the following steps:

1. Create a struct with a single data member that is itself a reference type, such as a pointer.

2. You may choose to use a private nested struct to hold the implementation, using `alias this` to forward methods automatically. The reference counted object in the previous chapter is a reference-type struct that uses this technique.

3. Use the struct normally—you should *not* use the `ref` storage class when passing it to functions.

How it works...

Structs are a compile-time collection of their contents. If a struct has only one member, it works almost exactly the same way as that member; if a struct's only member is a reference type, the struct works like a reference type too. Assigning a struct to another variable of the same type performs a simple memory copy of the contents:

```
struct Foo {  char[] c;  }
Foo a, b;
a = b; // conceptually performs memcpy(&a, &b, Foo.sizeof);
```

This is a shallow copy, and this has exactly the same semantics as assigning the members individually. This property builds the flexible foundation on which we can build all kinds of wrapped types with structs. Using structs with only one data member incurs little to no runtime cost compared to using a variable of the member's type directly.

There's more...

There is one major exception to the general rule that structs with one member are the same as the value they wrap: when you are returning a struct from a function. Consider the following functions:

```
int* returnPointer();
struct Ptr { int* p; }
Ptr returnWrapperPointer();
```

These two functions are *not* compatible on the ABI level despite the fact that both types have the same binary layout, because the struct wrapper may be subject to return value optimization (though it isn't actually an optimization in this case, which is why the D calling convention on 32-bit doesn't use it). This is a common compiler optimization to avoid the excess copying of object values by taking a pointer to the recipient object as a function argument, allowing the function to fill in the data directly instead of copying it through the return value to the destination.

This is permitted by the C++ spec even when the optimization may change the behavior of the function and is implemented across most C, C++, and D compilers for any struct passed with the C calling conventions and many structs passed by other conventions.

Since return value optimization may be performed by a C compiler, use caution when trying to substitute wrapped types for basic types in the `extern(C)` functions. It is likely that they will not work the way you expect when returned from a function. In these cases, stick to what you did in the C declarations and use wrappers once you are fully into D code.

Simulating inheritance with structs

Class inheritance can be broken up into three concepts: **subtyping**, **composition**, and **polymorphism**. With `alias this`, subtyping and composition are easy, providing a nonpolymorphic type of inheritance.

How to do it...

We will execute the following steps to simulate inheritance with structs:

1. Write a struct to use as the base object type.
2. Write the extended struct with a member of the base type.
3. Use `alias this` with the base type to allow easy access to base members and implicit conversion.

The code is as follows:

```
struct Base {
    int x;
    int y;
}
struct Derived {
    int dx;
    int dy;
    Base base; // a member of the base type - composition
    alias base this; // then use alias this for subtyping
}
```

```
void operateOnBase(Base base) {}
void operateOnDerived(Derived derived) {}
Derived d;
operateOnBase(d); // works
```

How it works...

The `alias this` method is invoked in two places: if a member is requested and not found in the outer struct and if implicit conversion to a specific type is attempted. `alias this` is implemented as a rewrite of the expression to automatically add a reference to the member.

For example, when you write `derived.x`, x is not found in the outer structure, so the compiler attempts to rewrite it as `derived.base.x`. Similarly, implicit conversion is implemented by the compiler rewriting it in terms of the `alias this` member—when you pass it to the `operateOnBase` function, the compiler rewrites the argument d into the `alias this` member. It works exactly as it would if you write `operateOnBase(d.base)`.

If the `alias this` member is a value type, the rewrite also yields a value. Thus, our call to `operateOnBase` will not update d—it will be passed by a value. If you want reference semantics in the function, you may write `ref Base base` in the function declaration. `alias this` has no runtime cost.

Creating a ranged integer

We saw in the previous chapter how we can make a `not null` type. We can use similar techniques to make an integer that is forced to stay in a particular range.

How to do it...

To create a ranged integer, execute the following steps:

1. Create a struct with an integer member.
2. Disable the default constructor.
3. Overload the arithmetic operators by using string mixins to automate most of the code generation process.
4. Insert range checks into the overloaded functions.
5. Use a getter property with `alias this` to allow implicit conversion to `int`.

Execute the following code:

```
struct RangedInt(int min, int max) {
    private int _payload;
```

```
    @disable this();

    this(int value) {
        _payload = value;
        check();
    }

    RangedInt check() {
        assert(_payload >= min);
        assert(_payload < max);
        return this;
    }

    RangedInt opUnary(string op)() {
        RangedInt tmp = _payload;
        mixin("tmp= " ~ op ~ "_payload;");
        return tmp.check();
    }

    RangedInt opBinary(string op)(int rhs) {
        mixin("return RangedInt(_payload " ~ op ~ "rhs);");
    }

    RangedInt opOpAssign(string op)(intrhs) {
        mixin("_payload " ~ op ~ "= rhs;");
        return check();
    }

    RangedInt opAssign(intrhs) {
        _payload = rhs;
        return check();
    }

    string toString() {
        import std.conv;
        return to!string(_payload);
    }

    @property int getPayload() { return _payload; }

    alias getPayload this;
}
```

```
void main() {
    import std.stdio;
    RangedInt!(50, 100) r = 80;
    r += 19;
    r++; // this will trigger an assertion failure
}
```

How it works...

Here, we wrapped and subtyped an integer while also changing its behavior with operator overloading. Before going to `alias this`, D will attempt to use member functions on the wrapped type, including operator overloads and constructors. By offering custom functions, we can hook or disable individual capabilities.

 We can disable individual operators, too. For example, add `@disable void opUnary(string op:"-")() {}` to the definition of `RangedInt`. Then, if you try to negate `RangedInt`, the compile will fail with the following message: `Error: functionsimpleranged. RangedInt!(0, 100).RangedInt.opUnary!"-".opUnary is not callable because it is annotated with @disable.`

The check function performs the range checks. We call it on every overloaded method to ensure that the result remains valid. To ensure that any mutation goes through one of the checked methods, we made `_payload` private and only exposed conversion to the base type of `int` through a getter property. To retain the operations expected from an integer, we implemented several operators:

 ▶ `opUnary`: This operator implements unary operators, that is, those with just one argument, for example, `-a`, `a++`, or `--a`. The postfix unary operators are automatically implemented in terms of the prefix forms, so we don't have to implement `a++` separately from `++a`. The operator is passed as the compile-time argument as a string.

 ▶ `opBinary`: This operator implements operators with two arguments, for example, `a + b` or `a / b`, `this`, the left-hand side of the expression `a` and the right-hand side of the expression `b` is passed as an argument. We could have also implemented `opBinaryRight`, where `this` is the right-hand side argument. The operator is passed as the compile-time argument as a string.

- ▸ `opAssign`: This operator implements `a` = `b`, where `a` is `this` in the function and `b` is given as an argument. The `b` argument can be of any type except `typeof(this)`, which is always handled automatically (a reference assignment for classes or a memory copy—optionally with `postblit`— for structs). The `opAssign` operator differs from constructors. Moreover, constructors are only called at the declaration point, even if you initialize it with `Foo f = 10 /* calls the constructor */`. The `opAssign` operator is called when you assign to it after the variable is declared: `f = 10`. We implemented both for `RangedInt` for easy interoperability with integer literals.

- ▸ `opOpAssign`: This operator is used for expressions such as `a += b`. Here, `a` is `this`, `+` is the operator, and `b` is passed as the argument. The operator is passed as the compile-time argument as a string.

Despite taking the operator as a compile-time string argument, operator overloading only allows us to implement operators predefined in the D language; it is not possible to define your own operators. This is because user-defined operators would break the D design goal of a context-free grammar—it would require the D lexer and parser to be aware of the user-defined context to identify the operator tokens and parse them with correct precedence. This would have an adverse impact on compile speeds.

Taking the operator as a compile-time string argument does have two advantages. We can use the symbol instead of having to remember a name and without using special syntax in the language, and we can use the string directly to form code to mix in.

There is one disadvantage of operator overloading being implemented with templates, though the operator overload functions cannot be virtual. In general, an interface or class may have a templated method, but they must always be final. This is because the compiler doesn't know what combination of compile-time arguments it may accept, and thus does not know how many slots to reserve in the virtual function table. To work around this, write the overload implementation as a final method that merely forwards the request to a virtual method, `intopBinary(string op : "+")(intrhs) { return add(rhs); }`, and then implement `add` in the subclass as a regular method. Now, the operator overload will work with the interface, which can be overridden by the child class!

We used the second property to concisely implement all the arithmetic operators for our wrapped type. Let's look at our implementation of `opBinary`:

```
mixin("return RangedInt(_payload " ~ op ~ "rhs);");
```

The `mixin` expression takes one argument: a string. It may also be a function that returns a string. The argument is evaluated at compile time, then pasted into the code and compiled normally. It is similar to `eval` in languages such as JavaScript, but with the important difference that the code is not interpreted at runtime—`mixin()` is wholly a compile time operation. The string passed to the `mixin` expression is not like C macros where the code must form a complete, compilable declaration, statement, or expression. It cannot mix an incomplete code fragment.

After performing the operation with the mixed-in code, we run the check. In `opBinary`, we depend on the `RangedInt` constructor to perform the range checking. In the other functions, we call it explicitly. If any operation upon the number causes it to go out of bounds, we will get an assertion failure.

There's more...

The `RangedInt` constructor presented here only performs limited checks. Since we used `assert`, the checks will disappear when the program is compiled with the `-release` switch. We could instead throw an exception or use the enforce function from `std.exception` to insert a check which will always be present. We may also accept default file and line arguments all the way up the call chain, so our thrown exception will tell where the out-of-range condition was entered in the user code instead of the library code.

The checks will not work if the limits are close to `int.min` or `int.max` because they do not handle wraparound. With the two's complement arithmetic mandated by the D spec (and, in practice, used by hardware on which D runs), `int.max + 1 == int.min`. This condition is called **integer overflow**. On x86, we can handle this with inline assembly, checking the overflow flag after performing the operation (or, the carry flag if we were using an unsigned type).

Since the flags can be lost in the process of a function call, we'd have to change two things to handle integer overflow with inline assembly: the check function itself and where the check is called. To avoid an actual function call, we'd use a `mixin`. The check function would be changed to return a string of code, and the usage site would be changed to mix in that code:

```
string check() {
    // returning a code string
return q{
  asm {
     // this code is x86 and dmd specific
     jo overflowed; // check the overflow flag…
  }
  if(_payload < min) goto overflowed; // check min
  if(_payload > max) goto overflowed; // and max
  return this; // still return the value
  overflowed: throw new Exception("Value out of bounds.");
 };
}
```

Each usage would be changed to the following code:

```
mixin(check());
```

Try using `RangedInt!(int.min, int.max)` and you will notice that it will throw an exception if you set the method to `int.max`, and then you can try to add a number greater than 1 to it. Why must we add a number greater than one? Adding just one may be optimized by the compiler into the `inc` instruction rather than `add`, which does not set the overflow flag! For a complete solution, we would also want to implement these operators and assembly language (asm) code ourselves to ensure we get exactly the behavior we want.

Creating an opaque handle type

Opaque handles are used to refer to an object, but are themselves not an object. They are often implemented in terms of pointers to a type that user code knows nothing about or a wrapped integer and can only be used by passing the handle to library-provided functions.

How to do it...

We will execute the following steps to create an opaque handle type:

1. Create a private struct with no data members and no methods in the interface to represent the opaque type. If you are implementing the library, you may use members and methods internally, but do not expose them to the public interface.

2. Either use `alias Impl* Handle;` or create a public struct with only one data member—a pointer to the private struct or the handle ID if you use integers—to represent the handle. Mark this member private. The alias method works better when interfacing with C libraries that do not use a handle struct. Otherwise, the struct gives more control.

3. Disable built-in functions on the public struct as desired to force the user to go through your library. You may disable the default constructor if it needs special initialization and/or `postblit` if you don't want the handle copied.

4. Provide public functions in the module that operate upon the only handle in their interface. Whenever possible, make the handle the first argument to the function.

5. Be certain that the same method, `handle` or `pointer`, is used in the library too. If the library is implemented with a naked pointer instead of a handle struct, also use the naked pointer at the usage point.

The code is as follows:

```
private struct OpaqueImpl{} // step 1
alias OpaqueImpl* OpaqueHandle; // step 2, pointer method
// or step 2, struct method
// struct OpaqueHandle{ private OpaqueImpl* item; }
// interface functions
```

```
OpaqueHandle createObject();
void freeObject(OpaqueHandleimpl);
void add(OpaqueHandleimpl, int);
void print(OpaqueHandleimpl);
void main() {
    // usage:
    auto handle = createObject();
    scope(exit) freeObject(handle);
    handle.add(10); // call using UFCS
    handle.print();
}
```

How it works...

Opaque handles are a technique to maximize binary compatibility. Since the user code doesn't need to know anything about the size or layout of the data, the library is free to change its implementation details at any time. It can add functions, add data, or remove data without breaking the client code. Opaque handles are also useful for interlanguage compatibility, since they only require an agreed method to pass basic data and call functions.

With D, we can use this technique directly and also build upon it, while maintaining similar syntax to other library writing techniques. There are four D features used here: `alias`, UFCS, an empty struct, and wrapper structs.

`alias` is a feature to give an entity an alternative name. It comes in two mostly equivalent forms: `alias oldnamenewname;` or `alias newname = oldname;`. Aliases can hide implementation details (the handle is a pointer, but this is not immediately visible at the usage point) and provide more specific names for your entities, but do not create a new type. This is why we defined the empty struct instead of simply `alias void* OpaqueHandle;`—the latter form would allow undesired implicit conversions since it does not define a unique type. This is similar to `typedef` in C++. D used to have `typedef` too, but it was deprecated in favor of the `struct`+`alias` combination to give better control over details. In Phobos, `std.typecons.Typedef` encapsulates this pattern in the standard library.

Next, we used an empty struct. On the implementation side, this struct would be populated with data; however, on the user interface side, it is empty to hide its details. In D, the implementation and interface may be separated logically using protection attributes or physically by writing two files, one with just declarations and the other with implementations (similar to header files in C or C++). The interface file may be automatically generated with `dmd -H`. Of course, the implementation may also be written in another language.

The .di files, meaning D interface files, may be hand-written or automatically generated with dmd -H. As far as the compiler is concerned, there is no difference between the .d and .di files—you may write implementations in a .di file or just write interfaces in a .d file. Partially as a result of this, an implementation file cannot import its corresponding interface file. The compiler will think the module is attempting to import itself.

Your first thought when declaring an opaque struct might be to write it without a body: struct OpaqueImpl; instead of struct OpaqueImpl { }. We chose the latter here because then the compiler will believe it to have no members instead of being a forward declaration of a struct with an unknown number of members. The advantage of this is we will avoid compiler errors when we try to pass it to functions using method call syntax (UFCS). The compiler will confidently believe it has no members and let you call other functions through it without error. The downside is that a user could also declare OpaqueImpl when it has an empty body, but we are able to prohibit that by simply making the structure private.

Lastly, if we can use a wrapper struct instead of an alias, we have the advantage of being able to add or disable methods, making the handle automatically reference counted, destroyed, or not null, as we've already done with other types in this chapter. If you are writing a library, use a wrapper struct. There's little runtime cost and it has the most potential for growth and control. If you are accessing an existing library, however, be sure to match the method they used. While wrapper structs are almost identical to the wrapped type on a binary level, there are subtle differences in passing them in return values. If you wrap a type you do not control, you should also wrap the functions that use that type.

There's more...

We looked briefly at the preceding alias syntax. There are two forms; what are the differences between them? Both work the same way; the only difference is the alias old new syntax (inherited from C) has slightly more compatibility with the function pointer attributes and the alias new = old syntax also functions as shorthand for a template, which lets you easily do pass-through or transformations of an argument list. This can be seen in the following code:

```
// the following two lines are equivalent
alias TemplateArgList(T...) = T;
template TemplateArgList(T...) { alias TemplateArgList = T; }
```

This is not possible with the other syntax. On the other hand, the C syntax allows you to define names that include function linkage and other attributes:

```
// this line will not compile with the equals based syntax
alias extern(C) void function() CallbackType;
```

When interfacing with C, this syntax can help define function pointers with the right linkage (calling convention) and attributes like `nothrow`. These differences may disappear with time. Currently, outside of these two cases, the syntax you use comes down to personal preference.

Creating a subtyped string for i18n

A specialized string is a type with a text representation. For example, user-visible text is a string, but not every string is user-visible text. When adding internationalization (often shortened to i18n) to an application, using a string subtype can help ensure that all messages are available to translators. Moreover, we'll use D's templates and compile-time string imports to efficiently load the translation file.

How to do it...

Execute the following steps to create a subtyped string for i18n:

1. Create a struct with a private string member and a public getter property for that string.
2. Add `alias this` to the string getting property.
3. Write a private function that loads the translation table and returns the string wrapped in our struct.
4. Write a template that takes a key, file, and line number that assigns the result of the translation function to a member with the same name. You may also use `pragma(msg)` to print out the whole list of translatable strings.
5. When you write functions to print strings to the user, accept the `TranslatedString` type rather than string.
6. Write a message using the translation template.

 On Windows, if you get garbled content in the console, you may need to enable UTF-8 output with `SetConsoleOutputCP(65001);` from the Windows API.

The following is the code to create a subtyped string for i18n:

```
struct TranslatedString {
    private string value;
    @property string getValue() { return value; }
    alias getValue this;
}

private TranslatedString localize(string key, bool requireResult =
true) {
```

```
            // we'll use an associative array for the translation
            // it would also be possible to load from a file, at
            // compile time
            enum string[string] translations =
                    [
                            "Hello!" : "¡Hola!"
                    ];

        if(auto value = key in translations)
            return TranslatedString(*value);
        if(requireResult)
            throw new Exception(key ~ " is not translated");
        return TranslatedString(null);
    }

template T(string key, string file = __FILE__, size_t line = __LINE__)
{
    version(gettext) {
            // prints messages at compile time with all strings
            // in the program, if requested
            import std.conv;
            pragma(msg, "#: " ~ file ~ ":" ~ to!string(line));
            pragma(msg, "msgid \"" ~ key ~ "\"");
            pragma(msg, "msgstr \""~localize(key, false)~"\"");
            pragma(msg, "");
        }

    enum T = localize(key);
}

void main() {
    auto p = T!"Hello!"; // translated string literal
    import std.stdio;
    writeln(p);
}
```

How it works...

Here, we utilize the type system to help us catch untranslated strings that are to be printed to the user and the compile-time features to help us translate them.

The `TranslatedString` type, if used throughout the library, would provide a degree of type safety to printing. Using `alias this` subtyping, it will easily convert back to string for integration with other functions without allowing implicit conversions from string to `TranslatedString`, which would defeat the purpose.

The T template provides concise syntax to access the localization function (without runtime cost; this pattern is how we can do user-defined literals in D, a topic we'll cover in greater depth in a later chapter) as well as a place to track all translatable strings in the application.

Using the version statement, we provide an optional code path that prints the locations, strings, and current translations of all the instantiations of this template. The version statement takes a single identifier. Unless that identifier is specialized on the compiler's command line or is predefined for the given target platform (for example, Windows or OS X), the code inside is not compiled. Here, we used version(gettext), so the code inside is only compiled if dmd is passed the –version=gettext argument.

If this code is compiled, it will run the pragma(msg) instructions. This will print out the given string at compile time. It is meant to give a compilation message to the user. The argument need not be a literal because it will be evaluated using compile-time function evaluation; ordinary D code will be run and the result printed.

The arguments to T, (string key, string file = __FILE__, size_t line = __LINE__), include another bit of D magic: the default arguments to file and line. Just like we saw with runtime function arguments back in *Chapter 1, Core Tasks*, when we looked at creating a custom exception type, the special tokens __FILE__, __LINE__, and a few others are automatically inserted at the call site. It works the same way with compile-time arguments. Using these, we can print out the list of strings (including the location of their appearance) for the translator to examine, without writing an external tool to parse the code to find the strings.

Once we have the strings, we put them into an associative array literal inside the localize function, which is wrapped in the TranslatedString type, and use that to get the translation to print to the user.

Forwarding methods with opDispatch

When writing wrapped types, you might want to forward methods without subtyping. The opDispatch method lets that happen with very little code.

How to do it...

To forward methods with opDispatch, we need to execute the following steps:

1. Write the wrapped struct.
2. Write a method called opDispatch, which takes variadic arguments: auto opDispatch(string name, T...)(T t).
3. In the body, write return mixin("member." ~ s ~ "(t)");.

The code has to be executed as follows:

```
class Foo {
    int test() { return 0; }
    void nop() {}
}

struct Wrapped {
    Foo f;
    this(Foo f) { this.f = f; }
    auto opDispatch(string s, T...)(T t) {
        return mixin("f." ~ s ~ "(t)");
    }
}

void main() {
    Wrapped w = new Foo();
    Int i = w.test();
    w.nop();
}
```

How it works...

We've been using `alias this` throughout the chapter to provide easy access to a wrapped data member or property. However, since this also enables implicit casting to the wrapped type, we don't always want it. Using `opDispatch`, we can provide access to a wrapped method without offering subtyping.

The `opDispatch` method works similar to the other operator overloads; it is a function with a special name that takes a compile-time string argument. Any time you try to access a nonexistent member with the dot operator, the compiler will try to instantiate `opDispatch!"name"` to handle the missing member. Execute the following code:

```
struct Foo {
    void test() {}
    void opDispatch(string s)() {}
}
Foo f;
f.test(); // it finds test in the object, so it is called normally
f.disp(); // disp is NOT found in the object, so it tries to call
          // f.opDispatch!"disp"(); before issuing an error
```

Once `opDispatch` is tried, the arguments are forwarded as well. Since we wanted to capture all possible arguments here to pass on to the wrapped type, we declared `opDispatch` as an unrestricted variadic template with `T...`. This will accept a list of any length, zero or more, of anything that can be passed as a compile time argument, including types.

Then, the runtime argument list, `(T t)`, is also variadic and may consist of several types. It accepts anything (given that the function body compiles).

Just like with `RangedInt` we implemented earlier, we will use a string `mixin` to concisely implement the forwarding. With the `auto` return value, the compile takes care of forwarding returns for us too, including returning `void`. The function just works.

 Wrapping the type might break some code that would otherwise work thanks to UFCS. Since the `mixin` is evaluated in the scope of the wrapped function and UFCS is evaluated at the call site, they may see different functions. The call site can import different modules than the wrapper function, thus enabling some functionality that doesn't work at the wrap site. This is a necessary consequence of using this method.

We can also forward to an array of objects with this same technique:

```
struct Wrapped {
    Foo[] fs; // an array instead of just one object
    this(Foo[] fs) { this.fs = fs; }
    Wrapped opDispatch(string s, T...)(T t) {
        foreach(f; fs) // simply loop over them
            mixin("f." ~ s ~ "(t)");
        return this; // for chaining
    }
}
```

This lets us work with arrays in the same way as jQuery's element collections:

```
Wrapped getElements() { return Wrapped([array, of, items]); }
getElements().addClass("foo").innerHTML("baz");
```

That code would compile, provided an `Element` class is wrapped and provides the individual `addClass` and `innerHTML` methods. You would not have to write wrapped methods manually to perform the looping.

Creating a tagged dynamic type

D's structs are a good foundation to create a dynamic type. We'll create a tagged union to serve as a starting dynamic type. This is the technique used to implement the library `jsvar` type that we used in a previous chapter. Here, we'll only support `int` and `string`.

How to do it...

We will execute the following steps to create a tagged dynamic type:

1. Write a struct with two members: a tag that holds the current type and a union that holds the possible types.

2. Make the data private and add checked getter and setter functions.

3. Add a constructor that takes the possible types. You may write it in terms of `opAssign`.

4. Add type coercion if you want weak typing in the getter function; otherwise, throw an exception on type mismatches.

5. Implement other methods or operators you want.

The following is the code to create a tagged dynamic type:

```
struct Dynamic {
   enum Type { integer, string }
   private Type type;
   private union {
      int integer;
      string str;
   }

   this(T)(T t) { // easy construction
      this = t;
   }

   // assignment of our supported types
   Dynamic opAssign(inti) {
      type = Type.integer;
      integer = i;
      return this;
   }

   Dynamic opAssign(string i) {
      type = Type.string;
      str = i;
      return this;
   }

   // getting our types back out into static variables
   // here, we used the coercion option instead of throwing if
```

```
      // we had the wrong type
      int asInteger() {
        final switch(type) {
          case Type.integer:
            return integer;
          case Type.string:
            import std.conv;
            return to!int(str);
        }
      }

      string asString() {
        final switch(type) {
          case Type.string:
            return str;
          case Type.integer:
            import std.conv;
            return to!string(integer);
        }
      }

      // we may also implement other operators for more integration
    }
```

How it works...

Dynamic types are usually implemented using the tagged union technique used here. A **union** is a group of variables which share a block of overlapped memory. Unless all the variables of the union are valid simultaneously (which we'll look at in the following recipe), it is important to know which member is currently active. That's where the `type` member comes into play.

The other parts of the code are things we've already seen. The `opAssign` function implements the = operator with other types. The constructor implements by declaring the struct with an argument list of other types. The `asInteger` and `asString` methods are just regular functions.

There's one interesting bit we use in those methods: the **final switch**. A final switch is guaranteed at compile time to cover every member of the `enum`. With an `enum`, this means the build will fail if a member is not handled by a case, making the final switch resilient to changes. If a new member is added to the `enum`, the compiler will help you remember to add a handling case to each and every switch that uses it.

There's more...

Phobos' `std.variant` provides a tagged union, `Variant`, that uses a large union as well as a pointer to an even larger type, making it capable of holding almost anything. `Variant` doesn't provide weak typing or full operator overloading. However, since it can hold and offer nearly any type with proper runtime checking, you may use it when you need a generic runtime variable, such as an array of mixed type elements.

`Variant` uses method templates and generated function pointers to handle the types rather than writing out a list manually. We'll look at these techniques in depth in *Chapter 9*, *Code Generation*, and *Chapter 8*, *Reflection*.

Creating a structure with two views into the same data

Sometimes, it is useful to have a structure with multiple representations. This may be achieved with properties, but there is also a more direct way of doing it: using **unions** and **anonymous structs**. We'll create a `Color` structure with both RGBA and array representations.

How to do it...

To create a structure with two views into the same data, we need to execute the following steps:

1. Write a struct to contain your type.

2. Add a union without a name to hold the alternative representations.

3. In the union, add the views. Be sure they match up in size and binary layout. For our `Colorstruct`, we'll want it to be represented by an array of `ubytes` with each byte also having a name.

4. For the names, write a nameless `struct` with each named member.

5. When using the structure, use the names directly.

To implement the preceding steps, we will have to execute the following code:

```
struct Color {
    union {
        ubyte[4] rgba;
        struct {
            ubyte r;
            ubyte g;
            ubyte b;
            ubyte a;
        }
```

```
        }
    }
    Color c;
    c.r = 100; // accessing the inner name is easy
    assert(c.rgba[0] == 100); // alternative view into same data
```

How it works...

D will permit you to group members inside an aggregate by wrapping them in other anonymous aggregates. Here, we wanted a struct that exposed two representations of the same data. A union is an aggregate type where all the members overlap in memory. This may be used to share memory between types where only one is valid at any time, as we did in the dynamic type, or it can be used to provide multiple equally legitimate views into the same data, which is what we're doing here.

The first view is an array of 4 bytes. The second view gives individual names to each byte. For that, we used a struct with four individual `ubyte` members. Thus, we have different views into the same memory.

Since we didn't give the inner union nor struct a name (this is only permitted inside another struct, union, or class), it serves to group the members in the implementation, but is invisible to the user. We do not need to use an additional dot member nor declare a separate variable of the anonymous type.

This technique would also be useful to access hardware-mapped memory or a task such as writing an x86 emulator, where the registers may be represented with several layers of nested anonymous structs and unions to provide access to each individual byte as well as the 16, 32, and 64 bit views (AX, EAX, and RAX, for example).

Let's execute the following code:

```
struct x86Accumulator {
    union {
        long RAX;
        // lowest items first because x86 is little endian
        struct {
            union {
                struct {
                    union {
                        struct {
                            byte AL;
                            byte AH;
                        }
                        short AX;
                    }
```

```
            short upperWord;
        }
        int EAX;
    }
    int upperDWord;
    }
  }
}

void main() {
    x86Accumulator a;
    import std.stdio;
    a.EAX = 50;
    // set the high byte of the low word independently
    // equivalent to adding 256...
    a.AH = 1;
    writeln(a.RAX); // should be 306
}
```

We can update or view individual parts, which simultaneously affects the whole object.

Simulating multiple inheritance with mixin templates

D does not have multiple inheritance like C++. Instead, it follows a Java-style pattern of one base class, multiple interfaces. However, using mixin templates, we can simulate all aspects of multiple inheritance.

How to do it...

We need to execute the following steps to simulate multiple inheritance with mixin templates:

1. Write an interface and mixin template instead of a base class.

2. Write your usage class, which inherits from the interfaces and mixes in the mixin templates to the body.

3. You may override functions from the mixin template by writing new ones with the same name in the `class` body.

The code is as follows:

```
import std.stdio : writeln;
interface Base1 {
```

```
        void foo();
}

mixin template Base1_Impl() {
   void foo() { writeln("default foo impl"); }
}

interface Base2 {
   void bar();
   void baz();
}

mixin template Base2_Impl() {
   int member;
   void bar() { writeln("default bar impl"); }
   void baz() { writeln("default bazimpl"); }
}

classMyObject : Base1, Base2 {
   mixin Base1_Impl!();
   mixin Base2_Impl!();

   void baz() {
     writeln("custom bazimpl");
   }
}

void main() {
   MyObjectobj = new MyObject();

   Base1 base1 = obj; // works on all interfaces
   Base2 base2 = obj; // works on all interfaces

   obj.foo(); // call methods through object
   obj.baz(); // note that the custom one is called
   base2.bar(); // or through interface
   base2.baz();
}
```

On running the preceding program, we will get the following output:

```
default foo impl
custombazimpl
default bar impl
custombazimpl
```

If you override one member of an overload set, you must overload them all.

How it works...

Inheriting and implementing multiple interfaces will allow your object to implicitly convert to the various interface types. The problem is they cannot have default virtual implementations. That's where the **mixin template** comes in.

A `mixin template` (not to be confused with the `mixins` string we used before) is a parameterized list of declarations which is inserted into the `mixin` site, almost as if you copied and pasted the code and compiled it.

Here, we paired a `mixin template` with each interface, putting the interface implementation in the template. An interesting feature of these templates is that they will not conflict with names written in the object. As a result, we can selectively override functions from the `mixin template`, as we did with the custom `baz` implementation.

 Since the customization is done by name, if you want to customize one member of an overload set, you must customize them all. That is, if we had `baz(int)` in addition to `baz()`, we'd have to write custom implementations of both.

When customizing functions, you may also wish to call the default implementation. To do this, give the `mixin template` a name and then refer to it by that name:

```
mixin Base2_Impl!() b2; // name it

void baz() {
   writeln("custom bazimpl");
   b2.baz(); // refer to the function by full name
   }
```

The other functions will still appear in the object—you will not have to refer to them by the full `b2.bar` name. The name is only used when disambiguating.

7

Correctness Checking

In this chapter, we will explore D's correctness checking and documentation features. We'll look at the following recipes:

- Using assertions and exceptions
- Using static asserts
- Using template constraints and static `if`
- Preventing memory corruption bugs with `@safe`
- Leveraging const-correctness
- Avoiding side effects of pure functions
- Verifying object invariants and pre- and post-conditions
- Unit testing your code
- Documenting your code with Ddoc
- Writing platform-specific code (versions) and per-client configuration modules

Introduction

D is designed to help make programs with fewer bugs. Its built-in support for assertions, contract programming, and unit tests help you verify your program at runtime. D's exception based error model helps us to ensure no runtime errors go unnoticed, without requiring return code to be checked after every function call.

D also provides numerous features to help you to prove correctness at compile time, from built-in function annotations to custom compile checks with static assert, which is capable of running D code with compile-time reflection to implement complex checks.

We'll also look at D's built-in support for documentation and platform versioning, which helps you to communicate that the code does what you intended, not just what you programmed.

Using assertions and exceptions

D has two features dedicated to error handling: **exceptions** and **assertions**. Exceptions are used to handle errors external to the program and assertions are used to verify assumptions inside the program. In other words, assertions are a debugging tool while exceptions handle situations that are beyond your control as a programmer.

How to do it...

Perform the following steps by using assertions and exceptions:

1. Any time you make an assumption about program state, explicitly express it with `assert`.

2. Whenever environmental or user data prevents your function from doing its job, throw an exception.

3. Write `assert(0);` on any branch that you believe ought to be unreachable code.

The code is as follows:

```
struct MyRange {
  int current = 0;
  @property bool empty() { return current < 10; }
  @property int front() {
    // it is a programming error to call front on an empty
      range
    // we assume current is valid, so we'll verify with
      assert.
    assert(!empty);
    return current;
  }
  void popFront() {
    // it is always a bug to call popFront on an empty
      range
    assert(!empty);
    current++;
  }
}
void appendToFile() {
  import core.stdc.stdio;
  auto file = fopen("file.txt", "at");
  scope(exit) fclose(file);
  // Files if not opening is not a bug - it is an outside
    condition
```

```
    // so we will throw an exception instead of asserting.
    if(file is null)
    throw new Exception("Could not open file");
    fprintf(file, "Hello!\n");
}
```

 You can never have too many asserts. If your code has a bug, you'll be thankful for all the assertions helping you narrow down the places it could be.

If you want to easily trigger the exception, try running this program in a read-only directory.

How it works...

The key factor to consider when deciding whether you should use `assert` or throw is: did this failure occur due to a program bug? Assertions are debugging tools. A correctly written program should never experience an assertion failure under any circumstances. Indeed, when compiled with the `-release` switch to `dmd`, assertions are removed from the generated code. Exceptions, on the other hand, do not indicate a bug in the program.

 You can use `version(assert)` to compile code on the condition that asserts are enabled.

Generally, exceptions should be thrown only when a program fails to complete its operation. For example, a function that checks whether a file exists should not throw an exception if the file is not found. Instead, it should simply return `false`. However, a function to copy or append to a file should throw an exception if the file is not found because it is impossible to copy a file that doesn't exist. The function could not do its job due to factors beyond the programmer's control, thus an exception is appropriate.

Any time you make an assumption about the state when programming, you should write it out explicitly with an assertion. Having too many asserts won't hurt you. They are removed from the release build so that there's no cost in your final build, and you can save a lot of debugging time if one of your assumptions proves to be invalid! For example, we demonstrated `assert` with a range earlier. Suppose we didn't correctly check empty before calling front. This would result in our program reading corrupted data, a problem that might not be discovered until it ruins a file or causes some other bug in production.

That's the power of `assert`; when used frequently, they help to find bugs as soon as the program's state becomes invalid. A failing assertion gives a location (file and line number in the source code), a stack trace, and optionally, a string message (the second argument to assert). An undetected bug gives a crash or corrupted result.

> Avoid functions that have side effects in assertions. Your program may inadvertently rely on those side effects when debugging, then break in release mode when those function calls are removed.

Exceptions are used for everything outside your control. If the condition can still fail even if you did a perfect job programming, use an exception instead of an assertion. Exceptions ought to use different types (child classes derived from Exception) to indicate different classes of problem. Phobos does not provide a generic exception hierarchy, instead opting to create `Exception` subclasses as needed. You should also do this because handling exceptions with the catch statement differentiates them by dynamic type; using subclasses will let the consumer of your function choose which types of exception they can handle, while leaving the others unchanged.

> It isn't wrong to throw an exception instead of using `assert`. It is slightly less efficient and may surprise the user. When writing a library, some people opt to use exceptions instead of assertions even when it is a programmer bug, since the user code is beyond the control of the library author. This defensive programming is not wrong, but typically, D style encourages assertions, even in libraries. However, if you are in doubt, exceptions are always a safe choice.

See also

▸ See the *Using a custom exception type* recipe in *Chapter 1, Core Tasks*

Using static asserts

A static assert is the main language feature for implementing custom compile-time checks. It can check any condition. If the static assert is compiled, the condition must be true; otherwise, it will issue a compile-time error. Here, we'll use it to verify whether our struct is of the correct size to interface with hardware.

How to do it...

Perform the following steps:

1. Write `static assert(condition, message);` in the code.
2. If your condition is too complex to represent as a simple condition, you may write a helper function and call it for the condition.
3. Remember that static assert must pass if the code is compiled, even if the path is not actually executed.

The code is as follows:

```
align(1) struct IDTLocation {
  align(1):
  ushort length;
  uint offset;
}
static assert(IDTLocation.sizeof == 6, "An IDTLocation must be exactly
six bytes with no padding.");
```

How it works...

The compile-time partner to `assert` is `static assert`. It functions in the same way, but instead of checking a runtime execution path, it checks a compile-time path. Whenever a static assert is compiled (specifically, this check occurs during the semantic analysis phase of compilation), its condition must pass or else a compile error will be triggered.

Compile errors do not necessarily cause the build to fail. Whether something compiles or not can be checked by the program. In these conditions, a compile failure is delivered to the program rather than being displayed to the user. Also, if a template fails to instantiate, the compiler may just use an alternate path, hiding the error. For example, if you are writing a wrapped type with overloaded operators and `alias this` and have a compile error inside the overloaded operator. Then, the compiler will see it as unsuitable and fall back on `alias this`, silently hiding your mistake! If you are in doubt that your code path is being attempted to compile, you can double-check by adding `pragma(msg, "any message here");` somewhere near your static assert.

Your compile-time assumptions should be checked by `static assert`, especially when interfacing with hardware or outside programs when binary layouts must be precisely correct to avoid memory corruption and other crashes. In our preceding example, we used it to verify the size of an `IDTLocation` struct that is loaded by the processor so that it can find interrupt handlers. If this is not loaded correctly, the CPU will almost immediately triple-fault when it tries to run the program, causing the computer to restart! These low-level bugs can be difficult to trace down and if driving real hardware, it could be physically damaging.

It is considerably cheaper and easier to double-check your assumptions at compile time. Even though this data structure looks simple enough to verify by simply looking at it, hidden issues such as data padding and alignment may catch you by surprise. If you remove `align(1)` from this structure, you'll see the assertion will fail because the compiler will align struct data members on native machine word boundaries by default. In this case, it would add an additional 2 bytes of padding.

One similar problem that can be caught by `static assert` is comparing struct sizes for C interoperation across platforms. For example, the Linux `xlib` library uses structs with C's `long` type to represent GUI events. C's `long` is not the same as D's `long`. In D, `long` is always a 64-bit integer. In C, `long` is 32 bits on all 32-bit platforms as well as 64-bit Windows; however, on 64-bit Linux, C's `long` is itself a 64 bit type.

When writing C bindings, binary compatibility is a must. A simple copy-and-paste of the C code will work on 64-bit Linux, but will crash on 32-bit systems! If we use a static assert to verify the size matches the C compiler's requirements (write a small program that simply prints `sizeof(The_Type)` and be sure to build and run it on the same platform to get the correct expected value). Our mistake will be caught at compile time instead of causing a crash. This may feel like tedium when checking it, but believe me, it will all be worth it the first time it catches a mistake.

> When writing bindings to C libraries, import `core.stdc.config;` and use the types `c_long` and `c_ulong` to do the correct translation. However, while this issue can be fairly easily fixed, the `static assert` still serves as a valuable sanity check to ensure you did do this correctly and to be a first line of defense against other translation mistakes.

Checking structure sizes is not the only thing done by `static assert`. It can check anything that can be run at compile time. We've used it before to verify our range objects adhere to a particular compile-time interface. Phobos' `std.random` also uses it to ensure parameters to a random number engine are good for pseudorandom number generation by checking the greatest common denominator and number of factors the integer parameters have.

It achieves these checks by simply writing regular functions to check the numbers and calling them in a series of `static assert` statements in the object as shown as follows:

```
struct LinearCongruentialEngine(UIntType, UIntType a, UIntType c,
    UIntType m) {
    private static bool properLinearCongruentialParameters(
    ulong m,  ulong a, ulong c)
    {
      /* snip some implementation */
      if (a == 0 || a >= m || c >= m) return false;
      // c and m are relatively prime
      if (c > 0 && gcd(c, m) != 1) return false;
      // a - 1 is divisible by all prime factors of m
      if ((a - 1) % primeFactorsOnly(m)) return false;
      // if a - 1 is multiple of 4, then m is a multiple of 4 too.
      if ((a - 1) % 4 == 0 && m % 4) return false;
      // Passed all tests
      return true;
    }
```

```
static assert(c == 0 || properLinearCongruentialParameters(m, a,
    c), "Incorrect instantiation of LinearCongruentialEngine");
/* Snip remaining object implementation */
}
```

The one thing to be aware of is that static assertions are run if they are compiled.
Even if it is put in a part of a function which is unreachable at run time, it still must pass.
Consider the following code snippet:

```
void foo() {
    return;
    // the following line is unreachable code, but still must
    // compile. Since the condition of zero is always false, this
    // assert will fail, and thus this function will not compile.
    static assert(0);
}
```

Using template constraints and static if

We saw template constraints and static `if` used in our range consuming functions in
Chapter 3, Ranges. There, they were used to selectively use range functionality for the
purpose of optimization and explicitly documenting our interface requirements. These
same features can also be used for producing custom compile-time errors.

Getting ready

To understand the problem we're trying to solve, compile the following simple program:

```
void main() {
    import std.conv;
    struct Foo {}
    Foo f;
    int i = to!int(f);
}
```

Also, observe the long error message with most of the locations being reported as inside
Phobos! (If you look at the very last line of the message, it will finally report the location in
your code.) It also doesn't tell you why it didn't match.

Similarly, try to call `std.algorithm.sort` with a range that lacks one of the requirements. It
may fail to provide swappable or assignable elements or might have a typo in a property name
like `emptty` instead of `empty`. The error message tells you no function matches, but it doesn't
say what, specifically, the problem is. (The typo problem is why we used static `assert` to verify
we correctly implemented the interface on every range we wrote in *Chapter 3, Ranges*. However,
even there, we would be informed of a problem early on to narrow the scope, but it was still up
to us to find what, specifically, the problem was.)

Also, try to compile this program:

```
string toString(T)(T t) {
    return t;
}
string toString(T)(T t) {
    return cast(string) t;
}
void main() {
    string s = toString(0.0);
}
```

Despite these functions not being semantically valid for the given type (`double`), which produces compilation errors (here, we're interested in the matching, not the specifics of actually implementing a conversion to string algorithm), it also produces an error that the given arguments match two different functions.

For simple templates or a small number of overloads or constraint requirements, the error message helps get to the point quickly. However, for a complex function with multiple requirements, the error messages can be of very little help at all. How can we improve the error message situation for our users?

How to do it...

Perform the following steps:

1. Write two functions for your constraints: one that returns a `bool` result and one that executes a series of `static assert` with appropriate error messages.

2. Use `if(!__ctfe) {}` to keep the code from actually running in the test.

3. Keep template constraints simple so that the error messages are readable. If required, refactor complex conditions into helper functions.

4. Use the template constraints for coarse requirements.

5. Perform other checks with argument specialization.

6. If the requirements still lead to complex error messages, use individual `static if` or `static assert` statements inside the function to customize the errors.

An improvement to Phobos' default `isInputRange` is shown as follows:

```
bool checkInputRange(T)() {
    if(!__ctfe) {
        // notice that this portion is the same as
            std.range.isInputRange
        T t = void;
        if(t.empty) {}
```

```
      t.popFront();
      auto f = t.front;
    }
    return true;
  }
  template isInputRange(T) {
    enum isInputRange = is(typeof(checkInputRange!T));
  }
  struct Test {
    int[] s;
    bool eempty() { return s.length == 0; } // typo intentional!
    int front() { return s[0]; }
    void popFront() { s = s[1 .. $]; }
  }
  // this tells it failed, but not why…
  //static assert(isInputRange!Test);

  // the error message here points out the typo!
  static assert(checkInputRange!Test);
```

Compilation results with the two styles are shown as follows:

cte.d(33): Error: static assert   (isInputRange!(Test)) is false

cte.d(4): Error: no property 'empty' for type 'Test', did you mean 'eempty'?

These messages aren't perfect, but they do point you in the right direction, toward the property `empty` on the type `Test`.

How it works...

Getting compilation errors is a great time saver compared to runtime problems; however, if they are difficult to read, they can be needlessly frustrating. D's metaprogramming capabilities enable a lot of patterns, but at the same time, can lead to complex or unhelpful error messages. By separating our concerns, we can help the compiler provide more help, or failing that, clean up the error messages ourselves.

To do this, we need to understand the way templates are chosen and how code can be test-compiled inside the program. There are two ways to try to compile code: with `is(typeof(` `/* a function that tries to use the code */))` and `__traits(compiles, the_code);`. Both return `true` if the code can be successfully compiled and `false` if the compilation failed. These return values may be checked in template constraints or the `static if` statements.

A template, unless it has obviously invalid syntax (such as a missing semicolon or mismatched parenthesis, in other words, it must successfully lex and parse) is not considered to have failed compilation until a particular set of compile-time arguments is passed to it and they fail semantic analysis.

The `is()` expression is a versatile tool for compile-time introspection. We'll explore it in detail in *Chapter 8, Reflection*. Here, we're using it to check whether a given type is valid. A function, if it compiles, is always a valid type, and if it does not compile, is an error type. The `is(typeof())` expression, thus, can be used to check if a function compiles. This is a very common pattern to check compile-time interfaces in Phobos.

Alternatively, we could use `__traits(compiles, some_code_here);`. This can be given in any block of code and simply sees if it compiles in-context or not, allowing us to achieve the same task as `is(typeof())`. `__traits(compiles)` is less often seen in Phobos simply because it was added to the D language after `is()`. Both patterns are acceptable to perform these interface checks. However, `is()` works better when comparing specific types, and `__traits(compiles)` is a better choice when checking whether a single expression compiles.

Now that we know how to check whether a piece of code is valid, we need to understand how templates (including types and functions with a compile-time parameter list) are chosen by the compiler.

Templates are matched based on their argument signature and constraint condition. If a given set of compile-time arguments matches the template's signature, it will be compiled, even if one overload doesn't actually work for the given arguments. This leads to the two errors we saw in the second exercise while getting ready. Although the function body was correct, the signature was and so the compilation was attempted.

This is where template constraints (or, in this case, argument specializations) come into play. When a template constraint fails, that template is taken out of the running entirely as a valid overload. Consider the following code snippet:

```
// this overload is only considered when the argument is NOT
convertible to double
string toString(T)(T t) if(!is(T : double)) {
  return t;
}
// this one is only considered when it IS convertible to double
string toString(T)(T t) if(is(T : double)) {
  return cast(string) t;
}
```

Attempting to compile will now only complain that our function doesn't actually implement a correct algorithm (with a specific line number of the problem and usage point!). The error about matching both functions is gone. Now, there is only one valid choice for the given type of `double`.

Our code now can be made to work and gives useful error messages. In this case, we could have also alternatively used argument specializations:

```
string toString(T)(T t) { /* the generic implementation */
string toString(T:double)(T t) { /* a specialized implementation for
double */}
```

With argument specializations, the compiler considers the best match for a given set of arguments, just like the traditional runtime overloaded functions, but with the option of a generic implementation to act as a catch-all.

The advantage of argument specialization is they are typically easier to write than template constraints, especially when the number of overloads becomes large. Since one and only one signature must match the given arguments, a list of specializations with constraints quickly becomes `if(cond_1 && !cond_2 && !cond_3)` on one, `if(!cond_1 && cond_2 && !cond_3)`, and so on to keep each option valid for only one condition. With specializations, on the other hand, you just write your requirements for this implementation in this signature.

The advantage of template constraints is they can become arbitrarily complex and serve as a gateway to remove an option entirely in order to ensure it isn't attempted to be compiled even if all other requirements is set. While specializations are limited to looking at one argument at a time and may not call helper functions to perform the matching, the condition in a constraint may call any number of functions by using any compile-time reflection options available in the language. These also inspect as many compile-time arguments as it wants, including looking at a combination of arguments.

You may mix constraints and specializations together. A coarse constraint with a fine-grained specialization, when possible, tends to give the best balance of control, concise code, and readable error messages.

The final tool we'll look at gives even finer control over compilation and is necessary to produce custom error messages: `static if` paired with `static assert`. This is the technique we can use to help clean up the error messages with `std.conv.to`.

The `std.conv.to` expression is even more complex than our example here. The reason the error messages haven't been improved in Phobos is because it was not written with these concerns in mind and would now require a massive refactoring with care to ensure none of its complex functionality is broken in the process. At the time this book was written nobody had the time to do the work. In your code, you may wish to consider using these techniques from the start to prevent the problem from becoming so massive down the line.

Both specializations and constraints depend on the compiler to produce the error message, which will come in the form of either **cannot deduce function from argument types** or **function called with argument types (list) matches both <options>**. If we want to customize it, we need to be permissive in the signature to get past the compiler gate. For example, consider the following code:

```
string toString(T)(T t) { /* no constraint here, no specialization */
static if(is(T : double)) {
  return null; // implementation not important
}
/* after doing our list of supported arguments, end with a custom
error message: */
else static assert(0, "toString only works on floating point types,
not " ~ T.stringof);
```

The following shows what happens if we try to compile while passing a string:

test.d(2): Error: static assert "toString only works on floating point types, not string"

test.d(5):   instantiated from here: toString!string

The custom error message is tailored for the function's needs, giving a custom error and a succinct location, in user code, where it originated.

Finally, in the `checkInputRange` function we wrote earlier, we used `if (!__ctfe) {}` to compile our code but not actually run it. The `__ctfe` variable is a magic variable that the compiler sets to `true` if the code is being run at compile time, and it is set to `false` once compilation is completed (allowing that code to be immediately removed from code generation). It can be used to do the following:

▶ Provide a special implementation for compile-time evaluation versus runtime evaluation. For example, using a generic algorithm at compile time and a hand-optimized assembler algorithm at runtime. The `asm` functions cannot be run at compile time at all.

▶ Remove the code generation functions from the compiled program (we'll see this in the following chapter).

▶ Provide a semantic check via compile-time evaluation without requiring the code to be run successfully, which is why we used it here.

By enclosing the implementation in `if (!__ctfe) {}`, we are saying that the function must compile, but it doesn't need to actually process any data.

Preventing memory corruption bugs with @safe

Memory corruption bugs are one of the most frustrating problems a C programmer can encounter. Memory corruption is writing to what you believed was memory owned by one object; it affects another object in unpredictable ways, leading to crashes. D aims to reduce the scope and occurrence of these bugs by providing a statically checked memory-safe subset which, ideally, exhibits no undefined behavior. In practice, @safe isn't perfect due to bugs in the specification and the implementation, but it nevertheless helps to significantly reduce the probability of memory corruption bugs.

How to do it...

Perform the following steps by using @safe:

1. Mark as many functions as possible with the @safe annotation and try to compile. The compiler will tell you which functions failed the test.

2. Use high-level constructs, such as foreach, references, and D array slices instead of low-level features such as pointers wherever possible.

3. Instead of pointer arithmetic, use array slicing. For example, replace ptr++; with slice = slice[1 .. $];.

4. Avoid the cast operator.

5. Delegate arguments to be used in the @safe functions must also be marked @safe.

6. If a function must perform prohibited actions, but can be manually verified to be correct, you may mark that function as @trusted.

7. Trust the garbage collector. Freeing memory manually is difficult to verify; if you free memory while there's still a reference to it, using that reference will result in memory corruption. So, unless all references are very carefully encapsulated, they should not be marked @trusted. The garbage collector will never free a reference prematurely.

8. To turn off @safe, mark functions @system. These attributes work on the function level, so you may have to re-factor code into additional functions to reach the level of granularity you need.

You may add @safe: to the top of your module and aggregate definitions to apply the annotation to all functions that follow, instead of writing it on each individual function.

Consider the following code snippet:

```
@safe void foo() {}
```

How it works...

The `@safe` annotation (sometimes called SafeD because that was the first-draft name of the concept) is an opt-in set of restrictions that aim to make D code have no undefined behavior and be memory safe, ensuring that memory is never unexpectedly corrupted.

The `@safe` annotation prohibits the use of several of D's lower-level features:

- Pointer manipulation is one such feature, since a pointer mistake is the most likely cause of memory corruption
- D's lower-level feature also include inline assembly, since the compiler cannot guarantee it is used correctly
- Casting between pointer types and using unions with pointers because type safety is lost
- Calling functions not marked `@safe` or `@trusted`, since the compiler cannot verify whether they are implemented correctly
- Taking the address of a local variable, since returning an address of a local can lead to stack corruption
- Catching any exception not derived from `Exception`, since the `Throwable` tree derived from `Error` signify unrecoverable errors
- Accessing globally shared data, since a race condition between threads may cause undefined behavior
- Explicitly casting between immutability or shared, since this potentially breaks type system guarantees by allowing modification of immutable data as well as violations of thread safety

`@safe` does not prevent null pointer dereferences. Since the program is terminated by a null pointer (through a segmentation fault or an unrecoverable Error being thrown), no memory corruption will occur. A crashing program might be annoying and may fail to release resources or leave a file half-written, but since the behavior of immediate termination is well-defined, it is not prevented by restrictions of `@safe`. It is recommended that you use early-and-often `assertions` and/or `NotNull` types to aid in debugging null reference issues.

The recurring theme is that @safe is about guarantees. If the compiler cannot guarantee it is correct, it is prohibited. What about the times when the compiler cannot make a guarantee, but the programmer can? This is where @trusted comes into play.

The @trusted functions violate one of the @safe rules, but is manually verified to do it correctly; the compiler trusts you to get it right. For example, using pointer arithmetic is memory safe, if and only if kept within bounds. If you can manually verify this is done correctly, you may mark the function @trusted. If you do, the function should be limited to returning a strongly-typed D slice (whose bounds are known to the D compiler and/or runtime and managed automatically), which is then worked with inside a fully @safe function. A @trusted function should be as small and as simple as possible.

Array bound checks may be turned off with the –noboundscheck flag to dmd, but only in non-@safe functions. In @safe functions, array bound checks are always present to ensure memory cannot be corrupted by writing past the array length.

It is a mistake to mark too many functions @trusted. It is better to rewrite functions to use higher level features whenever possible. Pointer arithmetic can be translated into array slice operations: slice = slice[1 .. $] generates the same code as ++ptr; (although with range boundary checks inserted when the compiler cannot statically ensure the operation is in bounds). The slice[0] = 0; statement generates the same code as *ptr = 0;.

The --ptr; value is a bit trickier to convert, since slice = slice[-1 .. $]; will generate an out-of-bounds error. To solve this problem, use two variables: a buffer slice and an index integer. Manipulate the integer instead of the slice or pointer.

The @system functions have no restrictions. It is the default safety level because of D's heritage from C. If you want to ensure your entire program is memory-safe, you may mark main @safe; though @safe is opt-in, this may limit your usage of libraries.

See also

- http://dlang.org/function.html#function-safety for the official specification of @safe, @system, and @trusted
- http://dlang.org/safed.html for a rationale of the feature

Leveraging const-correctness

As we saw in *Chapter 1*, *Core Tasks*, D's `const` and `immutable` methods provide strong guarantees. Sometimes, these strong guarantees make them difficult to use. Here, we'll look at how to make the most of `const` without letting it get in our way.

Getting ready

First, let's create a class to demonstrate the problem as shown in the following code:

```
class CachingObject {
  private int cache;
  private bool cacheSet;
  int getExpensiveComputation() {
    if(!cacheSet)
    cache = 31415927; // suppose this was an expensive calculation...
    return cache;
  }
}
```

We can use this method without trouble by simply passing the object around as a mutable instance. However, what happens if we want or have to use `const`? For example, while implementing the `toString` method, this is forced to be `const` by the base class signature as shown in the following code:

```
override string toString() { ... } // compile error, it must be const
override string toString() const { // this signature works...
  import std.conv;
  return to!string(getExpensiveComputation()); // but this won't
compile
}
```

How can we get the best benefits from caching while still being able to leverage the benefits of `const` and `immutable`?

How to do it...

Perform the following steps:

1. Mark as many member functions `const` as possible. Work from the inside out—start with methods that do not call other methods.

2. Whenever possible, also mark function arguments `const` or `immutable`, but do not try to force the issue. It is normal that `const` and `immutable` in D are less common than `const` in C++. When you want your code to break if the data is ever changed, use `immutable`. Otherwise, use `const`.

3. When consuming a `const` object cache expensive computations in a local variable because the object will likely not cache it internally.

4. Avoid casting to and from `const` or `immutable`. Casting away `const` in a method to modify a data member is undefined behavior in D and may lead to crashes, stale caches, or threading problems. Similarly, casting a mutable object to `immutable` may leave behind a mutable reference, thereby violating the immutability guarantee you just promised to uphold.

5. Overload the `const` and non-const methods to provide alternate implementations.

6. If a method returns a reference to a member variable, use `inout` instead of `const`.

7. To use immutable classes, provide an `immutable` constructor and create it with `new immutable`.

The code is as follows:

```
class ConditionalCaching {
  // support mutable construction
  this() {}

  // support immutable construction
  this() immutable {
   // we'll eagerly cache when immutable
   // since lazy caching is completely impossible
   cache = performExpensiveComputation();
   cacheFilled = true;
  }

  // our cache...
  private int cache;
  private bool cacheFilled;

  // helper function to perform the computation
  // this must be refactored into a const method to be
  // usable from all other methods.
  private int performExpensiveComputation() const {
    return 314159265;
  }

  // const getter: use the cache if we can, but if it isn't
  // already filled, we can't fill it now, so just perform the
  // computation now.
  int getExpensiveComputation() const {
    if(cacheFilled)
      return cache;
```

```
      else
        return performExpensiveComputation();
  }

    // mutable getter: we can fill in the cache, so we will.
    int getExpensiveComputation() {
      if(!cacheFilled) {
        cache = performExpensiveComputation();
        cacheFilled = true;
      }
      return cache;
    }
  }
}
```

You may also use a normal (mutable thread-local) associative array
to cache values in a const method, but you should prefer to use a
member cache variable for efficiency and purity. You may also pass
a cache helper to the method as a function argument.

How it works...

D's strong immutability guarantees to provide benefits, but also prohibit some patterns from
C++, necessitating new patterns in their place and some wholly new ones. A major difference
is the lack of anything like C++'s mutable keyword and the lack of a logical const member
field, which is commonly used to cache an expensive computation inside a const method.

There are three potential solutions. First, a global cache or a cache passed to the method as a
mutable argument, which works because the data is not reached through the reference; it isn't a
member variable so the restriction does not reply. The second potential solution is to cast to and
from const as needed. This invokes undefined behavior and thus is strongly discouraged. The
third potential solution is to use D's ability to overload methods based on constness to cache
internally when possible, and recommend the user to cache externally otherwise.

The idea is to break up the implementation into separate computing and conditional caching
functions. The computing method must be const so it can be called from other const or
immutable methods. Then, we implement the getter functions: one const that returns
the cache (if available) but is unable to update it, and one mutable, which does update
the cache.

While this will not cache as eagerly as a C++ mutable field, it does cache when possible
and does not break D's stronger guarantees. The D version will still be fully thread-safe and
may be usable in read-only memory. At the usage point, we can still conservatively assume
it does not cache and keep a copy of the result in a local variable instead of calling the
method multiple times when we know the object is const.

D never has `const` references to mutable data, unless you bypass the type system with `cast` or `union`. Anything reachable through a `const` or `immutable` reference must itself be `const` or `immutable`. If you want an unchangeable reference to mutable data, use a getter property that returns a mutable item without a corresponding setter property. On the other hand, a mutable reference to `const` data does exist, `const(int) *` or `immutable(char) []`, for example, but there is no such syntax for classes! Instead, import `std.typecons` and use `Rebindable!ObjectType`.

Another time overloading on constantness is useful in constructors. The default constructor (when you don't write one at all) works for both `mutable` and `immutable` objects, but once you write a constructor, you'll find it only works on `mutable` objects.

The usage-site code to create mutable or immutable objects is as follows:

```
// create a mutable object
ConditionalCaching c = new ConditionalCaching();
// this won't compile: we have to construct an immutable
// instance specially
// immutable(ConditionalCaching) i = new ConditionalCaching();

// create an immutable object properly. This calls the
// immutable constructor
immutable(ConditionalCaching) d = new immutable
  ConditionalCaching();
```

Notice that there are two different forms of the new operator and they call different constructors. Here, since caching is impossible for immutable objects, we added a special `immutable` constructor to pregenerate the expensive computation for us.

You can share one constructor for both immutable and mutable construction if you mark that constructor as `pure`.

Avoiding side effects of pure functions

A general principle of good programming is **encapsulation**. Functions should only access what they need to accomplish their task and should minimize side effects and action at a distance.

How to do it...

Perform the following steps to avoid side effects of pure functions:

1. Mark as many functions as possible with the `pure` annotation. It may go before or after the return type, name, and argument list.

2. Try to compile. The compiler will tell you which functions need your attention.

3. Take `const` or `immutable` objects whenever possible. Use the `in` or `scope` keywords on your parameters if you will not store a reference to them.

4. To enable the most functions to be pure, avoid the use of global (module-level or locals marked with `static`) variables.

5. If a function is conditionally `pure` based on compile-time arguments, you do not have to explicitly mark it with the `pure` keyword. Follow the rules and the compiler will infer its purity based on the purity of its arguments at the usage point.

6. If you need to call an impure function inside a `pure` function, for example, to debug, you may do so with the debug statement: `debug writeln("debug printing");`. Consider the following code snippet:

```
int foo(int a) pure {
    return a + 50;
}
```

 As with other annotations, you may also write `pure:` at the top of a module to have it apply to all functions or use curly braces to mark several functions pure at once. However, there is no impure keyword, so if you do this, you'll be locked into purity for the rest of the module!

How it works...

Pure functions in D are prohibited from accessing non-immutable global data or calling impure functions. There are two exceptions to these general rules: GC memory allocations with `new` are always allowed inside pure functions, and impure functions are allowed in `debug` statements. Other language features, including mutation of local variables, are allowed, the same as any other function. D treats functional programming as a big-picture design, not an in-function implementation style.

While pure functions may not modify global state, they may modify local variables, including its arguments. A pure function with all immutable arguments is called a strongly pure function. Like in many other programming languages, a strongly pure function may not modify any data external to the implementation and have no side effects.

A pure function with one or more mutable arguments is called a weakly pure function. Weakly pure functions are often a surprise for programmers coming from other languages because they allow mutation to data passed to it.

The benefit of pure functions is to statically enforce that the pure function's result is dependent only on the data you explicitly pass to it, making all its requirements obvious at the call point and limiting the amount of code you have to look at to understand the program's current state.

Verifying object invariants and pre- and post-conditions

D supports contract programming, which can help you ensure an object's state is always valid and object methods are passed with correct parameters and returns valid values, including while using class inheritance. Here, we'll see how to use these features and why they work the way they do.

How to do it...

Perform the following steps:

1. When writing an `interface`, `class`, or `struct`, add in and out blocks to methods, right after the signatures, and also add `invariant` blocks to the aggregate.

2. Put assertions in the `in` blocks to verify your preconditions.

3. Put assertions in the `out` blocks to verify your postconditions. The `out` block may take an argument to access the method's return value.

4. Add the `body` keyword before your method's body but after its `in` and `out` blocks (if it has them).

5. In child classes, also use `in` contracts to reassert your input requirements, even if they are the same as the parent class.

6. Put assertions in the `invariant` blocks to verify object conditions that are always true. The invariant must be valid as soon as the constructor returns.

7. Unless your data members may validly hold any value, make them private and only accessible through getter and setter properties.

8. Test your application by building without the `-release` switch and running the program.

The code is as follows:

```
interface Example {
    int negate(int a)
        in { assert(a >= 0); }
        out(ret) { assert(ret <= 0); }
        // note: no body since this is an interface
}
class ExampleImplementation : Example {
    int negate(int a)
        in { assert(a >= 0); } // same input restriction
        body { // note the body keyword following the contracts
        return -a;
    }
    invariant() {
        // we have no data, so no need for any invariant
            assertions
    }
}
void main() {
    auto e = new ExampleImplementation();
    e.negate(-1); // throws an assertion failure
}
```

How it works...

D supports contract programming, inspired by the Eiffel language, with three constructs: the in and out blocks on methods and invariant blocks in objects.

All contracts are run at runtime. Running contracts at compile time is not possible in D today. Like other assert statements, contracts are compiled out when compiling in release mode.

It's preferable to use the in and out blocks instead of writing assertions inside the function itself, because the in and out blocks understand inheritance. When overriding an inherited method in a class, the following points must be considered:

▸ Any one of the in blocks in the inheritance tree must pass (it may weaken preconditions by providing *alternate* checks). If there is no in block on a method, it is assumed to accept any input, and thus always pass. This is why child classes have to reassert their input requirements, even if they are the same as the interface.

▸ All of the out blocks in the inheritance tree must pass (it may strengthen postconditions by providing *additional* checks).

▸ All of the object invariants on the inheritance tree must pass (it must honor the parent's invariants).

These rules realize the **Liskov substitution principle** of object-oriented programming; a subclass should always be substitutable for its superclass or interface without breaking any code. When using an object through its interface, only the interface's in blocks are considered and it must pass (this is because the interface doesn't know which implementation it is forwarding to).

A limitation of contracts on methods in D is the lack of a pre-state in the out contract. There is no easy way to work around this limitation at this time. Instead, focus your out contracts on ensuring that your return value alone meets some requirements, such as not being null.

The current D spec does not permit contracts on abstract class methods as well (though they are permitted on interfaces). This limitation may be removed in the future.

Since contracts are logically part of the interface, when you write a library, you should also write your contracts in your D interface file (a .di file, which includes function prototypes but not the whole implementation bodies), if you choose to use them. This way, the user or compiler may choose to insert them in a debug build of a program, even when using a release build of the library. However, at this time, the compiler does not keep contracts. The common solution is to provide both debug and release builds of your library or to distribute full source code and let the user build it themselves.

Unit testing your code

Unit tests are blocks of code that verify the correct output of one small part of your code (a unit) at a time, such as an individual function or class. D has a built-in support for basic unit testing. Here, we'll see what we can do with it.

How to do it...

Perform the following steps:

1. Add unittest {} blocks to your modules, under your functions and inside your classes.
2. Put any imports needed by the test inside the unittest block.
3. You should write helper function and class definitions inside the unittest block.
4. Write assertions to perform your tests.
5. Use std.exception for additional helper functions.
6. Compile with dmd -unittest yourfiles.d.
7. Run the program.

Design your classes with dependency injection for easier mocking of tests. This is when instead of constructing child objects yourself, you accept them as arguments to the constructor. The unit test may then pass a dummy object to the class instead of, for example, a live network connection to test the code.

Consider the following code snippet:

```
unittest {
    assert(myFunction() == expected_value);
}
```

How it works...

D's specialized syntax for unit testing was added with a modest goal; to make writing basic unit tests so easy that there's just no excuse not to. They don't aim to do everything possible—there are third-party libraries to extend unit testing capabilities—but do aim to set a usable foundation.

Using them is very simple; you write a `unittest {}` block and fill it with `assert` statements to test your code. Use an alternate implementation or manual to figure out the expected values of your functions and compare the results.

Any types or imports you need should be local to the `unittest` block. This ensures you don't accidentally use these types or imports in non-tested code, which would cause the tests to pass, but the regular build to fail!

Outside the `unittest` block, you can use `version(unittest)` to conditionally compile code only if unit testing is enabled. This can be useful to provide an empty main function to allow your module to be used as a library import or be compiled alone to run its tests. You can also compile with `-unittest -main` for the compiler to automatically insert an empty `main` function for you.

You may also use any construct, including loops, conditionals, and exceptions. The unit testing code is just normal D code that is run upon request.

The Phobos module `std.exception` includes some helper functions to test functions in error conditions. For example, `assertThrown` can be used to ensure a function throws the proper exception when deliberately given invalid data.

See also

- ▸ `http://github.com/nomad-software/dunit` is an add-on unit testing library to extend D's built-in functionality

- ▸ `https://github.com/bgertzfield/deject` is a dependency injection and mock object library for D

- ▸ `http://dconf.org/2013/talks/gertzfield.html` is Ben Gertzfield's talk from Dconf 2013 about writing testable code in D

Documenting your code with Ddoc

To verify your code is working correctly, you must know what it is supposed to do. Like with unit testing, D has a built-in documentation generator called **Ddoc**. Ddoc is fairly simple, but it gets the job done and is always available.

How to do it...

Perform the following steps to document your code:

1. Attach documentation comments to declarations by writing `/** Docs */` or `/++ Docs +/` above them or `/// short description` directly after them.

2. Put documentation comments on both collections and members. For example, if you document a class member, ensure that there's a `doc` comment on the class itself too.

3. Document unit tests that you want to serve as usage examples.

4. Document function parameters by writing lines in the format: `name = meaning` under a section `Params:`.

5. Compile the module with the `-D` flag to `dmd` to generate the documentation's HTML file.

6. You may define and use macros. They are defined in a special section named `Macros:` with a `name=value` syntax and used with `$(name)` syntax to extend the textual capabilities of Ddoc.

7. Move macros that you use across several modules to a separate file with the `.ddoc` extension and pass it to the compiler when generating the documentation.

The following is an example of how to use Ddoc to document an object:

```
/++
    Example is a structure meant to demonstrate Ddoc
       documentation.

    In addition to the first one-line short description, we
       can also write
    longer multi-line descriptions to expand on the object's
       functionality.
+/
struct Example {
    int a; /// This integer is documented briefly.
    /**
       This function has documented parameters.

       We document all the parameters in a params section.
       The return value and exceptions can also be documented.

       Params:
         x = The x coordinate
       Returns:
         The y coordinate
       Throws:
         Exception if x is negative.
    */
    int getY(int x) { return 0; /* implementation irrelevant
       */ }
}
```

If you name the file ddoc.d, compile with:

dmd -D -c ddoc.d

The generated HTML (ddoc.html) looks like the following in a browser:

---

ddoc

struct <u>Example</u>;
      <u>Example</u> is a structure meant to demonstrate Ddoc documentation.

      In addition to the first one-line short description, we can also write longer multi-line descriptions to expand on the object's functionality.

  int <u>a</u>;
      This integer is documented briefly.

  int <u>getY</u>(int x);
      This function has documented parameters.

      We document all the parameters in a params section. The return value and exceptions can also be documented.

      Params:
      int x The x coordinate

      Returns:
      The y coordinate

      Throws:
      Exception if x is negative.

Page generated by <u>Ddoc</u>.

This screenshot uses the default HTML body and no CSS style sheet. You may customize the website's appearance with HTML and CSS by changing the DDOC macro to link to an external file.

How it works...

The D language and compiler has a built-in documentation tool that has a simple syntax, is easy to use, and has knowledge of the language. Thanks to the integration with the language, Ddoc comments do not need to repeat information that is already obvious from the code.

Ddoc has very little built-in syntax. A documentation comment consists of up to four parts:

- A one line summary, which is always the first line.
- A multiline description, which is any content after the first line, but before any labelled sections.
- The third part is the sections, starting with a label and a colon. Of the sections, `Params:` is special, because in that it also parses `name=description` lines. `Macros:` is special because it parses new macros in the format of `name=replacement`. Other section names serve to organize content without changing Ddoc's parsing.
- The fourth part is macros, which are sprinkled throughout.

Macros are Ddoc's tool for extension and customization. A macro works via textual replacement and is used with the syntax: `$(MACRO_NAME arg1, arg2, ...)`. Macros may span multiple lines. All of Ddoc's default output is defined as macros. You can see the defaults in the source code distributed with the `dmd` zip. The file is `dmd2/src/dmd/doc.c`, for example, the default HTML body is defined in the macro `DDOC`.

You may override this macro in your individual file (make a `Macros:` section at the top of your module) or with a separate file with the extension of `.ddoc` that you pass to `dmd` when generating the documentation.

> Leading stars or plusses are allowed and ignored:
>
> ```
> /**
>  *    The summary will not include the leading star.
>  */
> ```
>
> This will let you format your comments how you want without impacting the content.

Ddoc does not properly encode special characters for the output format. To work around this, you may replace special characters with macros, for example, `$(GT)` instead of `>` when generating HTML.

Macro syntax has three special forms in the replacement text: `$0`, which is all the arguments as a single string; `$1 .. $n`, which is one specific argument; and `$+`, which is all arguments beyond the first. Using `$1` and `$+`, we can create recursive macros to simulate loops:

```
Macros:
LIST_ITEM=<li>$0</li>
LIST_TAIL=$(LIST_ITEM $1)$(LIST_TAIL $+)
LIST=<ul>$(LIST_ITEM $1)$(LIST_TAIL $+)</ul>
```

If you write `$(LIST 1, 2, 3)` in your documentation somewhere, this will be generated: `<ul><li>1</li><li>2</li><li>3</li></ul>`, a well-formed HTML list with fairly concise syntax in the D code.

There's more...

As in the case of unit testing, the built-in facility is deliberately minimal to provide a baseline that there's just no excuse not to use. When additional features are needed, we'll turn to third-party documentation tools.

A pair of switches is possessed by dmd to help us with these: -X and -D. The -X switch generates a JSON file that lists all declarations it compiled. The -D switch generates the documentation. If you combine the two of them, the JSON file also includes the documentation comment attached to each declaration. This makes them easy to parse—no need to write a new compiler, as a JSON parser will suffice.

Writing platform-specific code (versions) and per-client configuration modules

Different platforms often need specialized code. D provides the version statement for this case, which is similar to but cleaner than C's #ifdef directives. In addition to platforms, special code may be needed when building customized versions of an application for a specific client or other special case. While version can do that job, it isn't ideal. So, we'll use another technique: configuration modules.

How to do it...

Writing platform-specific code and writing client-specific code is best done with two different techniques.

Platform-specific code

Perform the following steps:

1. Write version statements for all supported platforms.
2. Write else static assert(0, "Unsupported platform"); at the end of the version list.
3. Don't try to mix partial declarations for different platforms together, it will be more trouble than it is worth.

The code is as follows:

```
version(Windows)
void writeToFile(HANDLE file, in void[] data) {
  if(!WriteFile(file, data.ptr, data.length, null, null))
    throw new Exception("WriteFile failed");
}
```

```
else version(Posix)
void writeToFile(int file, in void[] data) {
  if(write(file, data.ptr, data.length) < 0))
    throw new Exception("write failed");
}
else static assert(0, "Unsupported platform");
```

Client-specific code

Perform the following steps:

1. Write separate files for each client, with all the files having the same module name.

2. Import the module by its module name in the rest of the application.

3. When compiling, explicitly pass the correct configuration file for the client you are building to the dmd command line:

   ```
   // company_x_config.d
   module myapp.config;
   enum bool wantFeatureX = false;
   enum string companyName = "FooBar, Ltd.";

   // company_y_config.d
   module myapp.config;
   enum bool wantFeatureX = true;
   enum string companyName = "Acme, Inc.";

   // yourapp.d
   import myapp.config;
   static if(wantFeatureX) { void implementFeatureX() {} }
   pragma(msg, "Compiling for client " ~ companyName);
   ```

   On compiling you will get the following output:

   ```
   dmd yourapp.d company_x_config.d # build for Company X
   dmd yourapp.d company_y_config.d # build for Company Y
   ```

How it works...

D supports conditional compilation with its version statement. A single simple argument is taken by version: a number or an identifier. Conditions cannot be combined. Version identifiers may be set in a module or on the command line, or preset for the compiler environment and target architecture. If the version is set, the code within is compiled. Otherwise, the code must be syntactically valid but is not actually compiled, and thus does not have to be semantically valid.

You may use `version(none)` to quickly disable a block of code. It may come directly before a declaration without curly braces, making it convenient to comment out a function without needing to trace down the end of the function.

The `version` statement has several limitations that make it less than ideal to customize an application for a client:

- It cannot cross module boundaries, so all client customizations must be present in the same file. This makes for messy code and may leak private details if one client buys a source license.

- Data cannot be passed on the command line. Custom strings and other values have to be done with another file of some sort.

- Boolean conditions cannot be expressed with version. For example, `version(a ||  b)` will not compile.

These limitations prompt us to look for alternatives. D presents two easily accessible options: data file imports or code imports. Data file imports are enabled with the `-J` switch to `dmd`. You must pass it a directory to search for the files. Then, in your code, you write `import("filename")`. The file's contents are brought into the code just like a string literal and may be manipulated. We'll use this facility later in the book.

Here, we'll use a regular module import instead. A regular module can consist of any code (since it is just code!), which gives us all the compile-time correctness checking possible in the rest of D.

The module system feature that enables this technique is the fact that the file name need not match the module name, as long as you pass the module explicitly to the compiler. By having multiple files with the same module name, we can use them the same way in the rest of your code, but swap them out at compile time in the make file or on the command line.

This also is preferable to versions because a missing configuration entry will result in a compile-time error, instead of silent acceptance.

See also

- `http://dlang.org/version.html` is the official specification for the `version` statement. The complete list of predefined version identifiers is available on this page.

8
Reflection

D supports limited runtime reflection out of the box as well as rich compile-time reflection that can be used in code generation efforts, custom semantic checks, building additional runtime reflection information, and more. In this chapter, we'll be covering the following recipes:

- ▶ Getting dynamic runtime type information
- ▶ Getting a list of child classes
- ▶ Determining whether a module is available
- ▶ Getting a list of all methods or fields in a module or an object
- ▶ Inspecting function overloads
- ▶ Determining names, types, and default values of function parameters
- ▶ Getting components of complex types
- ▶ Using user-defined attributes
- ▶ Implementing a custom lint-style check for virtual functions
- ▶ Extending the runtime type information
- ▶ Creating a command-line function caller

Introduction

Reflection is commonly associated with virtual machines of interpreted languages, but D proves it can work well with a natively compiled language too. D provides some built-in runtime reflection, a lot of compile-time reflection, and ways to make the compile-time information available at runtime to bridge the gap while only paying for what you use.

Getting dynamic runtime type information

The simplest form of reflection available in D is runtime type information, which is available through the `typeid()` operator. It is used extensively by the `druntime` implementation and is integral to the safe dynamic casting of classes.

How to do it...

Let's execute the following steps to get dynamic runtime type information:

1. In most cases, you only need to write `typeid(variable_or_type)`.
2. If you want to get a dynamic class type through an interface, first cast it to `Object`, check for `null`, and then use `typeid(the_casted_object)`.

The code is as follows:

```
TypeInfo typeInfoAboutInt = typeid(int);
typeInfoAboutInt = typeid(1); // also works
```

How it works...

The compiler and the runtime library automatically define type information for all types. This information is found in static `TypeInfo` objects, which is retrieved by reference using the `typeid()` operator. The definition of the `TypeInfo` interface is found in the automatically-imported `object.d` module of druntime, and thus it is always available to D programs.

`TypeInfo` is tailored for druntime's needs. It contains functions for:

▶ Hashing, equality, and comparison (needed for associative arrays).
▶ Construction, destruction, copying, and garbage collection flags (needed for the `new` operator and built-in array operators).
▶ Getting the next type out of a compound type. For example, `typeid(int*).next` is `typeid(int).typeid(int*)` gives information about a pointer, which points to the next type.
▶ An internal extension hook, intended for future garbage collection improvements.

Classes and interfaces have to get additional functions:

▶ The class' name
▶ The class' base class and interfaces
▶ The class' virtual function table
▶ The class' initial memory image
▶ Searching and creating the class, if it has a simple constructor

These methods are vital to the proper functioning of classes. They enable safe dynamic casting from base class to derived class, proper object construction, and automatic implementation of `toString`, which works without being explicitly overridden in every class you write.

The `TypeInfo` references are only stored with the data of class objects (specifically, the first hidden virtual function entry for each object stores a reference to the correct `TypeInfo` reference). With all other types, `typeid` yields a reference based on the static type. This means that you cannot retrieve the runtime type information from a `void*` or `void[]`, as shown in the following code:

```
void main() {
        int[] a;
        arrayType(a);
}
void arrayType(void[] arr) {
        // assert(typeid(arr) == typeid(int[])); // FAILS
        // The following passes because non-class typeid is based on
        static type
        assert(typeid(arr) == typeid(void[]));
}
```

If you want to work with `void*` in a type-safe way, it is important to explicitly pair a `TypeInfo` object with it. This is how the druntime functions work, also some of the language features' non-template D variadic functions work in the same way.

Templates are generally better at both type safety and efficiency than runtime information. You should only use `TypeInfo` based typing in functions when you have special ABI requirements. The `void*` and `TypeInfo` pairs are used in druntime primarily for legacy reasons; the library was designed before D had templates.

Static types are also used with interfaces: `typeid(some_object_via_interface)` and is `typeid(the_interface_you_are_using);`. In order to get the dynamic type of the object behind the interface, you will have to first cast it to an object, and then cast it from the object to the derived class.

Casting an interface to the object might fail because not all interfaces are D objects. It might also be a C++ or COM object. Thus, any time you cast an interface to object, you ought to check for the `null` value.

To compare types at runtime, you may use either the `==` operator or the `is` operator on `TypeInfo`. Since there's only one instantiation for each type, you can always rely on the comparison operators.

▶ Refer to the documentation on `TypeInfo`'s members at `http://dlang.org/phobos/object.html#TypeInfo`. Also, scroll down to `TypeInfo_Class` to see additional members available on classes.

Getting a list of child classes

Another form of runtime information available in D is a list of all classes in the program. Using this information, we can achieve tasks that will be impossible at runtime, such as getting a list of all child classes of a particular class. A potential use of this capability will be to load game objects, defined as classes inheriting a common base, from an XML file at runtime.

How to do it...

Let's execute the following steps to get a list of child classes:

1. Get the `typeid` of the parent class you're interested in.
2. Loop over `ModuleInfo` with the `foreach` loop.
3. Loop over the `localClasses` member of each loop value.
4. Add recursion if you want to get all descendants, including the children's children.

The code is as follows:

```
ClassInfo[] getChildClasses(ClassInfo c) {
    ClassInfo[] info;
    foreach(mod; ModuleInfo) {
        foreach(cla; mod.localClasses) {
            if(cla.base is c)
                info ~= cla;
        }
    }

    return info;
}

class A {}
class B : A {}
class C : A {}

void main() {
    foreach(cla; getChildClasses(A.classinfo)) {
```

```
        import std.stdio;
        writeln(cla.name); // you could also create the class with
        cla.create();
    }
}
```

Running the program will give the following output:

```
test.B
test.C
```

Notice that `test` is the name of the module containing this program. Also, try adding more modules to inherit from class A and observe that they still work.

How it works...

Similar to `TypeInfo`, the D compiler also automatically creates static instances of a type called `ModuleInfo`, tailored to the needs of druntime, which provides limited runtime reflection across the entire program. The definition is in `object.d`, so no explicit import is required to use it.

 Since `ModuleInfo` is undocumented on the official website, its interface may be subject to change without notice.

The members of `ModuleInfo` include pointers to the module constructor, destructor, unit tests, a list of imported modules, a list of local classes, and the module name. It also has a `static opApply` function that lets us perform a `foreach` loop over it.

The primary use of `ModuleInfo` is for the internal druntime code. The druntime is responsible for calling your `main` function. Before it runs your function, it loops over all modules in the application to run their module constructors, using the list of imported modules to run them in the proper order. So, dependencies are initialized before the modules that use them. If unit tests are enabled, druntime also runs those tests through `ModuleInfo` before running `main`.

A secondary use of `ModuleInfo` is to find and inspect classes present in the program. This is how the `Object.factory` function is implemented, and it is through these facilities that we achieved our task to find all the child classes.

Getting a list of all the available child classes is impossible at compile time. While a list of base classes is possible, the compiler must be aware of all base classes to form a working inheritance hierarchy—a list of child classes is a runtime task because two modules or shared libraries may both provide child classes and may be compiled separately, with no knowledge of one another.

The foreach(mod; ModuleInfo) loops over each module in the program, yielding ModuleInfo* on each iteration. Then, for each module, we loop over the localClasses member. The localClasses array is an array of the TypeInfo_Class objects (sometimes known by its alias, ClassInfo), the same type we retrieved with typeid in the previous recipe. The base member of this object also points to a TypeInfo_Class instance, and it may be null in the case of Object, which is the root of all D classes.

By comparing these TypeInfo instances with the is identity operator, we will build a list of each type we're interested in. It can be used with further runtime reflection operations, including to call the create method to construct a default object of that class type.

It is impossible to declare a variable, cast to, or to use any other compile-time operation on a ClassInfo object to learn more about or manipulate the class because compile time is longer than the time we're in this function. The ClassInfo objects aren't special in any sense other than the fact that they are automatically created at runtime; they are just another block of data. We'll cover a technique to enable extended runtime reflection later in this chapter.

> Note that the names returned are the full name of the class, including module and package name. All the runtime class functions work with full names, the most common mistake when trying to use Object.factory is forgetting to use the module name as well as the class name.

Determining whether a module is available

We might want to compile some extension features if and only if another module is available at compile-time to gracefully degrade when a dependency isn't installed. The most straightforward solution is to use the version statement, passing the appropriate identifier to the dmd command line. Can we also do it without extra compiler options from the user?

How to do it...

Let's execute the following steps to determine whether a module is available:

1. Try to compile an anonymous function that does nothing other than import a module.

2. Use it conditionally by wrapping any use of the module inside the static if statement.

3. Instruct the user to enable the module by placing it at a location where the compiler can find it automatically, or by adding the following module to the compile command line.

The code is as follows:

```
static if(__traits(compiles, { import test.foo; })) {
    import test.foo; /* safe to use */
} else {
    // module not available, work around
}
```

How it works...

This is an example of a common strategy to poke around D: conditional compilation. Instead of trying to find metadata, we can often simply try to compile a block of code to attempt the task we're interested in. If that compilation fails, assume the task cannot be done with the arguments we're given. Anything we can encapsulate in a small function can be tested with `__traits(compiles)`.

 This principle is also how the duck-typed interface checking for ranges works, as discussed in *Chapter 3, Ranges*, and *Chapter 7, Correctness Checking*.

Since imports can be local to a function, we can wrap it in an anonymous function (the `{ code }` syntax expands to `void delegate() { code }`) and see if it compiles. Once it does, the compiler has already loaded the module, so we can immediately use it.

Generally, any time you might get a compilation error and do not wish for it to be fatal, you may wrap the code in `static if(__traits(compiles))` to selectively enable or disable iffy features. However, be careful not to overuse this. It is easy to hide minor mistakes and completely disable the code that never actually compiles! Keep the conditional code as simple as possible and always run it normally when you change it. This ensures that it actually does work when it is supposed to.

The `__traits` function is a built-in language construct for special communication with the compiler. It always takes an operation identifier as the first argument, for example: `compiles`, `isSame`, `allMembers`, `getMember`, and others that can be found in the documentation. Subsequent arguments are specific to the operation. The `compiles` identifier takes only one argument; an expression that it attempts to compile.

The `__traits` function returns values in the form of compile-time constants that can be tested in `static if`, stored in `enums` or `aliases`, or used directly. In the generated code, they will be indistinguishable from data literals. When `__traits` returns a list, it does it as a `TemplateArgumentList` (sometimes also called a `TypeTuple`, though it can hold more things other than types). These lists may be looped over with the `foreach` loop at compile time to inspect individual elements with all compile-time tools.

See also

▸ Refer to the documentation for `__traits` at `http://dlang.org/traits.html`. It has a list of all the available operations, their arguments, and their return values.

▸ Refer to the specific documentation for the `compiles` trait at `http://dlang.org/traits.html#compiles`.

Getting a list of all methods or fields in a module or an object

To dig into an aggregate, the first step is to get a list of members. Then, we'll be able to look at each individual member and dig as deeply as we need to.

How to do it...

Let's execute the following steps to get a list of all methods or fields in a module or object:

1. Get a reference to the aggregate. For a `struct`, `class`, or `enum` type, you may use its name directly (or if it is passed to a template, the corresponding template parameter). To get a reference to a module, use `mixin("yourmodule.name")`.

2. Get a list of the names of all members with `__traits(allMembers)`.

3. Retrieve the member with `__traits(getMember)`. Use a helper template in the form of `alias helper(alias T) = T;` and an `alias` member in the loop to make referring to the member easier.

4. Using static `if` and the `is` expression, filter out any types: `static if(is(member)) { /* type */ }`.

5. Then, check for functions with the `is` expression on `typeof(member)`: `else static if(is(typeof(member) == function)) { /* function */ }`.

6. If the member is neither a type nor a function, it may still be a template, a module, a variable, or some other construct added to the language later. If it has a valid `.init` type, it is a variable; otherwise, some guesswork is needed. If the string value starts with `module`, you can tell it is a module. If nothing else matches, it is most likely a template.

7. You may use `__traits(compiles)` on the `getMember` function to filter out private variables if you need to.

The following is a program that defines some test structures and then drills down using the preceding steps to show details about all the members of the module:

```
struct S {
  // variables
```

```
    int a;
    int b;
    void delegate() c;
    string d;

    alias e = d;

    // functions
    void foo() {}
    int bar() { return 0; }

    // types
    struct Bar {}
    enum Foo { a, b }
}

template TestTemplate(string s) {
  enum TestTemplate = to!int(s);
}

// the helper for easier aliasing we'll need in step 3
alias helper(alias T) = T;

// This function writes details about all members of what it
// is passed. The string before argument is related to
// indenting the data it prints.
void inspect(alias T)(string before) {
  import std.stdio;
  import std.algorithm;

  // step 2
  foreach(memberName; __traits(allMembers, T)) {
    // step 3
    alias member = helper!(__traits(getMember, T, memberName));
    // step 4 - inspecting types
    static if(is(member)) {
      string specifically;
      static if(is(member == struct))
        specifically = "struct";
      else static if(is(member == class))
        specifically = "class";
      else static if(is(member == enum))
```

```
            specifically = "enum";

        writeln(before, memberName, " is a type (", specifically, ")");

        // drill down (step 1 again)
        inspect!member(before ~ "\t");
      } else static if(is(typeof(member) == function)) {
        // step 5, inspecting functions
        writeln(before, memberName, " is a function typed ",
        typeof(member).stringof);
      } else {
        // step 6, everything else
        static if(member.stringof.startsWith("module "))
          writeln(before, memberName, " is a module");
        else static if(is(typeof(member.init)))
          writeln(before, memberName, " is a variable typed ",
          typeof(member).stringof);
        else
          writeln(before, memberName, " is likely a template");
      }
    }
}
void main() {
  // step 1: we'll start with a reference
  // to the current module, gotten with mixin.
  // Note: __MODULE__ is a special symbol the
  // compiler replaces with the current module name.
  inspect!(mixin(__MODULE__))("");
}
```

When you run the program, you can see that it reflects the full structure of our code, including indented child members. This is shown in the following output:

```
object is a module
S is a type (struct)
        a is a variable typed int
        b is a variable typed int
        c is a variable typed void delegate()
        d is a variable typed string
        e is a variable typed string
        foo is a function typed void()
        bar is a function typed int()
        Bar is a type (struct)
```

```
        Foo is a type (enum)
                a is a variable typed Foo
                b is a variable typed Foo
TestTemplate is likely a template
helper is likely a template
inspect is likely a template
main is a function typed void()
```

 The output will also include the `module` object, which is automatically imported by all D modules.

How it works...

The `__traits` method and the `is` expression aren't limited to conditional compilation. Each feature has several operations to perform in-depth compile-time reflection. Moreover, the `.stringof` and `.mangleof` properties of the most D symbols can be used for a variety of purposes, including reparsing them to gather even more information.

The first and the foremost among them is `__traits(allMembers, Aggregate)`, which returns the names of each member of an aggregate (`struct`, `class`, `union`, `enum`, or `module`). Once we have the name of a member, we use `__traits(getMember, Aggregate, name)` to turn it into a symbol. A symbol is a specific name in the code, a class name, a variable name, and so on.

Working with symbols is different than working with variables. If you declared a new variable (for example, with `auto` or `const`), that will create a new symbol instead of working with the existing one. Instead, we alias the new names to the existing symbol. The `alias` term works in compile-time parameter lists or anywhere a declaration is allowed, including inside functions.

Due to a limitation of the D grammar and parser, we use a simple `alias helper` to enable its use with more parameters. For example, `alias a = __traits(getMember, Foo, bar);` will fail with a parse error saying **basic type expected, not __traits**. The `alias helper` allows us to easily work around this limitation, saving us from repeating the whole `getMember` expression every time we want to use it.

 The `alias` keyword also works when renaming the complex types, for example, binding compile-time parameters to a single name `alias toInt = to!int;` would let you use `toInt` anytime you would have used `to!int`.

Once we have the symbol aliased to a convenient name, we can start to learn more about it. First, we categorize it into three broad areas: types, functions, and others, using `static if` and the `is` expression. The first test, `static if(is(member))`, simply tests if a member represents a valid type, that is, it doesn't check whether it has a valid type; it checks if it is a valid type. This is an important distinction because it is how we differentiate types, including aggregate definitions that are types and can be drilled into directly with the `is` expression, from variables and functions, which have types that can be retrieved with `typeof()` to drill in to.

The next major category we test for is functions, with `is(typeof(member) == function)`. Functions get their own category because various special details are available for them that aren't available for other variables, such as parameter information.

Finally, we consider everything else to be other and use a variety of techniques to break it down. To differentiate modules from everything else, we perform a simple check on `.stringof` to see whether the name starts with the `module` keyword. If it isn't a module, we test the next broad category by checking if it has a validly typed `.init` property, which is a feature of all the D variables. If nothing has matched yet, we can assume it is most likely a template by process of elimination. Currently, reflection of templates is very limited, so we can't drill any more into it.

Once we break a symbol into one of the following broad categories, we can dig even deeper with consistent techniques:

- Types can be further categorized with the `is` expression, for example, `is(member == class)` tests whether it is a `class` declaration, and can also be tested for additional members with `__traits(allMembers)`.
- Functions can be drilled into by using the `std.traits` functions, or the prototype can simply be displayed to the user with `.stringof`.
- Modules can be drilled into by recursively calling `__traits(allMembers)` upon it. Keep in mind that the hidden import of objects is listed. So, if you drill down every member, you will also see D runtime code.
- Variables can be drilled into by examining their name or type at compile time or by value at runtime. Phobos' `std.traits` module has several members to categorize types as well, for example, `isIntegral!(typeof(member))` or `isSomeString!(typeof(member))`.

The categories have some overlap in techniques, but since there are several differences in what details are available and how to get to them. Categorizing before trying to dig into the reflection will help avoid compile errors.

 You can also call the `getMember` function on an instance if you want a directly usable reference, such as a member to call with a valid `this` pointer.

There's more...

Another way to get members of some types, mainly `structs` and `classes`, is with the `tupleof` property. The `tupleof` property yields a list of all the variables in the type in the same order that they appear in memory, including a hidden context pointer in the case of nested structures. The `.tupleof` property can be written to and looped over with `foreach`. Some code written before `__traits(allMembers)` was added to the language used `.stringof` in a loop over `obj.tupleof` to get the names of member variables.

The `.tupleof` property does not include child types or functions, but does, like other D tuples, have the interesting characteristic of automatically expanding function argument lists, as shown in the following code:

```
struct Test {
  int a;
  string b;
}

void test(int a, string b) {
  import std.stdio;
  writeln(a, " ", b);
}

void main() {
  Test t;
  t.a = 10;
  t.b = "cool";
  // test(t); // won't compile, Test is not int, string
  test(t.tupleof);// WILL compile!
}
```

So, while you can use the `.tupleof` property for reflection, its main strength is in variable manipulation and expansion.

See also

▶ Refer to the documentation for the Phobos `std.traits` module at `http://dlang.org/phobos/std_traits.html`, which encapsulates and expands upon many of the compile-time reflection capabilities provided by the compiler, often with more readable syntax. Check this first when trying to perform a new reflection-related task. It contains many more useful functions other than the ones mentioned here.

- ▸ Refer to the documentation for the `is` expression at `http://dlang.org/expression.html#IsExpression`. Notice that it has seven forms, each with unique capabilities.

- ▸ Refer to the documentation for the `__traits` feature of the language at `http://dlang.org/traits.html`.

Inspecting function overloads

When we handle functions by name, an important detail is left out; overloaded functions with the same name, but different arguments. How can we drill down into these overloads?

How to do it...

Let's execute the following steps to inspect function overloads:

1. Get the function name, whether from a string or by inspecting `__traits(allMembers)`.

2. Use `__traits(getOverloads, Aggregate, memberName)` to get a list of symbols.

3. Inspect the symbols with a loop and `is(typeof(overload))`.

The code is as follows:

```
struct S {
  void foo() {}
  void foo(int a) {}
}
void main() {
  import std.stdio;
  foreach(overload; __traits(getOverloads, S, "foo"))
    writeln(typeof(overload).stringof);
}
```

The following is the result of the preceding code:

```
void()
void(int a)
```

> It doesn't hurt to call `__traits(getOverloads)` on a name that isn't a function. It will simply return an empty set.

How it works...

The `__traits(getOverloads)` function works similar to `__traits(getMember)`, which we used in the previous recipe. However, instead of returning only one symbol, it returns a list of all the overloads in symbolic form. We may use these symbols individually with all the same reflection tools if we loop over the list.

Determining names, types, and default values of function parameters

In the previous two recipes, we got a list of functions, including overloads and signatures in the form of types. To do really interesting things with function reflection, we need to dig into the details, isolating the return type and function parameters.

How to do it...

Let's execute the following steps to determine names, types, and default values of function parameters:

1. Import `std.traits`. The Phobos module makes the task easier and is much more readable than the direct implementation.

2. Get the function symbol. You may use the name directly (do not take the address of it, as we want to work on the function itself, and not on the pointer) by using `__traits(getMember)` or `__traits(getOverloads)`.

3. Isolate the return value with `ReturnType!func`. You may use this in any context in which you will use a type.

4. Get the parameter types with `ParameterTypeTuple!func`. You may declare a variable with this type and fill arguments with it.

5. Get the parameter names with `ParameterIdentifierTuple!func`. You may alias this to a shorter name if you like.

6. Get the parameter default values with `ParameterDefaultValueTuple!func`. As with the identifiers, you may not declare a variable of this type, but you may alias it to another name.

7. Loop over or index the parameter tuples to inspect individual parameters.

The code is as follows:

```
import std.traits;

void showFunctionDetails(alias func)() {
```

```
import std.stdio;

writeln("         Name: ",
  __traits(identifier, func));
writeln("      Returns: ",
  ReturnType!func.stringof);
writeln("    Arguments: ",
  ParameterTypeTuple!func.stringof);
writeln("    Arg names: ",
  ParameterIdentifierTuple!func.stringof);
writeln("Arg defaults: ",
  ParameterDefaultValueTuple!func.stringof);
}
int testFunction(int arg1, string str = "value") { return 0; }

void main() {
  showFunctionDetails!testFunction();
}
```

Running the program will print the following output:

```
        Name: testFunction
     Returns: int
   Arguments: (int, string)
   Arg names: tuple("arg1", "str")
Arg defaults: tuple((void), "value")
```

 Inside a function, you may use `typeof(return)` to get the return type, even if it is inferred.

How it works...

Here, we drill into functions with four helpers from Phobos' `std.traits` module: `ReturnType`, `ParameterTypeTuple`, `ParameterIdentifierTuple`, and `ParameterDefaultValueTuple`.

`ReturnType` and `ParameterTypeTuple` both yield types with which you can declare variables (if the type is not `void`). All the tuple methods yield a loopable and indexable entity, but aside from `ParameterTypeTuple`, they give a list of symbols. Thus, they must be treated like a symbol, renamed, and passed around as aliases. The order of entries is the same as the order of parameters.

The implementation of these methods use combinations of advanced `is` expressions and `__traits` functions to get their information. First, they extract the specific type of the callable function given to it with a series of `is` expressions and `static if/else` statements, similar to how we categorized types in the earlier recipe. This is to support regular functions, delegates, and function objects (for example, `struct`s that implement `opCall`) uniformly. The function type it extracts is not the same as the function pointer. It instead extracts a particular function symbol because that gives most of the information for future compile-time reflection.

Then, the methods use a special form of the `is` expression to extract data. For example, the `ReturnType` template's source code is as follows:

```
template ReturnType(func...)
    if (func.length == 1 && isCallable!func)
{
    static if (is(FunctionTypeOf!func R == return))
        alias R ReturnType;
    else
        static assert(0, "argument has no return type");
}
```

First, it accepts any one symbol as long as it is callable. Then, it extracts the function type and gets the return value out of it.

This form of the `is` expression is similar to what we used previously, for example, `is(foo == class)`, but there's one item added here; the `R` parameter. In this form, if the condition passes, forming a valid type, then an alias named `R` will be introduced for the specific type that passed the test. Since we're checking for a return value, the type that passes is the return type, and as such, `R` becomes an alias for it.

The `alias R ReturnType;` line is an example of the eponymous template trick. If a template has one member (a function, a type, an alias, or anything else) with the same name as the template itself, that item acts like the template's return value. At the usage point, the template is replaced with that member. Thus, here, the usage of `ReturnType!func` will refer to the `alias R`, the return type extracted with the `is` expression.

The other methods have similar implementations, though `ParameterIdentifierTuple` and `ParameterDefaultTypeTuple` are a little more complex because they both extract specific data from the same source: `is(typeof(func) P == __parameters)`, which contains the names, types, and default values. The `std.traits` functions filter them out to one concern at a time to make the consuming code easier to read.

We'll return to these methods in the final recipe of this chapter, where we'll use them to build a dynamic function caller.

There's more...

Other information about functions is available through the `std.traits` module. For example, `ParameterStorageClassTuple` will tell you if arguments are `scope`, `out`, or `ref`. The `functionLinkage` method returns a string identifying the calling convention (for example, `"C"` or `"D"`). The `functionAttributes` method tells you whether the function is `nothrow`, `safe`, `@property`, and so on. You can also create new functions based on the old functions by using `SetFunctionAttributes`. Check the documentation at `http://dlang.org/phobos/std_traits.html` to learn more.

Getting components of complex types

We've seen how the `is` expression lets us match simple types, and how Phobos used it to extract function details previously. What about more complex types such as arrays or template instantiations? How do we break them down into details?

Getting ready

Let's define a concrete goal to accomplish. We'll make an arithmetic wrapper that should follow the same type conversion rules as built-in types, but only work with other members of the same wrapped family.

Such a type might be useful when creating a scientific units library, for example, where you want to use the type system to decorate the otherwise plain numbers with maximum flexibility. The following is an example of a complex type:

```
struct Number(T) if(__traits(isArithmetic, T)) {
  T value;

  this(T t) { value = t; }

  this(N)(N n) if(isSomeNumber!N) {
    this.value = cast(T) n.value;
  }
}

// convenience constructor
auto number(T)(T t) { return Number!T(t); }

template isSomeNumber(N) {
  // what's the correct implementation?
```

```
    enum isSomeNumber = !__traits(isArithmetic, N);
}

void main() {
    int b1 = 1;
    double b2 = 2.5;
    static assert(is(typeof(b1 + b2) == double));

    Number!int n1 = number(1);
    Number!double n2 = number(2.5);
    //Number!double n3 = n1 + n2; // how do we make this work?
}
```

There are two concrete challenges here; how can we tell if any random type is indeed an instantiation of the `Number` type, and how can we cause the addition operator to yield the same type we expect from the plain numbers, where `double + int = double` as shown by our `static assert` function? To do this correctly, we need to get the components of a complex type.

How to do it...

Let's execute the following steps to get components of complex types:

1. To determine the syntax of breaking down the type, write the declaration with as many or as few placeholders as you want. If we want to accept any instantiation of the `Number` type, we'll write `Number!T`.

2. Put a comma after it and list all the placeholders you used, optionally restraining them with `:` specialization or requesting for the `alias` symbol. So, in our case, we now have `Number!T, T`.

3. Put this together in an `is` expression with the type we have on the left-hand side, `:` or `==` as the operator (the `:` operator if you want implicit conversions to be allowed, and `==` if you want an exact match), and the type we wrote in the previous step on the right-hand side to form the matching condition. So, we can write `isSomeNumber` by using `is(N : Number!T, T))` to pattern-match the template instantiation, as shown in the following code:

   ```
   template isSomeNumber(N) {
       enum isSomeNumber = is(N : Number!T, T);
   }
   ```

4. Write an `opBinary` method inside `Number`, which pattern-matches the template with the same syntax as `isSomeNumber` and returns the result using the convenient constructor.

The code is as follows:

```
auto opBinary(string op, N: Number!T, T)(N rhs) {
    return(number(mixin("this.value " ~ op ~ " rhs.value")));
}
```

After adding the preceding code, both the required tasks will be complete. The compiler does the arithmetic calculation and yields the correct type for us automatically if we give the right input.

> When writing the pattern, keep your placeholders simple. If you want to match, say, an associative array of templates, first match an associative array. Then, inside that static if block, match the template separately. This will help to make your is expressions readable.

How it works...

Deconstructing complex types is done with the full form of the is expression. The full syntax of the is expression form we are using is as follows:

```
is(Check MatchAlias op SearchPattern, list, of, placeholders);
```

In the preceding code, the Check parameter is the type you are checking or deconstructing.

The MatchAlias parameter is always optional. If you choose to provide it, the type that matches the search pattern will be aliased to that name. Often, this is the same as what you passed in (the Check parameter). However, depending on the value of the SearchPattern parameter, it may extract details instead (see the previous recipe for the ReturnType implementation for an example).

The comparison operation is op. It can be either the == or : operator. The == operator checks for an exact match while the operator : checks for implicit conversions as well. You may think of the : operator as being related to inheritance, for example, class Foo : Interface will implicitly cast to Interface, so is(Foo : Interface) will be true. If you do not provide an operator, you must also not provide a SearchPattern parameter. This yields the simplest form of the is expression; it checks only if the type is valid without any specific requirements.

The SearchPattern parameter is what you're looking for. There might be a keyword such as class, function, or return if you are looking for those categories and details, or it may be a type, with as many or as few wildcard placeholders as you want to use.

Finally, you need to declare all the placeholders you used in the `SearchPattern` parameter in a comma-separated list. If you forget these, the compiler will issue an error about an undefined identifier. Since a template name is not a type itself, a template name must put the `alias` keyword before the placeholder name. Other types only need to list the name. The placeholders will be available for further inspection to find what they matched in the given `Check` type.

> You may also specialize on placeholder types with a colon followed by a type, but this can get to be difficult to read and lack the flexibility of subsequent expressions. Since they can be replaced by the nested `static if` statements that handle one step at a time, you may choose to rarely use this particular option.

Let's look at some examples. Previously, we used the `is(N : Number!T, T)` expression. Here, `Check` is `N`, the argument we passed in the template. We want to see if it implicitly converts to `Number!T`, which is a specific template with a placeholder parameter. If we used this expression with `static if`, inside that statement, we could also refer to `T` to see what exactly the parameter is on the type we're inspecting.

It is also instructive to look at a longer-form implementation of `isSomeNumber` type, which deconstructs any template, and then checks each piece for our match. This is shown in the following code:

```
static if(is(N : Template!Args, alias Template, Args...))
   enum isSomeNumber = __traits(isSame, Template, Number);
else
   enum isSomeNumber = false;
}
```

Here, we decomposed the entire template, which will work with any template's instantiation and not just the `Number` template. Then, we compared the deconstructed `alias` name to the original name by using `__traits(isSame)`, which tells us whether the two names are aliases for the same symbol. If `Template` is an alias for `Number`, that's a match. We also put an `else` branch on the `static if` statement because if the checked type didn't match the pattern at all, we know it certainly isn't what we're interested in here.

The `is` expression is not limited to templates. Another common use is to match or deconstruct arrays and associative arrays, as shown in the following code:

```
template isArray(T) {
   static if(is(T == E[], E)) {
      // Note: E is the element type of the array

      enum isArray = true;
   } else
```

```
        enum isArray = false; // didn't match the E[] pattern
    }
    template isAssociativeArray(T) {
        static if(is(T == K[V], K, V)) {
          // Here, K and V are the key and value types, respectively
            enum isAssocativeArray = true;
        }   else
            enum isAssociativeArray = false;

    }
```

We can get as complex as we want to match. You could write `is(T == K[V][][V2], K, V, V2)` if you wanted to match an associative array of arrays of associative arrays, and inspect each individual type (through `K`, `V`, and `K2`). However, if you specifically wanted `V2`, for example, to be an instance of `Number!T`, you should use a nested `static if` block to check that condition individually.

Back to our `Number` type, the other challenge we achieved was making `opBinary` work. In the `opBinary` compile-time argument list, we specialized out the right-hand side type using the syntax very similar to the `is` expression. Many pattern-matching capabilities of the `is` expression also work in a template argument list.

The implementation of `opBinary` is a bit anticlimactic. Since we wanted to match the language rules for arithmetic calculation of the constituent types, instead of trying to recreate those rules with a series of static `if` statements (which is possible, though tedious), we simple performed the operation and used the result. We could have also checked the result with `typeof` if we didn't want to use it immediately.

While compile-time reflection and `static if` statement give you the option of digging into the details, don't let them make you do more work than you have to. If the language itself can perform a task, let it perform that task and then simply inspect or use the result as required.

See also:

▶ Refer to the documentation for the `is` expression at `http://dlang.org/expression.html#IsExpression`

Using user-defined attributes

D supports user-defined attributes (sometimes called annotations), which are a way to add custom compile-time information to declarations that can be retrieved later by reflection. Here, we'll look at their capabilities and their limitations.

How to do it...

Let's execute the following steps to use user-defined attributes:

1. Create a `struct` or `enum` to use as the attribute. A `struct` attribute should have data members, as shown in the following code. An `enum` attribute is best used for a simple flag:

   ```
   struct MyNote { string note; }
   ```

2. Attach the attribute to a declaration with the `@` sigil, as shown in the following code:

   ```
   @MyNote("this is my note on foo") void foo() {}
   ```

3. Retrieve attributes by using the `__traits(getAttributes, symbol)` function. To pass the symbol to a function or template, use a compile-time parameter with the `alias` keyword.

4. Loop over the attributes, retrieving the one you want by identifying the type with the basic form of the `is` expression. For flags, check for the validity of the type and return `true` if it is present. For data annotations, such as `MyNote`, check the `typeof` parameter and then return the actual annotation so the data can be checked.

The code is as follows:

```
MyNote getMyNoteAnnotation(alias F)() {
    foreach(attr; __traits(getAttributes, F)) {
        static if(is(typeof(attr) == MyNote))
            return attr;
    }
    assert(0); // the annotation wasn't there
}
// get the note and print out the value
// (the member note is of the MyNote struct)
pragma(msg, getMyNoteAnnotation!(foo).note);
```

How it works...

D's user-defined attributes never modify a type or generate new code, but do allow you to attach data to declaration that you can use later through the compile-time reflection for code generation if you wish.

The attributes are regular D types, holding regular D data. Once you retrieve them, you use the value like any other variable. To attach them, you can write `@some_expression`, where `some_expression` can be almost anything, as long as it gives a result at compile time. Typically, the expression is a `struct` constructor `@MyNote("string")`, which attaches a value to the declaration similar to the `auto a = MyNote("string")` statement that assigns a value to a variable.

It is also legal to attach plain data to a declaration, such as `@1 int foo;` will have an `int` annotation with the value of 1. Since `int` is not a unique type and attributes are retrieved by type comparison, using naked attributes like this will lead to conflicts where one module interprets `int` in one way and another sees it as something entirely different. To avoid this situation, always declare a new type for your attributes.

The `__traits(getAttributes)` function returns a list of all the attributes attached to a symbol. Since the attributes may include data from other libraries about which you know nothing, it is best to loop through them and find only the ones that match your type. Once you have your data, you may do anything with it; but remember, it is just data. We'll look at a concrete example of a user-defined attribute flag in the next recipe.

 A common question is how to modify a type with an attribute. This is not possible in D. You may loop over a module, looking for types with an annotation, and then declare a new one with the transformation. However, there's already a tool in the language to modify types: templates and compile-time parameters! So, instead of trying to write `@NotNull Object`, use `NotNull!Object` and you'll find easier success.

Implementing a custom lint-style check for virtual functions

D's reflection capabilities can be used to perform some checks that the lint tools are needed to perform for the C or C++ code. Here, we'll implement the code to warn the user at compile time whether their class has an unmarked virtual function.

How to do it...

Let's execute the following steps to implement a custom lint-style check for virtual functions:

1. Define a plain `enum` called `Virtual` to use as the annotation to silence the warning.
2. Find classes in your program to test, either manually or with reflection.
3. Use `__traits(derivedMembers, Class)` to get all the members, excluding the base class members.
4. Use `__traits(isVirtualMethod, member)` to determine whether it is a virtual function.
5. Write a helper function that uses `__traits(getAttributes, member)` in a loop with `static if(is(Virtual))` to look for the annotation.

6. If it is not found, use `pragma(msg)` to warn the user.

7. Optionally, return a failure flag from your `check` function. The user may check this flag with `static assert` to turn the warning into an error. Alternatively, the user can write `enum virtualPassed = virtualCheck!item_of_interest;` to get warnings without errors.

The code is as follows:

```
// the UDA we should put on authorized virtuals
enum Virtual;

// alias helper for looping over members
alias helper(alias T) = T;

// Helper function to test for presence of @Virtual
bool isAuthorizedVirtual(alias member)() {
  foreach(attr; __traits(getAttributes, member))
    if(is(attr == Virtual))
      return true;
  return false;
}

// Loop over all members, looking for classes to drill
// into and virtual functions to test.
bool virtualCheck(alias T)() {
  bool passes = true;
  foreach(memberName; __traits(derivedMembers, T)) {
    static if(memberName.length) {
      alias member = helper!(__traits(getMember, T, memberName));
      // drill down into classes
      static if(is(member == class))
        passes = passes && virtualCheck!member;

      // check overloaded functions (if any) for
      // unmarked virtuals
      foreach(overload; __traits(getOverloads, T, memberName))
        static if(__traits(isVirtualMethod, overload)) {
          static if(!isAuthorizedVirtual!overload) {
            // and warn if we find any
            pragma(msg, T.stringof ~ "." ~ memberName
              ~ " " ~ typeof(overload).stringof
              ~ " is virtual");
            passes = false;
          }
```

```
            }
        }
    }
    return passes;
}

class Test {
    @Virtual void foo() {} // specifically marked, ok
    void foo(int) {} // virtual but not marked = problem
    final void f() {} // final, ok
}

// We'll use static assert to run the test and cause a compile
// error if any tests fail.
static assert(virtualCheck!(mixin(__MODULE__))); // test all classes
in the module
```

The following is the compilation result of the preceding code:

```
Test.foo void(int) is virtual
virt.d(51): Error: static assert   (virtualCheck!(virt)) is false
```

How it works...

D's reflection gives us access to other information about items beyond their name and type. We can also retrieve other details, such as whether a function is virtual, its calling convention, and other attributes.

The rest of the implementation is a fairly straightforward application of what we already learned. We use compile-time reflection to drill down into all members of the module, check the information we're interested in, and then use `pragma(msg, "string")` to print the warning, if necessary. Since it is currently impossible to get the exact file and line numbers of a declaration with reflection, we instead print the full name and type so that the user can identify the function from the message. Finally, we return a flag instead of using the `static assert` statement in the test so that compilation doesn't fail immediately with the first note.

 If you need to perform checks that cannot be fully completed at the compile time, consider calling the check functions in a unit test block so they run at runtime.

Extending the runtime type information

D's built-in `TypeInfo` doesn't provide nearly as much information as we can get from the compile-time reflection tools. Here, we'll create an extended type info with custom data.

How to do it...

Let's execute the following steps to extend the runtime type information:

1. Create an interface with methods exposing the information you want to make available at runtime.

2. If your method works with the data, remember that RTTI is typically used with very little compile-time type information. Thus, methods should take a generic runtime type, such as `Object` or `void*` in the generic interface.

3. Create an associative array of your interface keyed on `TypeInfo`.

4. Write helper functions to retrieve the information from the associative array. Use `typeid()` to get the lookup key from a given variable or type.

5. Write a template class that will implement your generic interface for each supported type. The `std.traits` Phobos module will help with our implementation.

6. Write a `mixin` template that loops over all the types to which you wish to add support for extended type information. Alternatively (or additionally), you could provide a `registerType` function to be called explicitly or on request in the extended info lookup functions.

7. On the user side, register the types you wish to support and use the information.

The code is as follows:

```
/// stores the information
immutable MoreInfo[TypeInfo] moreTypeInfo;

/// Gets extended info from a value
public immutable(MoreInfo) extTypeInfo(T)(T t) {
  if(auto ptr = typeid(t) in moreTypeInfo)
    return *ptr;
  return null;
}

/// Gets extended info from a type
public immutable(MoreInfo) extTypeInfo(T)() {
  if(auto ptr = typeid(T) in moreTypeInfo)
    return *ptr;
```

```
      return null;
  }

  /// The interface we provide to more info
  public interface MoreInfo {
      immutable:
    /// is it an integral type?
    bool isIntegral();

    /// given a pointer to this type, return it as a string
    /// Be sure the pointer is actually the correct type!
    string getAsString(in void*);
  }

  /// The implementation of the interface for any type
  private class MoreInfoImpl(T) : MoreInfo {
      immutable:
    // std.traits offers reflection helpers
    import trait = std.traits;

    bool isIntegral() {
      return trait.isIntegral!T;
    }

    string getAsString(in void* ptr) {
      import std.conv;
      auto t = cast(T*) ptr;
      return to!string(*t);
    }
  }


  /// This creates all the instances we want to enable
  public mixin template EnableMoreInfo(types...) {
    /// A static constructor is run at thread startup
    shared static this() {
      foreach(type; types)
        moreTypeInfo[typeid(type)] = new immutable MoreInfoImpl!type();
    }
  }

  /* User code */

  class A { } // a random custom class

  // enable more info for built-in ints and our class
```

```
  mixin EnableMoreInfo!(int, A);

void main() {
    import std.stdio;
    // test
    writeln(extTypeInfo(1).isIntegral()); // true
    writeln(extTypeInfo!(A).isIntegral()); // false

    int a = 34;
    writeln(extTypeInfo(a).getAsString(&a)); // prints 34
}
```

How it works...

We used three features to make information from compile-time reflection available at runtime: classes with interfaces, static module constructors, and associative arrays with the `TypeInfo` keys.

First, the interfaces were used to provide a consistent base type that always works at runtime. Sometimes, it is tempting to think of templates as being almost magical—if we could only write `cast(runtime_type)` it will all work. However, this is impossible because templates and types only exist at compile time. If you had enough information to successfully perform a downcast, you'd have enough information to use compile-time reflection and thus have no need for runtime information anyway!

So, while the class that implements the interface is a template, allowing us to use compile-time reflection to fill in the information, saving a lot of manual work. The interface itself is what must be used at runtime and it must all work with generic types. To get a type's value generically, we put `getAsString` in the interface. No matter what the underlying data is, we can convert it to one uniform type, string, and use that. Since the interface itself isn't a member of the type we're converting, `getAsString` must take a pointer to the data so it knows what to convert. Given the limitations of the generic MoreInfo interface, the data pointer must also be generic, so we use `void*`.

Other interface methods that operate on the data will need to work the same way; return a consistent type and take a generic pointer to the data.

Once we've defined and implemented the interface, we need some way to access it at runtime. That's where the associative array comes in. Using `TypeInfo` as a key, we can look up our extended information any time we are given a `TypeInfo+void*` pair elsewhere in the code, including generic classes. We can work with classes with a generic base type of `Object` instead of `void*` if you prefer, and we can always retrieve their `TypeInfo` with the `typeid` operator, but that only works on class objects. Remember, class objects are unique and they always carry their `TypeInfo` reference with the actual data.

However, how do we populate the associative array with data coming from several sources, possibly across modules and compilation units? That's where the static module constructor comes in.

A static module constructor is declared with one of two syntaxes: `static this()` or `shared static this()`, both in module scope. The `static this()` constructor declares a thread-local module constructor. Each new thread spawned will run its code to initialize thread variables. The `shared static this()` constructor declares a module constructor for the data shared across all threads, including the immutable data. A `shared static` constructor is run only once, automatically upon program start-up, before `main` is run.

You can also write static constructors for your classes and complex types by using the same syntax in the object's scope. It is important that you write the definition exactly as it is seen here; the literal keywords `static this` or `shared static this` must appear, in that order, for the compiler to recognize the constructor.

Since our extended type info never changes, we made it immutable. Immutable data normally cannot be modified, but the compiler makes an exception for constructors to allow them to be initialized. Since it is immutable, it can also be shared across threads, so we initialized it in a `shared static` constructor. Thus, the cost of initialization is minimized because it is done once and only once.

What happens if you have multiple calls to `EnableTypeInfo` in the same module? Try it, you'll find it works. The compiler will combine multiple module constructors together automatically.

Once the array is built, we can use it like any other collection of data. The `extTypeInfo` helper functions give us an easy interface to use a given type or variable, or we can access the array directly with a `TypeInfo` key. Since our extended type information is opt-in, these functions may return a `null` value, indicating that the extended information is not available for the given type. Here, we used a small manually curated list of types that will be enabled. We could have also used compile-time reflection to search the module for all types it defines.

Why don't we construct the extended information lazily in the helper function? Immutability of the array notwithstanding, that will actually work for some types. The problem is lazy construction only works where compile-time reflection will work anyway, defeating the point of enabling runtime reflection. An example where it will not work correctly is when you give it an instance of a child class through a base class. The lazy function will construct information for the base class, unaware of the child class.

There's more...

The D runtime and compiler also includes a feature we could use to make extended type information for all user-defined types automatically. In the documentation of `TypeInfo` at `dlang.org`, you might have noticed a member `rtInfo`, which provides implementation-specific type extensions for the garbage collector.

Every time the compiler encounters a new type definition, it invokes a template called `RTInfo` on that type. The `RTInfo` template is found in the automatically imported core library file, `object.d`. The `RTInfo` template can return a pointer to the implementation-defined data that is accessible through `TypeInfo`, and it can also define new module constructors to build additional lists, exactly as we did here.

The same feature could, in theory, be used for user-defined type extensions too. However, since customizing it means customizing your core runtime library, it isn't very practical today. There's ongoing work in the D community to make this feature more accessible to end users.

Creating a command-line function caller

One useful application of reflection is that it builds dynamic interfaces automatically. Reflection can be used to help the code that interacts with a scripting language, a network protocol, and more. Here, we'll write a command-line program that calls functions and displays information about them when help is requested. We'll need to be able to add new functions without needing any boilerplate code to be added along with it.

How to do it...

We can create a command-line function caller by performing the following steps:

1. Loop over all members of the module.
2. Find functions with a protection level of export (alternatively, you may look for the presence of a user-defined attribute).
3. If the user requested help, list the possible functions or details about a particular function, by performing the following steps:
    1. Use a user-defined attribute for documentation.
    2. Use `std.traits'` `Parameter*Tuple` family of functions to get details about the function.

4. If the user wants to run a function, prepare a function call as follows:

   1. Use `std.traits.ParameterTypeTuple` to build the argument list.

   2. Check `std.traits.ReturnType` to see if the function has a return value (in other words, if it doesn't return `void`). If it does, store the return value as a string. Otherwise, call the function without trying to store the return value.

5. Format the result or the error message for presentation to the user, as shown in the following code:

```
// The functions we want to make available
export {
  @doc("Say hello to the user", ["the user's name to greet"])
    string hello(string name = "user") {
      return "Hello, " ~ name ~ "!";
    }

  @doc("Adds two numbers together.")
    int sum(int a, int b) {
      return a+b;
    }
}

// alias helper for reflection
alias helper(alias T) = T;

// Our user-defined attribute for documentation
struct doc {
  string value;
  string[] argDocs;
}

// Helper function to find a generic value UDA
auto getAttribute(alias mem, T)() {
  foreach(attr; __traits(getAttributes, mem))
    static if(is(typeof(attr) == T))
    return attr;
  return T.init;
}
// Function to do the reflection and call
int runWithArgs()(string[] args) {
  import std.traits, std.conv, std.stdio;

  string name;
  if(args.length) {
    name = args[0];
```

```
        args = args[1 .. $];
    }

    // look over the whole module for callable functions
    alias mod = helper!(mixin(__MODULE__));
    foreach(memberName; __traits(allMembers, mod)) {
      alias member = helper!(__traits(getMember, mod, memberName));
      static if(
          // Is it a function marked with export?
          is(typeof(member) == function) &&
          __traits(getProtection, member) == "export")
      {
        if(name == "--help") {
        // user requested help
          if(args.length) {
            if(memberName == args[0]) {
              // print the details of this function
              writef("Usage: %s", memberName);
              foreach(argName; ParameterIdentifierTuple!member)
                writef(" %s", argName);
              writefln("\n\t%s", getAttribute!(member, doc).value);

              if(ParameterTypeTuple!member.length)
                writeln("Arguments:");

              auto argDocs = getAttribute!(member, doc).argDocs;

              foreach(idx, argName; ParameterIdentifierTuple!member)
{
                string defaultValue;
                bool hasDefaultValue;
                static if(!is(ParameterDefaultValueTuple!member[idx]
                == void)) {
                  defaultValue = to!string(ParameterDefaultValueTupl
                  e!member[idx]);
                  hasDefaultValue = true;
                }
                string argDoc = "?";
                if(idx < argDocs.length)
                  argDoc = argDocs[idx];

                writefln("\t%s (%s): %s %s",
                    argName,
                    ParameterTypeTuple!member[idx].stringof,
```

```
                    argDoc,
                    hasDefaultValue ? "[default=" ~ defaultValue ~
                    "]" : "");
            }
        }
    } else {
        // no details requested, just show the full listing
        writefln("%16s -- %s", memberName, getAttribute!(member,
        doc).value);
    }
// the user did NOT ask for help, call the function if
// we have the correct name
    } else if(memberName == name) {
        // Prepare arguments
        ParameterTypeTuple!member arguments;
        alias argumentNames = ParameterIdentifierTuple!member;
        alias defaultArguments = ParameterDefaultValueTuple!member;

        try {
            foreach(idx, ref arg; arguments) {
                // populate arguments, with user data if available,
                // default if not, and throw if no argument provided.
                if(idx < args.length)
                    arg = to!(typeof(arg))(args[idx]);
                else static if(!is(defaultArguments[idx] == void))
                    arg = defaultArguments[idx];
                else
                    throw new Exception("Required argument " ~
                    argumentNames[idx] ~ " is missing.");
            }

            string result;

            // We have to check the return type for void
            // since it is impossible to convert a void return
            // to a printable string.
            static if(is(ReturnType!member == void))
                member(arguments);
            else
                result = to!string(member(arguments));

            writeln(result); // show the result to the user
            return 0;
        } catch(Exception e) {
```

```
            // print out the error succinctly
            stderr.writefln("%s: %s", typeid(e).name, e.msg);
            return 1;
        }
      }
    }
  }
  return 0;
}

int main(string[] args) {
  return runWithArgs(args[1 .. $]);
}
```

6. Run it with the following options to look at the results:

```
$ ./command --help
        hello -- Say hello to the user
          sum -- Adds two numbers together.
$ ./command --help hello
Usage: hello name
        Say hello to the user
Arguments:
        name (string): the user's name to greet [default=user]
$ ./command hello "D fan"
Hello, D fan!
```

Also, try adding new functions and see how they work with no additional boilerplate code.

 Since Ddoc comments are not currently available through compile-time reflection, we had to define our own doc structure to use as an attribute instead.

How it works...

We brought together the following techniques we learned earlier in the chapter to form a complete program:

▶ Looping over the module using __traits(allMembers) and finding functions with the is expression

▶ Locating the user-defined attributes with a helper function and then using the value like a regular data type

- Getting function details with the `std.traits` module from Phobos and `__traits(getProtection)`, which returns a string with the protection level (for example, private, public, protected, export, or package)

- Using runtime type information to get the dynamic name of the `Exception` subclass used to print errors

The new part is using the reflection data to actually locate and call the function's given information at runtime.

The first thing to notice is that the compile-time reflection is done the same way, as if the name of the function we want to call doesn't even exist. The reason is that at compile time, the name indeed doesn't exist yet—it comes from the user at runtime! All the reflection information needs to be there just in case the user wants to call it.

Another consequence of this is that we need to make sure that all the possible function calls compile. If `name != memberName`, the code won't run, but it will be still compiled just in case it does run the next time.

The next new thing is actually calling the function. We learned about `ParameterTypeTuple` previously and saw how to get information from it. Here, we're using `ParameterTypeTuple` to actually declare a variable that holds the function arguments. We loop over it, by reference, filling in those arguments from our runtime strings. Using `typeof` in the loop, we can determine what type of value the function expects and automatically convert our strings appropriately.

Notice that we checked the length of the runtime `args` argument against the index of the parameter loop instead of looping over the runtime arguments and assigning them to the parameters. It is important to always loop over compile-time constructs when available, since that maximizes the potential for compile-time reflection.

If we try to write `foreach(idx, arg; args) arguments = to!(typeof(arguments[idx]))(arg)`, the compiler will complain about not being able to index a compile-time construct with a runtime variable—it won't even know the limits until the user provides an arguments' string! Remember, compile-time data can always be used at runtime, but runtime data can never be used at compile time.

Once the arguments are prepared, we pass them to the function. As we saw in the discussion of `.tupleof` previously, compile-time tuples or template argument lists have the special ability to expand to fill argument lists.

The last notable aspect of the function call is checking the return value. We want to assign it to a string so that we can print it to the user. Almost any type can be converted to a string, but there is one major exception: `void`. When a function doesn't have a return value, we cannot do the conversion! If we want to store the return value in a variable, we will have to perform this check too, since variables cannot have no type or `void` type.

A simple call to `ReturnType` inside `static if` lets us handle the special case without breaking the build.

There's more...

The generated code for these loops looks like the following:

```
if(name == "hello")
    hello(to!string(args[0]);
if(name == "add")
    add(to!int(args[0]), to!int(args[1]);
```

It is a linear list of function names. If you had a very large number of functions, searching this list for the right function to call may be slow. A potential optimization for this program will be to put each function call into a helper function or a switch case statement, and then generate the code to perform a hash table lookup with a `mixin` expression. We'll learn about code generation in the next chapter.

9

Code Generation

In this chapter, we will explore D's code generation capabilities and cover the following recipes:

- ▶ Creating user-defined literals
- ▶ Parsing a domain-specific language
- ▶ Generating data structures from text diagrams
- ▶ Automating dynamic calls with multiple dispatch
- ▶ Building a lookup table
- ▶ Using string parameters to change functions
- ▶ Wrapping instance methods
- ▶ Using `opDispatch` to generate properties
- ▶ Duck typing to a statically-defined interface

Introduction

Code generation is a central feature of the D programming language. In fact, it is so important that we've already used it extensively throughout this book! Templates perform code generation. They are a block of code with placeholders which are filled in to form the generated code. With compile-time function evaluation and the `mixin` expression, we can build D code out of strings and have them compiled.

Here, we'll look at some specific examples of how to use these techniques to generate code from various inputs.

Creating user-defined literals

D doesn't have specialized syntax for user-defined literals, but using the template syntax with the right implementation, we can generate the same code as if it did. A distinguishing factor of user-defined literals is that there must be zero runtime cost to use them. Here, we'll write the code to enable integer literals written in octal, a simplified version of the implementation of `octal` in Phobos' `std.conv` module.

Getting ready

First, let's write an octal number parser, converting from string to integer. The algorithm is simple: read a digit, multiply our accumulator by eight, and then add the value to the accumulator until we're out of digits. Any invalid digit is an exception. All these steps are shown in the following code:

```
int readOctalString(string n) {
    int sum = 0;
    foreach(c; n) {
        if(c < '0' || c > '7')
            throw new Exception("Bad octal number " ~ n);
        sum *= 8;
        sum += c - '0';
    }

    return sum;
}

unittest {
    assert(readOctalString("10") == 8);
    assert(readOctalString("15") == 13);
    assert(readOctalString("4") == 4);
    import std.exception;
    assertThrown!Exception(readOctalString("90"));
}
```

How to do it...

Let's execute the following steps to create user-defined literals:

1. Write a regular function to get the value you want from a string.
2. Write a template that takes a string parameter and whose body consists of one line:
   `enum myname = yourFunction(s);`.

3. Write templates that take other types of literal, if appropriate, and convert them to string to forward them to the template discussed in the preceding step.

The code is as follows:

```
// step 2:
template octal(string s) {
  enum octal = readOctalString(s);
}
// step 3: octals also make sense with some int literals
template octal(int i) {
  import std.conv;
  enum octal = octal!(to!string(i));
}
// usage test:
void main() {
  import std.stdio;
  writeln(octal!10);
  writeln(octal!"15");
  writeln(octal!4);
}
```

It prints 8, 13, and 4, matching our preceding unit test. Let's also confirm the compiler outputs the same code as it will for a normal integer literal by looking at the following disassembly:

```
$ objdump -d -M intel simpleoctal | grep _Dmain -A 30
0808f818 <_Dmain>:
 808f818:       55                              push   ebp
 808f819:       8b ec                           mov    ebp,esp
 808f81b:       b8 08 00 00 00                  mov    eax,0x8
 808f820:       e8 e3 7d 00 00          call   8097608
<_D3std5stdio14__T7writelnTiZ7writelnFiZv>
 808f825:       b8 0d 00 00 00                  mov    eax,0xd
 808f82a:       e8 d9 7d 00 00          call   8097608
<_D3std5stdio14__T7writelnTiZ7writelnFiZv>
 808f82f:       b8 04 00 00 00                  mov    eax,0x4
 808f834:       e8 cf 7d 00 00          call   8097608
<_D3std5stdio14__T7writelnTiZ7writelnFiZv>
 808f839:       31 c0                           xor    eax,eax
 808f83b:       5d                              pop    ebp
 808f83c:       c3                              ret
```

The relevant lines are mov eax, 0x8, mov eax, 0xd, and mov eax, 0x4. They are indistinguishable from any other integer literals, and there are no calls to octal or readOctalString in sight! (The calls after those lines are to writeln.)

How it works...

This is an example of the general pattern we'll be exploring in this chapter. We will write a regular function to convert input from one form to another, and then use D to evaluate that function at compile time to generate code or data.

The enum keyword is central to our result. In D, the enum keyword is used for all named constants that do not have a memory address. This, of course, includes traditional enumerations such as enum Color { red, green, blue }, and it also works as a single value. In both cases, the value works just like a literal value at the usage site, as if you copied and pasted the value straight to the usage point.

 An enum structure is similar to a #define statement in C. The difference is that the value of an enum structure is always determined at compile time, even if it is assigned to a function, and enum values in D always have a specific type; they are not just text to be transplanted into code.

When you declare an enum structure with a value, the right-hand side of the equation is immediately evaluated at compile time, regardless of complexity, and it will cause a compile-time error if this is unsuccessful for any reason. This is an extension of constant folding as seen in almost all the compiled languages, where if you write 1 + 2, the compiler automatically translates that to 3 instead of a literal adding an instruction in the compiled program. D simply takes that concept much farther.

Therefore, the enum keyword is the D idiom to force a compile-time function evaluation to create a literal in the generated code.

 The enum keyword is not the only way to trigger compile-time evaluation, and it is not always the best way. It is also run for a static initializer, such as a static variable or an initializer in a class or a struct definition, or anywhere else where the regular code can not be immediately run. Since the enum array literals always allocate at the usage point, they are often better represented as a static immutable variable.

The next task is to ensure we get the enum keyword's behavior without being forced to do the following tedious two-step process:

```
enum ourOctalPermissionLiteral = readOctalString("755");
chmod("my_file", ourOctalPermissionLiteral);
```

Since the compile-time evaluation and literal behavior only happens in specific contexts like enum, trying to call the readOctalString function directly will produce a plain runtime function call. We need to use the enum keyword as an intermediary. That's where the short octal template comes into play.

A template is fundamentally a block of code with parameters which act as placeholders that are replaced at the usage point to generate new code. We've used them extensively throughout this book to create new types and functions. Here, we're using a template to create an enum value from a string placeholder.

When the octal template is used, the enum structure is created on the spot and substituted for the template, giving us the convenience of template usage syntax with the behavior of enum literals, achieving our goal.

See also

▸ A blog post by Walter Bright describing this technique after it was first discovered can be found at http://www.drdobbs.com/tools/user-defined-literals-in-the-d-programmi/229401068. Templates and compile-time function evaluation with enum were both designed features, but the usefulness of the combination was only realized later.

▸ The documentation for Phobos' octal template can be found at http://dlang.org/phobos/std_conv.html#octal. It is similar to but more complex than the one we did here because it also obeys the language's typing rules across several types of integers and their edge cases.

Parsing a domain-specific language

D can embed domain-specific languages as strings. By writing a compiler for your specialized language to D in D, you can convert code in any language to a D code string, which can then be mixed in and compiled to the optimized machine code by the D compiler.

To demonstrate the technique, we'll write a small stack-based arithmetic program here.

How to do it...

Let's execute the following steps to parse a domain-specific language:

1. Write a regular parser for the language, making it work when compiled normally at runtime. For the stack language, this is very simple: we just need to split the string. For a more complex language, we will need to build abstract syntax trees out of classes.

2. Ensure the parser works at runtime by creating a main function that outputs its result.

3. Write methods that return strings of the D code from your language's data structures. The stack language will output calls to D functions for `push`, `pop`, and calling an operation.

4. Write the generated code out at runtime to make the debugging easier.

5. Once you are happy with the results, use the `mixin` expression to compile the code as D.

The code is as follows:

```d
import std.stdio, std.string;
string[] parse(string code) {
  return code.split(" ");
}

string convertToD(string[] pieces) {
  string code;

  foreach(piece; pieces) {
    if(isNumeric(piece)) {
      code ~= "push(" ~ piece ~ ");\n";
    } else {
      code ~= "push(call!'"~piece~"'(pop(), pop()));\n";
    }
  }

  return code;
}

void runDslCode(string code)() {
  int[16] stack;
  int stackPosition;
  void push(int p) {
    stack[stackPosition++] = p;
  }

  int pop() {
    return stack[--stackPosition];
  }

  int call(string op)(int a, int b) {
    return mixin("b"~op~"a");
  }

  mixin(convertToD(parse(code)));
```

```
    writeln(stack[0 .. stackPosition]);
}

void main() {
    enum code = "5 5 + 3 - 2 * 1 + 3 /";
    // writeln(parse(code)); // to aid with debugging
    // writeln(convertToD(parse(code)); // debugging aid
    // usage:
    runDslCode!"5 5 + 3 - 2 * 1 + 3 /"();
}
```

The intermediate debugging aid will print the generated D code as follows:

```
push(5);
push(5);
push(call!'+'(pop(), pop()));
push(3);
push(call!'-'(pop(), pop()));
push(2);
push(call!'*'(pop(), pop()));
push(1);
push(call!'+'(pop(), pop()));
push(3);
push(call!'/'(pop(), pop()));
```

The end result of the program is to print [5], the result of our DSL expression. If you disassemble the generated binary, you will see that the compiler was able to optimize the DSL. With dmd, the calls to the push, pop, and call operations can all be inlined. With gdc, the GNU D compiler, and ldc, the LLVM D compiler, their full optimizations go even further, doing the calculations at compile time and simply filling in the final values directly to the result buffer!

How it works...

There's nothing special about the compile-time D code. It is often literally the very same code you will write for any program, including complex cases such as parsing another programming language. Unlike with a regular compiler or interpreter though, the goal of a domain-specific language in D is simply to generate the D code, neither to directly run or necessarily to analyze or optimize it—because the D compiler can do those tasks for you.

The majority of the D language and library works at compile time, enabling straightforward implementations of DSL lexers and parsers. In our stack language example, the bulk of the work was done by simply calling the Phobos split function.

Generating the actual D code can be messy work. Adding white space to the generated code will help when debugging.

 If you need to refer to a type in a `mixin` expression, always refer to the local alias. For example, `void generateCodeForT(T)() { mixin("return T.sizeof"); }` is always preferable to `"return " ~ T.stringof ~ " .sizeof"`; because otherwise the name may be ambiguous at the usage location.

Sometimes, we can cut corners on our language implementation knowing that the D compiler can make up the gaps, or in the worst case, it will cause a compile-time error with a difficult-to-read error message.

 If you have a lot of code written in DSL or any other kind of datafile that you want to be available at compile time or embedded in your executable, you may use the `string s = import("filename");` expression instead of using string literals. The file's contents will be available just as if you copied the content into your D code and fixed any needed escaping yourself. Enable the import expression by passing `-Jpath` to dmd, where `path` is the directory where the datafiles can be located.

There's more...

The `std.regex` Phobos module uses this technique with its `ctRegex` function. The result is a regular expression engine that performs exceptionally well because it generates customized and optimized code for each pattern it is given at compile time.

I also wrote a small Lisp translator to show how the technique can be used with a more complex language, but it was too long to reprint in this book. You can see that code at `https://github.com/adamdruppe/book/blob/master/lisp.d`.

It implements a four-stage compiler by performing the following steps:

1. First, it tokenizes the input string.
2. Then, it parses it (a simple job for a Lisp-like language).
3. Next, it performs semantic transformations, handling special forms like defining functions.
4. Finally, each AST node has a method to generate the D code, completing the transformation.

See also

▶ `http://dlang.org/function.html#interpretation` is the official
documentation on the rules for compile-time function evaluation

Generating data structures from text diagrams

Data structures are often defined with text diagrams. Like domain-specific languages,
D can parse these strings and generate data structure definitions at compile time.
We'll briefly demonstrate the technique by writing a parser for a simple diagram.

How to do it...

Let's execute the following steps to generate data structures from text diagrams:

1. Start by writing a regular program to parse the diagram into structured fields.
   For our diagram, we'll want to split it into lines and then split the data lines into
   individual fields. The name will be the text within and the length will be one byte
   per four characters.

2. Take the structured data and generate the D code from it with string concatenation.
   Here, we'll build an anonymous structure with each field from the diagram, using
   simple integral types to match the size. Write out your code with `pragma(msg)`
   or at runtime while debugging until the code looks right.

3. Use the `mixin` expression to compile your code in a `struct` block. If you use this
   pattern often, you may encapsulate it in a `struct` block with a compile-time string
   parameter and then alias that parameter to a final name.

This is shown in the following code:

```
enum diagramString = '
+------------------+
|LEN |  ID | MSG    |
+------------------+
';

struct DiagramField {
    string name;
    int length;
}
```

```
DiagramField[] readDiagram(string diagram) {
  DiagramField[] fields;
  import std.string;
  auto lines = diagram.splitLines();
  foreach(line; lines) {
    if(line.length == 0) continue; // blank line
    if(line[0] == '+') continue; // separator line

    auto parts = line.split("|");
    foreach(part; parts) {
      if(part.length == 0) continue;
      DiagramField field;
      field.name = part.strip;
      field.length = part.length / 4;
      fields ~= field;
    }
  }

  return fields;
}

string toStructDefinition(DiagramField[] fields) {
  string code = "struct {\n";

  foreach(field; fields) {
    string type;
    switch(field.length) {
      case 1: type = "ubyte"; break;
      case 2: type = "ushort"; break;
      case 4: type = "uint"; break;
      case 8: type = "ulong"; break;
      default: assert(0);
    }
    code ~= "\t" ~ type ~ " " ~ field.name ~ ";\n";
  }

  code ~= "\n}";
  return code;
}

struct StructFromDiagram(string diagram) {
  mixin(toStructDefinition(readDiagram(diagram)));
}
```

```
alias Message = StructFromDiagram!diagramString;

/*
// an alternative way to form to the struct
struct Message {
  mixin(toStructDefinition(readDiagram(diagramString)));
}
*/

void main() {
  import std.stdio;
  debug writeln(toStructDefinition(readDiagram(diagramString)));
  Message m;
  m.ID = 5;
  writeln(m);
}
```

The output will be as follows:

```
StructFromDiagram!("\x0a+-----------------+\x0a|LEN | ID | MSG     |\
x0a+-----------------+\x0a")(0, 5, 0)
```

Since we used the `alias` method, the internal type name (used in the automatic `toString` implementation) is made from compile-time arguments, including the diagram. The alternate way results in a different name, but the same data.

How it works...

Whereas we made data and code in the previous two recipes, here we finished our demonstration of the technique discussed in the previous recipes by creating a data structure from a string at compile time. The pattern is similar: parse the string and then output what it represents in D with the help of templates and mixins. We simply generate a `struct` definition with appropriate data members. This definition can be mixed into an existing `struct` type or aliased to a more convenient name and used directly. While parsing a diagram looks different, the code is basically the same as any other domain-specific language.

See also

▸ A D solution that uses this technique on a more complex diagram to generate bit fields is available at `http://rosettacode.org/wiki/ASCII_art_diagram_converter`

Automating dynamic calls with multiple dispatch

Multiple dispatch is an extension of the concept of virtual functions. With a virtual function, the exact function called depends on the runtime type of the `this` object. With multiple dispatch, the exact function called depends on the runtime type of two or more objects. D does not have support for multiple dispatch built into the language, but with some code generation, we can add it ourselves.

Getting ready

Let's consider how we will do it manually. Given two or more class objects and a list of functions, we will need to call the most specific function possible for their dynamic type.

To determine if a class is more specific than another, we look at the inheritance hierarchy. If class A is a parent or an ancestor of class B, class B is more specific than class A. This makes the generic root class, `Object`, which has no parents, the least specific of all.

To determine if an object is an instance of a more specific class, we attempt to cast it and test for the `null` type.

What if there are two matching functions of equal specificity? You should avoid writing functions like that, but ultimately, the choice is pretty arbitrary. Just pick one.

Now, we'll see how we can automate this process.

How to do it...

Let's execute the following steps to automate dynamic calls with multiple dispatch:

1. Get a list of overloads with compile-time reflection.
2. Ensure the input arguments are not null, since null objects have no runtime type and checking for them may crash the system.
3. Declare a delegate to hold the current best match. The return type should be the common type of all possible function overloads so that there's a consistent return value for any dynamic type combination. Use `std.traits.CommonType` and `std.typetuple.staticMap` to extract the common return value from all overloads.
4. Loop over each argument, determining the specificity and attempting a dynamic cast.
5. If and only if all the arguments cast successfully, consider this as a successful match.
6. Call the best match after examining all possibilities.

The code is as follows:

```d
class A {}
class B : A {}
class C : A {}

import std.stdio;

void test(Object b, Object c) { writeln("Object, Object"); }
void test(A b, C c) { writeln("A, C"); }
B test(B b, C c) { writeln("B, C"); return b; }
void test(B b, B c) { writeln("B, B"); }
void test(C b, C c) { writeln("C, C"); }

/*
   The goal is to call the overload of func that best
   matches the *dynamic types* of the passed argument.
*/
auto dynamicDispatch(alias func, T...)(T t) {
  import std.traits;
  import std.typetuple;

  // step 1: getting all overloads of the given function
  alias overloads = TypeTuple!( /* TypeTuple is like our alias helper
  but it works with multiple arguments and is found in the standard
  library module std.typetuple */
     __traits(getOverloads, // get all overloads…
        __traits(parent, func), // from the parent of the function…
        __traits(identifier, func))); // that share a name with it.

  // step 2: ensure we weren't given null
  foreach(a; t)
    assert(a !is null);

  // step 3: the variable that will hold our match
  CommonType!(staticMap!(ReturnType, overloads)) delegate() dg;
  int bestSpecificity = int.min; // and the best match's score

  overloads:
  foreach(overload; overloads) {
    // step 4: loop over each one and find a match
    ParameterTypeTuple!overload args;
    static if(T.length == args.length) {
      int specificity = 0;
      bool isExactMatch = true;
      foreach(idx, ref arg; args) {
        arg = cast(typeof(arg)) t[idx];
```

```
            if(arg is null)
              continue overloads;
            // We check for an exact match - where the typeid we have
            // is a perfect match for the typeid we need
            if(isExactMatch && typeid(typeof(arg)) !istypeid(t[idx]))
              isExactMatch = false;
            // The specificity is the distance from Object; the number
            // of base classes. We multiply by the argument length to
            // help get an average of all arguments.
            specificity += BaseClassesTuple!(typeof(arg)).length * args.
            length;
          }

          specificity /= args.length; // average specificity
          // Debugging info, printing out the options we found
          writeln("specificity of ", typeof(overload).stringof, " = ",
          specificity);

          if(specificity > bestSpecificity) {
            // If it is a better match than we have, it becomes the
            // new best
            bestSpecificity = specificity;
            // the cast ensures we get a consistent type
            dg = { return cast(ReturnType!dg) overload(args); };

            // found an exact match, no point continuing to search
            if(isExactMatch)
              break overloads;
          }
        }
      }
    }

    // if a suitable function was found, call it
    if(dg)
      return dg();

    // otherwise, throw an exception
    throw new Exception("no dynamic match found");
  }

  void main() {
    Object a = new A();
    Object b = new B();
    dynamicDispatch!test(a, b);
  }
```

Play with the new lines in the `main` function to see how it works with other combinations too.

How it works...

We once again visit compile-time reflection over functions to automate a task that requires working with individual function arguments. With the help of `std.traits.ParameterTypeTuple`, we can inspect the types of arguments as well as build an argument list to pass to the function.

The `cast` operator on class objects when going from a base class or interface to a more derived class attempts a dynamic cast. It uses runtime type information attached to the object itself to see if it is a good match, returning `null` if it is not.

The rest of the code implements the algorithm we figured out while getting ready: find the best matching function by looking for arguments that work with the most specificity by looking at the number of base classes. The determination is done at runtime using the compile-time data, which is possible because a new dispatch function will be automatically generated by the compiler for each overload set it is passed with.

The trickiest part of the algorithm's implementation is defining the delegate that holds the current best match. The arguments are left empty because we generated a simple wrapper in the loop previously, which captures the arguments from the outer function in a closure. The return type needs to be consistent, even if the return types of the overloads are not, because the type needs to be known at compile time, and the exact function chosen will not be known until runtime.

To solve this problem, we use `CommonType` from `std.traits` to extract the best common type from all the possibilities. `CommonType` takes a list of types. Since we needed the common return type, we couldn't just pass it the list of overloads. Instead, we had to extract the return type from each overload. Phobos has the magic we need in the `std.typetuple` module: `staticMap`. `staticMap`. Like its runtime partner function, `std.algorithm.map`, it takes two arguments: a transformation function and a list of inputs. It applies the transformation to each item in the input list, generating a new output list.

`staticMap!(ReturnType, list...)` thus generates a new list of just the return types of the input functions, all at compile time, giving us exactly what we need to determine the common return type for our delegate. Inside the wrapper function, we force the use of the common type with an explicit `cast` object completing the implementation.

See also

▸   The official documentation on the `std.typetuple` module is found at
    `http://dlang.org/phobos/std_typetuple.html`

Building a lookup table

In the final recipe of the previous chapter on reflection, we built a command-line function caller that did a linear search through all the available functions to find the right one for the command. Here, we'll revisit that concept and generate more efficient code.

How to do it...

Let's execute the following steps to build a lookup table:

1. Create a `switch` statement.

2. If you are looping over a tuple of strings, such as one from a template argument list or returned from `__traits`, you can write the `case` statements inside the `foreach` loop.

3. Otherwise, build the code as a string and use the `mixin` expression to add it to your `switch` statement.

4. Let the compiler optimize the `switch` statement.

All the preceding steps are mentioned in the following code:

```
void callFunction(string functionName) {
  s: switch(functionName) {
     default: assert(0); // can add defaults or cases outside the loop
     foreach(methodName; __traits(allMembers, mixin(__MODULE__))) {
        case methodName:
           // implement the call
        break s; // break the switch specifically to clarify intent
        inside loop
     }
  }
}
```

> If you want a custom hash function, you can use CTFE by calling regular hash functions in the `case` statements: `int hash(string s) { ... }` `switch(hash(s)) { case hash("foo"): /* ... */ break; case hash("bar"): /* ... */ }`. Ensure that your hash is well-distributed, because `switch` will not handle collisions automatically.

How it works...

When a `switch` statement is compiled, all possible case values are known to the compiler, allowing it to generate more efficient code than a plain list. All the possible string cases are sorted by length and by content at compile time. This list is sent to a runtime function which performs a binary search to find the case that handles a given input value.

We can often take advantage of these optimizations by creating a `switch` statement and populating the cases with compile-time `foreach` loops. The code is pretty straightforward.

Another strategy to make lookup tables is with compile-time function evaluation. CTFE is often used with enums, but it also works with static immutable arrays to create data tables. To do this, write a function that calculates the data and returns a table. Then, use that function to initialize the table. It is important that you mark the table `static immutable` to ensure it is only initialized once, at compile time, and can be shared across all threads implicitly.

Using string parameters to change functions

Suppose you have two functions that are identical in most respects but differ in some minor aspects. You need them to be separate functions, but would like to minimize code duplication. There's no obvious type parameterization, but you can represent the difference with a value.

How to do it...

Let's execute the following steps to use string parameters to change functions:

1. Add a compile-time parameter to your function.
2. Use `static if` or `mixin` to modify the code based on that parameter.
3. Then add `alias` specific sets of parameters to user-friendly names using
   `alias friendlyVariation = foo!"argument";`.

The code is as follows:

```
void foo(string variation)() {
        import std.stdio;
        static if(variation == "test")
                writeln("test variation called");
        else
                writeln("other variation called");
}

alias testVariation = foo!"test";
alias otherVariation = foo!"";

void main() {
```

```
        testVariation();
        otherVariation();
}
```

How it works...

This is a very straightforward application of the `static if` block. Since a different function is generated for each set of compile-time parameters, we can change the code with compile-time functions and get pointers or call each individual one with certain bound compile-time parameters, which is similar to a partial application in functional programming languages.

Be careful not to write difficult-to-understand code with this technique. It may often be better to split the function into smaller, more reusable pieces.

Wrapping instance methods

Earlier, we looked at a dynamic type in D which included the capability to wrap native functions with dynamic typing and property replacement. Now, it is time to see exactly how that works and how automated code generation makes it a lot easier.

 By unifying types, we enable both dynamic transformations as well as create an array of delegates to access functions of varying types. We cannot declare an array of function pointers that all take different arguments, but we can declare an array of pointers to helper functions that take one input array and transform the values for use.

How to do it...

Let's execute the following steps to wrap instance methods:

1. Write a generic conversion function to and from your consistent type. You should use `std.variant.Variant` or `std.conv.to` directly, if possible, and use type families with `std.traits` if working with a custom type.

2. Write a helper function generator that takes an existing function as a runtime delegate and returns the wrapped type. Constrain the compile-time argument with `std.traits.isDelegate`.

3. Use `std.traits.ParameterTypeTuple` to loop over the function arguments and set them from the input data, using your conversion function to set the types.

4. Use `static if(is(ReturnType!func == void))` to branch on the presence of a return value. If it is of the `void` type, call the function with the `args` argument. If it is not of the `void` type, transform the return value.

5. Pass methods to the helper with `&__traits(getMember, object, memberName)`. Do not use an `alias` helper in this step, and be sure to get the member of an object and not the type.

6. Test it by building an associative array of all the methods on an object and try calling them through it.

The code is as follows:

```
import std.traits;

// this alias represents the unified type our wrapper yields
alias WrapperFunctionType = string delegate(string[]);

// step 2: this returns the wrapped function, given the original
WrapperFunctionType wrap(Func)(Func func) if(isDelegate!Func) {
        // it immediately returns the wrapped function here
        return delegate string(string[] args) {
                import std.conv;
                ParameterTypeTuple!Func funcArgs;

                // step 3: populating the arguments
                foreach(idx, ref arg; funcArgs) {
                        if(idx >= args.length) break;
                        // the cast allows us to write to const
                        // arguments. to!() performs conversions.
                        cast() arg = to!(typeof(arg))(args[idx]);
                }

                // step 4: call the function, handling the
                // return value.
                string ret;
                static if(is(ReturnType!func == void))
                        func(funcArgs);
                else
                        ret = to!(typeof(return))(func(funcArgs));
                return ret;
        }; // remember, this is a return statement, needing ;
}

WrapperFunctionType[string] wrapAll(T)(ref T obj) {
        WrapperFunctionType[string] wrappers;

        foreach(memberName; __traits(allMembers, T)) {
                // only wrapping methods
                static if(is(typeof(__traits(getMember, T,
                memberName)) == function))
                        // wrap with a delegate from obj
                        wrappers[memberName] = wrap(&__
                        traits(getMember, obj, memberName));
```

```
                }

                return wrappers;
        }

        // a test structure with various method types
        struct Test {
                int a;
                void foo() {
                        import std.stdio; writeln("foo called");
                }

                int setA(int a) { return this.a = a; }
                int getA() { return this.a; }
        }


        void main() {
                Test t;
                // Wrap functions into a uniform array with string keys
                auto functions = wrapAll(t);

                // call foo with no arguments
                functions["foo"](null);

                functions["setA"](["10"]); // calls t.setA(10);
                import std.stdio;
                // confirm we can get the value and that it matches
                // the original object too.
                writeln(functions["getA"](null), " == ", t.getA());
        }
```

Running the program will confirm that foo is called and the getter and setter functions work correctly.

How it works...

The code generation here barely looks like code generation. It works very similar to any regular closure that you can write in D and many other languages. The difference is that the wrapper here is aware of the specific type of the delegate passed to it, and thus it can customize its behavior. A separate wrapper will be automatically generated for each different type passed to it, allowing us to use all the compile-time features such as static if, introspection on types, and generic functions such as std.conv.to.

The function wrapper uses `ParameterTypeTuple` and `ReturnType` to perform the transformations needed to present a uniform interface. `ParameterTypeTuple` yields a list of all the function's arguments in a form that we can use to declare a variable. Looping over it with `foreach` and `ref` lets us set each value from the input array. Using `typeof` with the generic function `to`, the type conversion is performed quickly, easily, and generically. The cast on the left-hand side of the assignment is used to remove `const`. Generally, casting away `const` is a bad idea, but here it can be necessary to populate the full argument list on some functions.

The `ReturnType` check is necessary because `void` can never be converted to any other type. If a function returns `void`, we must not try to use its return value. This is the same as we did in the compile-time function caller previously.

The major difference between wrapping an object method and the compile-time function caller we wrote in the previous chapter is that the object wrapper needs an object which is only available at runtime. Thus, this function needs to work with compile-time data and runtime data together. It works with delegates instead of the `alias` arguments, while still templating the outer function on the type of the delegate given.

Not all information about a function is available through a delegate type. If we needed more information such as the parameter names or default values, they will need to be passed to the wrapper function from the outside along with the delegate.

If we tried to use an `alias` argument, the compiler will issue an error saying `need this to access member foo` when we tried to call it. An `alias` parameter doesn't include a pointer to the `this` object; it will only be a reference to the function itself. A delegate, on the other hand, includes both the necessary pieces of information to call an object method.

Similarly, we have often used an `alias helper` function in the past to refer to a member when doing compile-time reflection. Here, it is not important because the `alias helper` function will also lose the reference to this, yielding a plain function instead of a delegate. The plain function that it gives doesn't know that the `this` pointer is even necessary, so while the code may compile, it will crash when it tries to actually use the object! This is also why `wrap` is specifically constrained to the `isDelegate` method instead of the `isCallable` method, to catch this mistake at compile time by means of a type mismatch error. We specifically need a delegate because only delegates keep a reference to the object instance.

Once the wrapper is working, we can use it to populate arrays. Here, we used compile-time reflection to get all the methods on a `struct` type and populate an associative array. Since the wrapper interface is the same for all functions, this can now be used to consistently call any method on the given object.

Using opDispatch to generate properties

opDispatch is a good hook for code generation of all kinds. Here, we'll use it to generate properties to access an associative array of keys in a different format in order to mimic the style property in the JavaScript DOM, which translates foo.style.backgroundColor, for example, to the background-color CSS property.

How to do it...

Let's execute the following steps to use opDispatch to generate properties:

1. Write a function to transform the camelCase string to a dash-separated string.
2. Create a struct type with two opDispatch @property methods: a getter that takes no runtime arguments and a setter which takes a string runtime argument. Both the opDispatch methods should take one compile-time string argument.
3. Use the enum keyword with the transformation function to ensure it is done at compile time.
4. Constrain opDispatch to work only on the properties you want to enable, or if you want it to work on everything, set it minimally to not work on popFront.
5. Add a member and constructor that points to the associative array it will manipulate.
6. Test it by creating a small DomElement class with a style property that returns the Style struct and a main function which tries to use it.

The code for the preceding steps is as follows:

```
// transformation function
string unCamelCase(string a) {
  import std.string;
  string ret;
  foreach(c; a)
    if((c >= 'A' && c <= 'Z'))
      ret ~= "-" ~ toLower("" ~ c);
    else
      ret ~= c;
  return ret;
}
```

```
private struct Style {
  // pointer to the associative array we'll modify
  string[string]* aa;
  this(string[string]* aa) {
    this.aa = aa;
  }

  // getter
  @property string opDispatch(string name)() if(name != "popFront") {
    enum n = unCamelCase(name); // step 3
    return (*aa)[n];
  }

  // setter
  @property string opDispatch(string name)(string value) if(name !=
"popFront") {
    enum n = unCamelCase(name); // step 3
    return (*aa)[n] = value;
  }
}

class DomElement {
  string[string] styles;
  // step 6
  @property Style style() {
    return Style(&styles);
  }
}

void main() {
  auto element = new DomElement();
  element.style.backgroundColor = "red";
  element.style.fontSize = "1em";

  import std.stdio;
  writeln(element.styles);
  writeln(element.style.backgroundColor);
}
```

By running the preceding program, we will get the following output:

```
["background-color":"red", "font-size":"1em"]
red
```

This shows that the properties transformed properly for both reading and writing.

How it works...

`opDispatch` is invoked whenever a non-existent member is requested of an aggregate with the dot syntax. It is passed with the name of the requested member as a compile-time parameter. Otherwise, it is just a regular template and may provide code or data.

 It is strongly recommended to always put a constraint on `opDispatch`, because without it, the compile-time duck typing will be completely thrown off. For example, the `isInputRange` function will return `true` because the missing methods of `empty`, `popFront`, and `front` will be provided by `opDispatch`. This will result in functions such as `writeln` trying to iterate over the object as a range and print its contents. However, since they weren't intentionally written, it is unlikely that the object will actually work as a range.

Since the name is passed as a compile-time parameter, it can be used for all kinds of compile-time transformations, including changing the string into a new kind of literal and even mixing it in as a domain-specific language.

Here, we used it to change the format of a string to generate thin accessor properties. The code is very straightforward; a regular function manipulates the string. Then, we use the `enum` keyword to force the manipulation to be done at compile time for maximum runtime performance and use it to look up data in the associative array.

We also wanted the generated properties to work on the child property, `style`. Since `opDispatch` only works with one level at a time, we created a helper object and property function to expose it. The helper object needs a reference to the data it modifies, which we pass in the constructor as a pointer. We could have also passed a reference to the `DomElement` class. Even if the `Style` struct were nested inside the `DomElement` class, it will still be necessary to explicitly pass it a reference to avoid compile errors.

When dot syntax is used on the `style` property, the child properties are generated transparently and on demand by `opDispatch`.

Duck typing to a statically-defined interface

A distinguishing feature of the Go programming language is static interfaces that do not need to be explicitly inherited. Using D's compile-time reflection and code generation capabilities, we can do something similar.

Getting ready

Let's start by defining a goal. We'll write an interface and a `struct` block that could implement the interface, but which does not explicitly inherit from it (the `struct` blocks in D can not inherit from the interfaces at all). We'll also write the following brief function that uses the interface to perform a task:

```
interface Animal {
  void speak();
  void speak(string);
}

struct Duck {
  void speak() {
    import std.stdio;
    writeln("Quack!");
  }
  void speak(string whatToSay) {
    import std.stdio;
    writeln("Quack! ", whatToSay);
  }
}

void callSpeak(Animal a) {
  a.speak();
  a.speak("hello");
}

void main() {
  Duck d;
  // callSpeak(wrap!Animal(&d)); // we want to make this line work
}
```

The `callSpeak` function will not work out of the box with `Duck`, because `Duck` does not statically inherit from the interface. If we wanted to do this manually, we could write a small class that implements the interface by forwarding all the required methods to a member, `Duck`. Let's see how to do this automatically.

How to do it...

Let's execute the following steps to use duck typing in a statically-defined interface:

1. Write a `wrap` function that loops over all the virtual methods of the interface and builds code based on it.

2. Use `std.traits` or `.stringof` to extract the signature of each method and reproduce it as a code string.

3. Write the body of each method as a string which calls the corresponding method on the `struct` block.

4. Print out the code with `pragma(msg)` or `writeln` (running it at runtime) to check it against what you write manually to help while debugging.

5. Create a class which inherits from the static interface and use mixin to compile your generated code inside that class.

6. Return the new object for use.

The code related to the preceding steps is as follows:

```
T wrap(T, R)(R* r) {
    static string wrapperImpl() {
        if(__ctfe) {
            // this helper function will find matching parentheses
            // to navigate the string. It does not handle parentheses
            // in string literals, which may occur with a default
            // argument (which  be seen in this string too), but
            // that's rare enough that we can ignore it for many cases
            int matchParens(string s, int idx) {
                if(s[idx] == '(') {
                    // search forward for match

                    int count;
                    for(int i = idx; i < s.length; i++) {
                        if(s[i] == '(') count++;
                        else if(s[i] == ')') count--;
                        if(count == 0)
                            return i;
                    }
                    assert(0); // unbalanced
                } else if(s[idx] == ')') {
                    // search backward for match

                    int count;
                    for(int i = idx; i >= 0; i--) {
                        if(s[i] == '(') count++;
```

```
            else if(s[i] == ')') count--;
            if(count == 0)
              return i;
        }
        assert(0); // unbalanced


    } else assert(0);
}

// loop over the interface and find functions...
string code;
foreach(memberName; __traits(allMembers, T)) {
  static if(is(typeof(__traits(getMember, T, memberName)) ==
  function)) {
    foreach(overload; __traits(getOverloads, T, memberName)) {
      // the string gives the return value, arguments list, and
      attributes
      // const pure @safe const(char)*(int, string)
      auto str = typeof(overload).stringof;

      // pragma msg can help a lot to see the strings
      // you're working with
      //pragma(msg, typeof(overload).stringof);

      auto argIdx = matchParens(str, str.length - 1);
      string argList = "";
      string argsStr;
      int count = 0;

      // we'll build strings to make the class code
      // and forwarding function call
      argsStr = "(";

      const argStrInput = str[argIdx + 1 .. $ - 1];
      // loops each character, looking for commas which
      // separate arguments
      foreach(idx, argc; argStrInput) {
        if(argc != ',')
          argsStr ~= argc;
        if(argc == ',' || idx == argStrInput.length - 1) {
          import std.conv;
          auto part = " a" ~ to!string(count++);
          argsStr ~= part;
```

```
            if (argList.length)
                argList ~= ",";
            argList ~= part;
            }
            if (argc == ',')
                argsStr ~= argc;
        }
        argsStr ~= ")";

        code ~= str[0 .. argIdx] ~ " " ~ memberName ~ " " ~
        argsStr;
        code ~= "{ return r." ~ memberName ~ "(" ~ argList ~ ");
        }\n";
        }
      }
    }
    return code;
  } else return null;
}

//pragma(msg, wrapperImpl()); // for debugging help
// create a class that statically inherits the interface
static class Wrapped : T {
  R* r;
  this(R* r) {
    this.r = r;
  }
  // finally, add the code we generated above to the class
  mixin(wrapperImpl());
}
return new Wrapped(r); // pass it a reference to the object
}
```

How it works...

The most difficult part of the `wrap` function's implementation is reproducing the same function signatures the interface uses. Here, we took the shortest path: as simply as possible, using the string the compiler provides with the `.stringof` property of each method.

The `.stringof` property on a function gives its signature, including the return type, arguments, and any modifiers that affect its type. To successfully override the method, all these details need to be correct—except argument names, which do not need to match (indeed, function arguments don't need names at all, especially in the interfaces where the names are not referenced anyway).

Since the string returned by the compiler is always well-formed, we can depend on matching parentheses to navigate to the string. The only thing that can complicate this is the presence of a default string argument value containing the unmatched parentheses. We could also watch for quotes to handle this case. The example skipped this to keep the code shorter, since it is not needed for most of the functions.

Starting from the right-hand side, we match the parentheses to isolate the argument list. The `.stringof` property always puts modifiers on the left-hand side, so we know the last character is always the closing parenthesis of the argument list. While this kind of assumption could be labelled a hack, it also gets the job done with the minimum of hassle.

Once the argument list, return type, and attributes are isolated, we start to build the string that implements the interface. The code generation method here is to build the D code as a string. This can result in a very messy implementation, but focus on just one part at a time: split the interface argument string using commas to get the types of each argument, and then build the new function's argument list by piecing them back together with new commas and a consistent pattern of argument names. Simultaneously, build a call argument list by putting together only the names. Here's what we aim to generate:

```
void foo(int, string); // the interface we need to match
// the implementation must match types in the argument list,
// but the names need not match. So we'll use a simple numbered
// pattern
override void foo(int arg1, string arg2) {
    // when calling the function, we only want the names, no types
    // in this string.
    return r.foo(arg1, arg2);
}
```

The constructed strings build this code, one piece at a time.

> While the `void` values cannot be assigned to values or used as function arguments, they can be used in a `return` statement. When forwarding to another function, we can therefore always use `return f()` and the compiler will do the right thing without error, even if `f()` returns `void`. This greatly simplifies the generation process.

Once the code is built, we use the `mixin` expression to compile it into our implementation class. This works like copying and pasting the string into the class at compile time. While the `mixin` expression cannot create partial declarations, it can create a list of complete methods to be added to an incomplete class.

Here, we created a static nested class with a constructor that takes a pointer to the object we're wrapping and mixes in the methods needed to implement the interface. Finally, the instance of that class is returned via the interface. As far as the outside world is concerned, the specifics of this class aren't important, it just needs to implement the interface.

If it is impossible to implement the interface successfully by wrapping the input object, the class will not compile, causing the build to fail. It is still static compile-time duck typing, and not a dynamic type wrapper.

There's more...

Phobos' `std.typecons.wrap` function does this same job more thoroughly than we do here; however, it has the caveat that it currently only works on classes. With our `wrap` function, we took the structure by pointer, allowing the wrapped class to operate on the original data and matching most user expectations since interfaces are expected to be able to act on the object. However, this has a potential trade-off that the `struct` block might go out of scope and be destroyed while an instance of the wrapped class still exists, leaving a dangling reference.

A solution to that problem would be to have a private copy of the `struct` block in the generated class. However, this no longer updates the original data, limiting the potential of duck typing to several interfaces at once. Neither solution is perfect, but both can be automatically generated, so you may pick the strategy that is right for your use case.

10
Multitasking

In this chapter, we will look at D's multitasking capabilities with threads, fibers, and processes. We'll learn about the following:

- ▶ Using threads
- ▶ Passing messages with `std.concurrency`
- ▶ Processing parallel data with `std.parallelism`
- ▶ Using fibers
- ▶ Creating new processes
- ▶ Exploring thread-safe, single-locking singletons
- ▶ Using asynchronous I/O

Introduction

Multitasking has several uses in modern computer programs. It can accelerate speed by utilizing multiple processor cores or continuing to crunch numbers while waiting on a file to load from secondary storage, such as a slow hard drive. It can improve scalability by spreading a task across several servers. Also, it can improve reliability by putting buggy components in separate processes that will crash independently of the main application.

D has support in the language and library for various forms of multitasking, including processes, threads, fibers, and single-instruction and multiple-data CPU features. By accessing operating system APIs, D can also utilize asynchronous I/O, among other features.

Using threads

Threads are a common building block for multitasking inside a single process. A thread is an independent stream of program execution that has access to the memory of other threads.

How to do it...

To start using threads, we will have to execute the following steps:

1. Write the command `import core.thread;`.
2. Write a function to perform your independent task.
3. If the thread needs to pause, use the static method `Thread.sleep` from the thread to be paused.
4. Create an additional thread with `auto thread = new Thread`, passing it as a pointer to your function.
5. Call `thread.start` to begin execution.

Take a look at the following code:

```
import core.thread;
import core.atomic;

import std.stdio;

int count = 0;
shared(int) sharedCount = 0;

// this is the function that will run in our threads
void threadedFunction() {
    foreach(i; 0 .. 5) {
        writeln("thread running ", count++, " global: ", sharedCount);
        Thread.sleep(1.seconds);
        atomicOp!"+="(sharedCount, 1);
    }
}

void main() {
    auto thread = new Thread(&threadedFunction);
    thread.start();

    Thread.sleep(1500.msecs);

    auto thread2 = new Thread(&threadedFunction);
    thread2.start();
}
```

Running the program will result in the following interleaved output:

```
thread running 0 global: 0
thread running 1 global: 1
thread running 0 global: 1
thread running 2 global: 2
thread running 1 global: 3
thread running 3 global: 4
thread running 2 global: 5
thread running 4 global: 6
thread running 3 global: 7
thread running 4 global: 9
```

How it works...

The D runtime library encapsulates threads in a `Thread` class, one of which is created automatically when a program starts up, representing the program's main thread of execution. So, any operation that can be done by a child thread can also be done by the main thread, such as `Thread.sleep`, which pauses execution for the specified duration.

A thread's constructor takes a pointer to a function, which they execute to completion. This is similar to how the program as a whole runs `main` and terminates when it returns. A new thread is created in the paused state. To begin its execution, we must call its `start` method.

All started threads will run simultaneously and automatically spread out across multiple processor cores, if available. Multiple threads running simultaneously means nonatomic operations (that is, operations that consist of more than one machine instruction) may be interrupted at any time. Thus, working with shared data must be done carefully.

To alleviate the difficulty of working with shared data, D takes a different approach than most other languages. Whereas in C, for example, all global and static variables are assumed to be shared unless specifically marked as __thread, in D, all global and static variables are assumed to be thread-local unless specifically marked as `shared`. Shared then becomes part of the variable's type, forcing you to think about the ramifications of sharing data between threads before you use it.

You can also declare nontyped shared data with the __gshared storage class, which creates globally shared data without using the separate `shared` type. However, you should avoid this whenever possible because it gives up the additional checks that `shared` provides.

Our example program had both `count` and `sharedCount` to illustrate the difference. The `count` variable is thread-local, so each thread has an independent count and the variable can be used normally. The `sharedCount` variable, on the other hand, is shared across all threads and needs to be properly synchronized to avoid race conditions (where one thread reads a value, another thread writes a value, and the first thread writes back the old value, saving over the second thread's write).

To address this problem, instead of using the regular increment operator, we used `core.atomic.atomicOp`. An atomic operation is one that cannot be broken down into interruptible pieces—it is done all at once, without giving another thread a chance to intervene before it is finished. `atomicOp` takes an operation as a compile-time string argument, a piece of shared data to act upon, and the value by which to modify it.

In the next recipe, we'll look at a higher level of abstraction on top of the low-level threads seen here, which simplifies some of the details of data sharing.

There's more...

Threads in D, by default, are known to the garbage collector and will prevent the termination of the program until they are all completed.

To create a thread that doesn't prevent process termination, you want a daemon thread. Creating a daemon thread is easy: simply create a regular `Thread` and then set the `isDaemon` property to `true`, as shown in the following snippet:

```
auto thread = new Thread(&threadedFunction);
thread.isDaemon = true; // make it a daemon thread
thread.start();
```

Now, if `main` returns before this thread is complete, the process will terminate immediately without waiting for the thread to finish.

Creating a thread that is not known to the garbage collector is more difficult and very tricky to get right. To do this, you will have to create a thread using operating system primitives like you would in C instead of the D library. Doing this is not recommended and should only be used when you are certain about what you are doing.

See also

▸ The concurrency chapter of the book *The D Programming Language* by Andrei Alexandrescu, who explains the language features and library in greater depth

▸ The official documentation of the core thread module is `http://dlang.org/phobos/core_thread.html`

▶   The official documentation of the atomic operations used for lock-free programming
    is `http://dlang.org/phobos/core_atomic.html`

▶   The official documentation of the time types, including the durations used by
    `Thread.sleep`, is `http://dlang.org/phobos/core_time.html`

Passing messages with std.concurrency

Passing data to and from threads correctly can be difficult to get right. Phobos provides an
abstraction to make passing messages much simpler.

How to do it...

Execute the following steps to pass messages with `std.concurrency`:

1. Use the command `import std.concurrency;`.

2. Spawn a thread with an independent function. You may pass arguments to the
    function as long as they can be safely shared across threads. You can pass an
    instance of `thisTid` to the child thread so that it knows who its parent is for
    communication, or the child can use `std.concurrency.ownerTid` to get
    the handle of the thread that spawned it.

3. Define a struct to serve as a message to communicate across threads.

4. Send a message with the `send` function and your struct from the child thread
    when it has completed its task.

5. In the parent thread, use `receive` with a delegate to handle your message type.

6. Add additional threads to the program as needed or more message handlers to the
    receive call if you want to receive more messages.

Review the following code:

```
import std.concurrency;

struct MyMessage {
    int a;
}

void writeToFile(string filename, string text) {
    import std.stdio;
    auto file = File(filename, "wt");
    file.write(text);
}
```

```
void doSomething(Tid parent, Duration sleepDuration) {
  import core.thread; // for sleep
  Thread.sleep(sleepDuration);
  send(parent, MyMessage(sleepDuration));
}

void main() {
  // writing to files can be slow, let's spawn a thread
  // so the rest of the program doesn't have to wait
  spawn(&writeToFile, "text.txt", "writing some text");

  // we'll also make another worker thread to do a slow
  // operation
  auto tid = spawn(&doSomething, thisTid, 3.seconds);

  // we'll now wait until the child sends us a message
  receive((MyMessage msg) {
    import std.stdio;
    writeln("Got my message: ", msg.a);
  });
}
```

How it works...

The `std.concurrency` feature builds on the `core.thread` model to provide an easy-to-use and correct-by-default message passing API. The key functions for the basic operation are `spawn`, `send`, `receive`, and `thisTid`.

The `spawn` function takes a pointer to a function, just like `new Thread()`, and then takes a list of arguments to pass to that function. Among the arguments we passed was `thisTid`, a reference to the current thread for use with message passing. Remember, the main thread is created automatically, so a `Tid` is always available, even before spawning any new thread. The `spawn` function automatically starts the new thread and returns its `Tid`, which can be used to send messages to it from the parent thread.

The `spawn` function will statically reject any data that may be written from two threads at a time. This rejects mutable arrays, but does not include any `immutable` data or value types such as integers. To spawn a thread with a mutable array, it must be explicitly marked as `shared` in both the variable declaration and the function argument lists.

The `send` function sends a message to the specified thread, identified by its `Tid`. The message is plain data, identified by its type. The implementation will append the message to a thread-local mailbox in the target thread until it is handled by calling `receive`.

Similar to user-defined attributes, you can also send plain data, such as built-in strings; however, I recommend against this because a basic type can mean anything without looking at the context. By always using a user-defined struct for messages, the intended usage can be made clear on both the send and receive sides.

The `receive` function performs type matching against a list of delegates. You give it a list of handlers for various message types. The type of the argument is the message it handles. Message type matching is performed from the first delegate given to `receive` to the last, with the first match being called. Any unreachable handler, for example, a repeated type or a more specific type after a more generic handler, will cause a compile-time error. A handler that takes an argument of type `std.variant.Variant` acts as a catch-all for messages.

If you want two-way communication, you can include a `Tid from;` field in the message struct, which the `receive` handler can then use to send a reply. The parent thread may run `receive` in a loop to process several messages.

See also

> ▸ The documentation for the module can be found at `http://dlang.org/phobos/ std_concurrency.html`, which covers the functions we saw here as well as many others; these include variants for receiving with a timeout value, receiving only a specific message, using out-of-band communication, and more.

> ▸ The free chapter on concurrency from Andrei Alexandrescu's book, *The D Programming Language*, is available at `http://www.informit.com/ articles/article.aspx?p=1609144`

Processing parallel data with std.parallelism

Concurrency can be thought of as doing several tasks in the same time frame, hiding the implementation of putting one task on hold while it waits for something and another task is running concurrently. Parallelism, by contrast, is spreading a task out across several processors to be executed simultaneously. Parallelism is ideally suited to numeric computations, where one portion of the result does not immediately depend on another, for example, when multiplying several smaller factors to divide and conquer the multiplication of a large number or performing one calculation on several independent values of an array.

How to do it...

To process parallel data with `std.parallelism`, execute the following steps:

1. Use the command `import std.parallelism;`.
2. Write a normal `foreach` loop that works on an array.
3. Make sure that each loop iteration is independent.
4. Call `parallel()` on the array you're looping.

Take a look at the following code:

```
import std.parallelism;
import std.math;

// just to populate the initial array
int[] generateNumbers() {
  int[] a;
  a.length = 50000;
  foreach(idx, ref i; a)
    i = cast(int) idx; // cast needed for 64 bit compiles
  return a;
}

static int[] numbers = generateNumbers();

void main() {
  foreach(i; 0 .. 1000) // run several times for benchmarking
// foreach(ref num; numbers) // linear loop
  foreach(ref num; parallel(numbers)) // parallel loop
    num *= sqrt(abs(sin(num) / cos(num))); // arbitrary per-item work

  import std.stdio;
  writeln(numbers[0 .. 20]); // display some results
}
```

The execution time for this program will be cut by approximately the number of processor cores your computer has when you switch to the parallel loop. On my dual-core computer, the execution time was cut from six seconds down to three, giving the same results.

How it works...

The `std.parallelism` feature provides functions and objects that easily spreads a loop across multiple processors, automatically selecting a recommended number of threads based on the number or processor cores detected.

 The `std.parallelism` feature's implementation utilizes objects with `opApply` overloaded to take input data and spread it out across a task pool using the user-friendly `foreach` syntax. It uses `opApply` instead of implementing an input range because it needs to change the looping structure itself, not just the data and advancement method.

The `std.parallelism` feature has limited checks to ensure that your code is correct; your loops are subject to low-level data issues without compile-time errors. While adding parallelism to your `foreach` loop is a very easy way to parallelize it, it is still your responsibility to ensure that each iteration of the loop is indeed independent. Taking the argument by `ref` and operating only on the current element in the loop, reading or writing to no other data, is an easy way to accomplish this.

The `std.parallelism` feature also has the `map` and `reduce` functions, which are automatically parallelized versions of the `map` and `reduce` functions in `std.algorithm`. With these, you can succinctly and efficiently implement many parallel algorithms without necessarily writing any explicit loops.

See also

▶ The official documentation of the parallelism module can be found at
   `http://dlang.org/phobos/std_parallelism.html`

Using fibers

Fibers are similar to threads, but are more lightweight and cooperative rather than pre-emptive. That is, a fiber must explicitly yield to pass control to another fiber, either by calling the `yield` function directly or through a function that yields for you (such as an I/O function). On the other hand, threads will be scheduled automatically by the operating system and may be interrupted at any time.

How to do it...

Let us execute the following steps:

1. Create a fiber with `new Fiber`. You do *not* have to create a special storage location for your state because fibers automatically save and restore their own stacks, so regular local variables will work.

2. Call `Fiber.yield` periodically inside your fiber to let other fibers run. The `yield` function will return control to the function that called the fiber.

3. Pass messages to worker threads to perform long computations.

4. The `main` function is responsible for scheduling the fibers. It should call the `call` function on the fibers when it is ready to resume their execution.

Take a look at the following code:

```
import core.thread;

int count;

void testFunction() {
    import std.stdio;
    count++;
    writeln("Fiber run count: ", count);
    Fiber.yield();
    writeln("Fiber recalled after yielding!");
}

void main() {
    auto fiber1 = new Fiber(&testFunction);
    auto fiber2 = new Fiber(&testFunction);

    // Call the fiber, this will return when it calls Fiber.yield
    fiber1.call();
    fiber2.call();

    // now it will resume execution from the last yield call
    fiber1.call();
    fiber2.call();
}
```

Running the program will print the following:

```
Fiber run count: 1
Fiber run count: 2
Fiber recalled after yielding!
Fiber recalled after yielding!
```

How it works...

A `Fiber` represents the execution context of a function that can be paused and resumed. It is created similar to a `Thread`, by first importing `core.thread` and then creating the `Fiber` by passing the constructor a pointer to the function.

However, after creation, Fibers and Threads work very differently. Whereas a Thread is started and then executes concurrently with other threads, a Fiber is called, like a function, with the flow of execution transferring to it. Unlike just any function though, a fiber can call `Fiber.yield()`, which returns the execution to the caller while remembering the exact state it had when it yielded. Next time the fiber is called, it picks up where it left off the last time.

Since fibers are cooperative when multitasking, they `yield` rather than being interrupted by the operating system. There is no need for memory synchronization or shared data. In the example, we used a thread-local variable, `count`, to represent a value across two separate fibers, and it was effortlessly updated by both. The downside to this model is that they do not utilize multiple CPU cores the way threads can, and thus do not help with parallelism. Nevertheless, fibers can sometimes outperform threads depending on the task. Asynchronous I/O is an example where fibers shine because they are not bound by the CPU.

See also

- The official documentation of the `Fiber` class can be found at `http://dlang.org/phobos/core_thread.html#Fiber`
- To see the use of fibers with a scheduler geared toward asynchronous input and output, visit `http://vibed.org/`

Creating new processes

Processes are the main isolation unit in a multitasking operating system. Separate program instances run in separate processes, giving each one an isolated memory space and execution context which can never accidentally step on the toes of another.

Processes can also be a useful concept in the context of a single logical program. Creating a child process can allow you to use a separate program to help you complete your task or can isolate a subtask inside your program from the rest of it, giving you resiliency against crashes as well as concurrency and parallelization across several processors, even across several different physical computers in some cases.

How to do it...

Here, we'll briefly explore using processes for two tasks: creating crash-resistant plugins, which will work well across platforms, and forking execution to handle independent tasks, which uses Posix functions.

To create a crash-resistant plugin, we need to execute the following steps:

1. Write the plugin as a separate program that communicates with the parent through the `stdin` and `stdout` streams.
2. In the parent program, use the command `import std.process;`.
3. Call `pipeProcess` to spawn the plug-in program.

To fork execution to handle independent tasks, we need to execute the following steps. These steps will not work in Windows.

1. Use the command `import core.sys.posix.unistd, core.sys.posix.sys.wait;`.
2. Call `fork` in an `if` statement.
3. If `fork` returns zero, proceed with your task, terminating the process when you are finished.
4. If `fork` returns nonzero, you are in the parent process. Perform your independent task, then wait for the child thread to finish before terminating.

The following is the code:

```
import core.sys.posix.unistd;
import core.sys.posix.sys.wait;

void main() {
  if(auto pid = fork()) {
    if(pid < 0) throw new Exception("fork failed");
    // this is the parent, continue doing
    // work here
    int statusCode;
    wait(&statusCode); // wait for the child to finish
  } else {
    // this is the child, it can do independent work
    // here
  }
}
```

How it works...

Crash-resistant plugins are separate programs that adhere to a communication protocol. Since they are separate processes and have totally isolated memory spaces and execution flows, a bug in the plugin will not be able to overwrite the memory or otherwise crash into the parent program.

The `fork` function is the main multitasking function in the Unix family of operating systems. When it runs, the process immediately splits into two: parent and child. Each is fully independent after the call, using separate copy-on-write memory spaces and execution contexts.

 The `fork` function is not efficiently implemented on Windows, so it should not be used on that operating system. Instead, use threads and minimize shared data to get the same result.

The return value of `fork` tells you if you are in the parent or the child process. If it returns 0, you are in the child branch. If it returns a negative number, an error has occurred, and if it returns a positive number, you are in the parent branch and the return value is the ID of the new process. The processes execute independently, but the parent can keep track of the child's progress and wait for its termination. The child process will inherit data and open files from its parent, allowing them to communicate.

There's more...

Using reflection and code generation, we can automate most of the communication process between the two cooperating programs. Serializing and deserializing data can be automated with the reflection facilities, such as `tupleof`, and the messages may be represented by the functions' names (like we did in the command-line function caller in *Chapter 8, Reflection*) or numbers (using facilities such as `__traits(getVirtualIndex)`), called automatically with `__traits(getMember)`.

Memory can be shared across processes using the operating system functions, such as `shmget` on Posix located in `core.sys.posix.sys.shm`. These functions work the same way in D as they do in C; however, ensure that the shared resources are properly released upon abnormal program termination. Using a destructor alone is not enough—you must also install signal handlers to ensure that the program is not terminated without giving your destructors a chance to run.

Use the `sigaction` function from `core.sys.posix.signal` to install signal handlers for any signal that can terminate the process, such as `SIGINT` and `SIGPIPE`. In the signal handler, set a flag or send a message for your event loop, which should reply with a normal return or by throwing an exception. If the program is terminated by a signal, the scoped cleanup functions will not run, but when an exception is thrown, all cleanup code is run before the program ends.

See also

▸ The *Communicating with external processes* recipe from *Chapter 4, Integration*, discusses how to create processes for separate programs and communicate with them through pipes using the Phobos standard library

▸ The official documentation of the process module can be found at `http://dlang.org/phobos/std_process.html`

▸ To see the D implementation of Apache Thrift, a cross-language remote procedure call and serialization framework that can be used to simplify communication across processes, visit `http://klickverbot.at/blog/2012/03/thrift-now-officially-supports-d/`

Exploring thread-safe, single-locking singletons

Lazy initialization in a multithreaded environment poses an interesting problem: how do you avoid a race condition where the variable is initialized by two different threads, which would defeat the purpose of using a singleton in the first place?

The most straightforward solution is to always use synchronization when getting the singleton instance. This correctly solves the race condition, but comes with a significant performance cost. Clever programmers devised a way to avoid synchronization with a double-checked locking mechanism, checking if the object needs initialization both before and after entering a synchronized block. This has good performance, but has a major problem: it is buggy. Optimizing compilers or different memory models across platforms meant that the double check cannot be relied upon to do the right thing in all cases.

D's built-in thread-local variables offer an elegant solution to the problem that brings the correctness of the straightforward solution and the performance of the double-checked solution together, without the need for complicated code.

How to do it...

To explore thread-safe, single-locking singletons, execute the following steps:

1. Define a singleton class with a `shared` instance.
2. Define a thread-local initialized variable.
3. In the `get` function, if it is not initialized, enter a synchronized block that creates the instance, if necessary.
4. Set the `initialized` value to `true`.
5. Return the `shared` instance.

The following is the code:

```d
class ThreadLocalSingleton {
  private static bool initialized;
  private static shared(ThreadLocalSingleton) instance;

  static shared(ThreadLocalSingleton) getInstance() {
    if(!initialized) {
      synchronized(ThreadLocalSingleton.classinfo) {
        if(instance is null) {
          instance = new shared ThreadLocalSingleton();
        }
      }
      initialized = true;
    }
    return instance;
  }

  int count = 0;
  void foo() shared {
    import std.stdio;
    count++;
    writeln("foo ", count);
  }
}

void useSingleton(shared(ThreadLocalSingleton) s) {
  s.foo();
}

void main() {
  auto i = ThreadLocalSingleton.getInstance();
  useSingleton(i);

  // you can also spawn new threads that use the singleton
}
```

The program will compile and run, printing a count. You can add additional threads and see that it continues to work efficiently.

How it works...

Since locking is expensive, avoiding synchronized blocks can often improve performance. Using D's built-in thread-local storage, we can efficiently bypass all but the first lock for any thread, without using bug-prone double-locking mechanisms.

▶ David Simcha's DConf 2013 discourse is available at `http://dconf.org/2013/talks/simcha.html`, where he presented the pattern used here. He discusses it at about 28 minutes into the video.

Using asynchronous I/O

The D standard library does not include asynchronous I/O functions, but we can still use them by calling C functions or with third-party libraries.

How to do it...

We will execute the following steps to use asynchronous I/O:

1. Find a C API you like, either the operating system functions or a third-party library such as `libuv` or `libevent`, bindings to which can be found at `http://code.dlang.org/`.

2. Use the C functions instead of the Phobos functions.

Here's an example of how to get an asynchronous input from a text file on Windows using the Win32 API:

```
import core.sys.windows.windows; // basic Windows headers
import std.conv;

 // Not all necessary functions are defined in core.sys.windows.
windows
 // but that's never a dealbreaker: we can just define the prototypes
ourselves
// ReadFileEx is specialized for asynchronous reading
  extern(Windows)
    BOOL ReadFileEx(HANDLE, LPVOID, DWORD, OVERLAPPED*, void*);
// SleepEx will pause the program, allowing our async handler to be
called when the data is ready
  extern(Windows)
    DWORD SleepEx(DWORD, BOOL);
// This function will be called when the operation is complete
extern(Windows) void readCallback(DWORD errorCode, DWORD
numberOfBytes, OVERLAPPED* overlapped) {
  // hEvent carries user-defined data. We load it with a pointer to
the buffer below.
```

```
    auto data = (cast(ubyte*) overlapped.hEvent)[0 .. numberOfBytes];
    import std.stdio;
    writeln("Received: ", cast(string) data);
    // we may issue another read here to get more data
}

void main() {
    // We need to open the file with the Windows API too, so we can set the
    // required FILE_FLAG_OVERLAPPED for asynchronous access
    auto handle = CreateFileA("test.txt", GENERIC_READ, 0, null, OPEN_
EXISTING, FILE_FLAG_OVERLAPPED, null);
    if(handle is null) throw new Exception("Couldn't open file.");
    scope(exit) CloseHandle(handle); // always cleanup C resources with
scope guards

    OVERLAPPED overlapped;
    ubyte[1024] buffer;
    overlapped.hEvent = buffer.ptr; // This is allowed to be user-
defined data, we'll fill it with a pointer to the buffer for use in
the callback
    // issue the async read request
    if(ReadFileEx(handle, buffer.ptr, buffer.length, &overlapped,
&readCallback) == 0)
        throw new Exception("ReadFileEx failed " ~
to!string(GetLastError()));

    /* Do other things while the operating system loads the data for
us…. */

    SleepEx(500, true); // wait for the operation to complete
}
```

If you create a file called test.txt and then run the program, it will display its contents.

How it works...

Since D has full access to C libraries and operating system APIs, we can use functionality that is not yet available in Phobos when we need it. Asynchronous I/O is an example where this is necessary. The example is virtually identical to what you might see in an example in the C language.

On Windows, a flag must be set when the handle is created to enable asynchronous operations (called **overlapped** operations in the Microsoft documentation). On Posix, a flag may be set with `fnctl` after the file is opened, or you may use an event loop that triggers on file readiness to avoid blocking operations.

These operations require full access to the file handle, which limits the amount of Phobos calls you can use. For example, `std.process.pipeProcess` conveniently creates the pipes for you, but that precludes setting the overlapped flag. If you want to use asynchronous I/O on a pipe to communicate with another process, it will be necessary to perform all the operations yourself at the operating system API level. (Indeed, on Windows, you cannot even use the `CreatePipe` function that the `std.process` implementation uses to create the pipes because it does not allow you to set the overlapped flag either; you must use the lower-level `CreateNamedPipe` function instead.)

In some cases, you can create a Phobos object from an operating system handle. For example, you can create `std.socket.Socket` from an existing low-level handle, but in most cases, you are on your own to write the code as you would in C. When in doubt, you can search the Internet for C asynchronous I/O documentation and examples and apply that same knowledge to D.

See also

▸ The website `http://code.dlang.org/` has wrappers for C libraries to ease the use of cross-platform asynchronous I/O

▸ To see the D framework that uses asynchronous I/O internally, visit `http://vibed.org/`

11
D for Kernel Coding

Let's turn our attention to using D to start writing bare metal code—the origin of an x86 kernel in D and laying some groundwork for bare metal in other environments. We'll start with the following:

- ▸ Running D on bare metal x86 with a stripped runtime
- ▸ Adding interrupt handling to the bare metal x86 code

Introduction

Most D users today use D to program traditional computers with operating systems such as Windows, OS X, or Linux. However, with custom runtime code and the open source GRUB bootloader (a program which boots the computer and loads our program), we can also run D programs compiled with an unmodified copy of the DMD compiler on Linux with bare metal to form the basis of writing an operating system kernel in D.

Running D on bare metal x86 with a stripped runtime

D can do most of what C can, including writing bare metal code (without an operating system) with minimal runtime library requirements. While most D libraries (including the Phobos standard library) will not work in such a minimal environment, we can still use the majority of the core language if we opt for enough library support.

Getting ready

Running experimental bare metal programs on physical hardware is a slow and time consuming process. Instead, I recommend that you set up an emulator or virtual machine. In this book, we'll use **QEMU**; this may be available in your Linux distribution's package manager, or you can build it from a source by downloading the code from `http://qemu.org/`. We'll also use Linux to build the application. To follow along, you'll need a Linux computer with the DMD compiler installed.

How to do it...

To run D on bare metal x86 with a stripped runtime, we need to execute the following steps:

1. Create a new directory for the project.

2. Create a `multiboot.S` file that declares a section of the executable file, `.multiboot`, containing the multiboot magic ID number, multiboot flags, and multiboot checksum (in that order). It should have the following contents:

```
.section .multiboot

# Multiboot magic ID number
.set MAGIC,     0x1BADB002

# request alignment and memory map
.set FLAGS,     1 | 2

.align 4
.long MAGIC
.long FLAGS
.long -(FLAGS + MAGIC) # Checksum
```

3. Create a `linker.ld` file that sets the program entry point to `_d_run_main`, starts placing sections at the 1 megabyte point, and puts the `.multiboot` section first. The following contents will do the job:

```
ENTRY(_d_run_main)

SECTIONS {
        . = 1M;

        .text BLOCK(4K) : ALIGN(4K) {
                *(.multiboot)
                *(.text)
        }
}
```

4. Create a `Makefile` that assembles the multiboot header, compiles the D code with no default library and minimal runtime checking, and links them all together using the linker script. Ensure that the commands use a leading tab, *not* a space. The following is the content:

```
all:
        gcc -m32 -c multiboot.S -o multiboot.o
        dmd -c -m32 test.d object.d –defaultlib
          = -noboundscheck -release
        gcc -m32 –omy_kernel test.o object.o
          multiboot.o -T linker.ld –nostdlib
```

5. Create a file, `test.d`, to say hello. To write on the screen, we will directly access the video memory through a pointer. Use the following contents:

```
void main() {
        clearScreen();
        print("Hello, world, from bare metal!");
}

void clearScreen() {
        ubyte* videoMemory = cast(ubyte*) 0xb8000;
        foreach(idx; 0 .. 80*25) {
                videoMemory[idx * 2] = ' ';
                videoMemory[idx * 2 + 1] = 0b111;
        }

}

void print(string msg) {
        ubyte* videoMemory = cast(ubyte*) 0xb8000;
        foreach(char c; msg) {
                *videoMemory = c;
                videoMemory += 2;
        }
}
```

6. Create a file named `object.d` to provide the minimal runtime library functions needed for the basic language to work without the compiler issuing errors about a corrupted runtime library. It will include our program entry point, which calls `main` and then loops forever, as well as a number of necessary support classes, which we will not use initially but are required by the compiler. This file must be named `object.d` and should contain the following contents for `dmd`. (Note that this may be different for other compiler versions, including `ldc`.)

```
module object;

static assert((void*).sizeof == 4); // must be 32 bit
```

```
alias string = immutable(char)[];
alias size_t = uint;
alias ptrdiff_t = int;

extern(C)
void _d_run_main() {
        asm {
                naked;
                call _Dmain;
                loop_forever:
                        cli;
                        hlt;
                        jmp loop_forever;
        }
}

extern(C) void _d_dso_registry() {}
extern(C) __gshared void* _Dmodule_ref;
extern(C) void _Dmain();

// required support classes by the compiler

class Object { }

class Throwable {}
class Exception : Throwable {}
class Error : Throwable {}

class TypeInfo { }

class TypeInfo_Struct : TypeInfo {
        void*[13] compilerProvidedData;
}

class TypeInfo_Interface : TypeInfo {
        TypeInfo_Class info;
}

class TypeInfo_Class : TypeInfo {
        void*[17] compilerProvidedData;
}

struct ModuleInfo {}
```

7. Run `make`.

8. Test the program by running `qemu -kernel my_kernel`. You may add other commands to QEMU as well, such as curses if you do not have a graphics display available.

 When you run `make`, the compiler will run *very* quickly. This is normal because it doesn't have to parse any of the runtime or standard library; the compiler's workload is greatly reduced compared to most programs!

You should see the emulator pop up with the hello message:

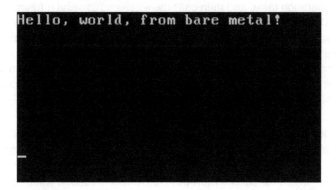

Hello, world, from bare metal!

The text cursor may be anywhere. Moving the cursor must be done separately from writing to the screen on bare metal! If you run `strip my_kernel; ls -lh my_kernel`, you will see that the file is only about 7 KB in size.

How it works...

Before running the "hello world" program on bare metal, we have four important aspects to set up: booting support, a custom entry point, a minimal library to use instead of `druntime`, and finally, the meat of our program itself.

Booting up an x86 PC can be a fairly involving task. If you were doing it yourself, you'd have to write a small bootloader program that loads your main file, switches the processor to the 32-bit mode (it initially boots to the 16-bit mode for backward compatibility), and transfers the execution to the D code.

However, thanks to the **multiboot** standard supported by QEMU in the test environment and the GRUB loader on a physical computer, we don't have to worry about all those details. Instead, we put a multiboot header in our file consisting of flags, a magic number, and a checksum. Then, we command the linker to put that section at the beginning so that the loader can find it.

Since multiboot requires low-level control over linker sections, we could not write it in D. Instead, we wrote a small file in the GNU assembly language, `multiboot.S`, to define the section and header data. It contains no executable code, which brings us to the custom entry point.

All the code executed by our program is found in the D files. There is no need for a separate assembly language bootstrapper—when we need assembly in D, we can use the inline assembler. By default, the linker looks for a symbol called `_start` to serve as the program entry point.

> In normal code, `_start` is located in the C runtime library. It performs preparation tasks and then calls the `extern(C)` `main` function, which in D programs is automatically generated by the compiler to call the `_d_run_main` function, which is located in the D runtime library. You can see the original source code for `_d_run_main` in `dmd2/src/druntime/src/rt/dmain2.d`, found in the dmd zip download. You can also find the definition of the C `main` function in the compiler's source code in the `dmd2/src/dmd/mars.c` file.

Since the D compiler forces us to define `_d_run_main`, and we defined a linker script for the multiboot header anyway, we can easily change the program entry point to go directly into our code. In `linker.ld`, the line `ENTRY(_d_run_main)` instructs the linker to set the entry point to our `_d_run_main` function. When the program is loaded, it will begin execution at the beginning of that function.

Now that we have the linker set up, it is time to start writing code. First, we focused on what we wanted to accomplish and wrote our `test.d` file to that effect—we wanted to print a message to the screen. This code is pretty normal looking—it is just plain D with a regular `main` function and helper functions to loop over an array and write it to the video memory.

Interacting with hardware often follows the same principle of writing to a specific memory location. The video hardware is **memory mapped**, meaning a portion of the memory space is reserved for communication with it. One such address is `0xb8000`, mapped to the text screen buffer.

Since from the program's perspective it is just a block of memory, we can access it through a simple pointer. The text buffer is 80 x 25 cells in size, with each cell represented by two bytes: first, the extended ASCII character to display, and second, the attributes of that cell, including foreground color (the lower 4 bits, each representing red, green, blue, and one as a brightness flag), background color (the next 3 bits), and a blink flag (the highest bit).

When we clear the screen, we look through the entire buffer, setting the character to a space and the attributes to `0b111`, a gray foreground on a black background. Try changing that number to see a more colorful message!

When writing our message, we write our characters at the beginning of the buffer, leaving the attributes alone. A future exercise may be to define a __gshared variable to keep track of your current position so that two consecutive prints do not overwrite each other. Be careful not to write out of bounds of the video memory! Since D's bound checking requires runtime library support, we disabled them. Since we're running the processor in the kernel mode, there's no hardware memory protection either. We're on our own to use the pointers correctly.

 This print function will not work correctly if the string contains non-ASCII characters, but for the sake of simplicity, we will ignore this—writing most non-ASCII characters to the hardware text buffer is a nontrivial task, and supporting the whole Unicode character set in this environment is impossible.

Now that our program is written, we must provide a minimal runtime library so that the compiler will actually accept it. Enter object.d.

object.d is the required module that provides the foundational bridge between the compiler's world and that of the runtime library. It is also automatically imported to every D module and provides global aliases and symbols, which the rest of the D code takes for granted. The string type, for example, is not a keyword in D. Instead, it is defined as alias for immutable(char)[] in object.d; something we do here too.

The first thing our object.d does, after declaring itself to be the special object module, is issue static assert to ensure it is actually being compiled for a 32-bit target (the size of a pointer is 4 bytes). Since the processor is in the 32-bit mode when control is passed to our program, we need to ensure that our program has generated code it can actually run. The static assert will cause the compile to fail if we forget to pass the -m32 flag.

Next, we define aliases for the three most common pseudo-built-in types in D: string, size_t, and ptrdiff_t. We can also define wstring and dstring here if we wanted to use them. None of these aliases are strictly necessary to compile the D code; however, since these types are typically used in the D code as though they are built-in, defining them lets us carry over our habit of writing string to the bare metal world. The size_t and ptrdiff_t types normally change their type based on the target platform; however, since we are specifically targeting 32-bit x86, we will ignore this detail.

Next is our program entry point, which is the definition of _d_run_main. It is defined as extern(C) because the compiler communicates with the runtime through functions without name mangling. We wrote this function with the naked inline assembly to ensure that we have precise control over what is run. Though we don't use it here, the flag we set in the multiboot header to request a map of available memory will make that data available to us by a pointer stored in the EBX register. If we wanted to expand on this program to use the memory allocation, this pointer will be valuable information that we don't want to lose.

In the `naked` function, the compiler does not add additional instructions to set up a stack frame, preserve registers, or even automatically return from the function. It gives us complete control over everything that happens.

With that control reserved for later use, we proceed to the rest of the function. First, we call `_Dmain`, which is a symbol created by the compiler to represent the `main` function written in D. The `main` function is not used directly because the D symbol is not in the scope; this function is found in a separate file that the runtime is not aware of. Under the function, we declared the prototype `extern(C) void _Dmain();` to bring it into the local scope.

After `main` returns, since we have no operating system to return to, we disable interrupts with the `cli` instruction, then halt the CPU with the `hlt` instruction. Just in case it ever resumes execution, we can also use the `jmp` instruction to go to a previous label, forming an infinite loop. The user will have to restart the computer to use it again.

If we enabled exception handling—this is possible even on bare metal, although it takes several lines of code in `object.d`—we would want to call a helper function that calls `_Dmain` inside a `try/catch` block instead of calling it directly. In this case, exceptions thrown but not caught by the program will be gracefully handled. You can see how the real `druntime` does this by checking `dmd2/src/druntime/src/rt/dmain2.d`.

The next thing our `object.d` does is define an empty function called `_d_dso_registry`. This function is currently specific to D on Linux, but since we used the Linux compiler, it expects it to be there. The compiler passes information related to registering D-shared objects. We don't care about this information, so we simply defined an empty function to ignore it without causing a compile error. You can see the `druntime` definition of this function in `dmd2/src/druntime/src/rt/sections_linux.d`. Similarly, the compiler may reference `_Dmodule_ref` to provide a hook for runtime module information, and if it is missing, it can cause the link to fail; so, we define it but never use it. It is `__gshared` because trying to make a thread-local variable would result in either a link error due to the changing definitions of TLS and non-TLS data, or worse yet, a runtime crash because of the compiler-generated code that our system doesn't actually support.

Finally, we define the minimal support classes required by the compiler. It expects `class Object` and `TypeInfo` to be available, even if we don't actually use them; this list of classes will grow somewhat as we use more D data types (although much of that code can be automatically generated).

The compiler doesn't particularly care about the methods these classes provide, but it does provide the `TypeInfo` data in a specific format and expects there to be enough room for that data. Since we aren't actually using that data currently, instead of reproducing the actual types of the data to form usable variables, we simply defined an array of `void*` to pad out the space.

The size expected can be found in the compiler's source code in dmd2/src/dmd/typinf.c and the expected layouts can look at the definitions in dmd2/src/druntime/src/ object_.d. Finally, we compile the program and run it in the emulator to test it. If all goes well, your program will say **Hello, world, from bare metal**!

There's more...

Much of the D language will not work with this minimal runtime. To re-add language features, you'll need to bring in more of the D runtime. If you try to use a feature and get an undefined symbol error from the linker, search the druntime source code for that symbol. You may be able to copy and paste it into your own object.d to enable that portion of the language. However, there are some features you will not want because they complicate memory management. Array concatenation, for example, is prone to memory leaks without the garbage collector's help, so it may be best to leave them disabled and use manually written alternatives instead.

You can write the D programs for regular operating systems using a minimal runtime library too. To try this, start with your custom object.d. Change _d_run_main to import core. stdc.stdlib and call exit(0) from the C standard library instead of looping forever (the cli and hlt instructions will cause a segmentation fault on Linux anyway, as they are protected CPU instructions). When compiling, use the -defaultlib= option for dmd, but do not use the -c option or the link manually; let dmd automatically link the program normally.

The result will be a small file, about 12 KB in size, with no dependencies except the system C library. You can write programs in the C-like subset of D, paying only for the small requirements in object.d and what you decide to use beyond that.

I don't recommend that you do this as a matter of course because you'll lose compatibility with most other D code as well as many of the value-added features of the D language; the smaller file size isn't worth those costs! But the option is available to test your minimal runtime without going to the emulator or other specialized tasks.

See also

▶ My DConf 2014 talk is available at http://dconf.org/2014/talks/ruppe. html. I discuss this topic as well as how to bring in more of the D runtime to enable more language features.

▶ The documentation for the multiboot standard is available at http://www.gnu. org/software/grub/manual/multiboot/multiboot.html.

▶ Visit the home page of the GRUB bootloader at http://www.gnu.org/ software/grub/, which can be used to boot our kernel on a physical PC.

▶ A wiki link with a lot of bare-metal-related articles is http://wiki.osdev.org/ Main_Page. Many of the C examples can also be used in D.

▶ *Running on bare metal ARM* in *Appendix*, *Addendum* will show you how to apply these principles in programming ARM boards with D.

Adding interrupt handling to the bare metal x86 code

In the previous recipe, we displayed the "hello world" program on bare metal. Next, we'll add interrupt handling and enable keyboard support.

Getting ready

Get the code from the last recipe and ensure that it still compiles and runs. We will be adding to it here.

How to do it...

Execute the following steps to add interrupt handling to bare metal x86 code:

1. Declare the constants and data structures needed to communicate with the hardware. The definitions can be translated from the hardware manuals.

2. Write an empty interrupt handler with a `naked` inline assembly that does nothing except return with the `iretd` instruction.

3. Write a keyboard interrupt handler with a `naked` inline assembly. We'll need to read the byte using the keyboard from I/O port `0x60` using the `in` assembly instruction. Then, store it in a global variable, acknowledge the interrupt, then clean up. (The stack and all registers must be left in the same state they were in when we entered this function.) Then, resume normal execution with the `iretd` instruction. It is very important that you do *not* use the `return` keyword in D because interrupt handlers must return with the special instruction.

4. Declare the `__gshared` variables to hold the data tables for interrupt handlers and memory protection data.

5. Write helper functions to set the hardware data structures. Load the empty interrupt handler in the whole table and set the keyboard handler for IRQ 1, which is located at the interrupt number `1 + IRQOffset`.

6. Prepare a global descriptor table with separate descriptors for code, data, and a task state selector. We don't care about the specifics, so we'll just load the entire memory space; however, we do need to know the descriptor numbers for the interrupt handler.

7. Load the global descriptor table with the `lgdt` assembly instruction.

8. Load the interrupt descriptor table with the `lidt` assembly instruction.

9. Enable IRQ1—the keyboard's interrupt request line—by writing the appropriate mask to the programmable interrupt controller's data I/O port with the inline assembly.

10. Enable interrupts with the `sti` assembly function.

11. In your `main` function, write an endless event loop. It should ensure interrupts are enabled with the `sti` instruction, then use the `hlt` instruction to stop the CPU, and then wait for the next interrupt. After one arrives, temporarily disable interrupts with `cli` so that we can handle the data without it being overwritten as we work, write a message if a key was pressed, then start the loop over again.

This is quite a bit of code, but once you get the keyboard working, adding other interrupt handlers is relatively easy. The following is the code:

```
// The following values are defined by the hardware specs.

enum PIC1 = 0x20; /* IO port for master PIC */
enum PIC2 = 0xA0; /* IO port for slave PIC */
enum PIC1_COMMAND = PIC1; /* Commands to PIC1 */
enum PIC1_DATA = (PIC1+1); /* IO port for data to PIC1 */
enum PIC2_COMMAND = PIC2; // ditto for PIC2
enum PIC2_DATA = (PIC2+1);


// This is the interrupt number where the IRQs are mapped.
// 8 is the default set by the system at boot up. We can
// also change this by reprogramming the interrupt controller,
// which is recommended to avoid conflicts in real world code,
// but here, for simplicity, we'll just use the default.
enum IRQOffset = 8;


// This is a data structure defined by the hardware to hold
// an interrupt handler.
align(1)
struct IdtEntry {
  align(1):
  ushort offsetLowWord;
  ushort selector;
  ubyte reserved;
  ubyte attributes;
  ushort offsetHighWord;
}


// This is a hardware-defined structure to store the location of
// a descriptor table.
align(1)
struct DtLocation {
  align(1):
  ushort size;
  void* address;
}
```

```
// Ensure the hardware structure is sized correctly.
static assert(DtLocation.sizeof == 6);

// Hardware defined data structure for holding
// the Global Descriptor Table which holds
// memory protection information.
align(1)
struct GdtEntry {
  align(1):
  ushort limit;
  ushort baseLow;
  ubyte baseMiddle;
  ubyte access;
  ubyte limitAndFlags;
  ubyte baseHigh;
}
/* End of hardware data definitions */

// This is an interrupt handler that simply returns.
void nullIh() {
  asm {
    naked;
    iretd;
  }
}

// stores the last key we got
__gshared uint gotKey = 0;

// This is a keyboard interrupt handler
void keyboardHandler() {
  asm {
    naked; // we need complete control
    push EAX; // store our scratch register

    xor EAX, EAX; // clear the scratch register
    in AL, 0x60; // read the keyboard byte

    mov [gotKey], EAX; // store what we got for use later

    // acknowledge that we handled the interrupt
    mov AL, 0x20;
    out 0x20, AL;
```

```
    pop EAX; // restore our scratch register
    iretd; // required special return instruction
  }
}


// Now, we define some data buffers to hold our tables
// that the hardware will use.

// This global array holds our entire interrupt handler table.
__gshared IdtEntry[256] idt;
__gshared GdtEntry[4] gdt; // memory protection tables
__gshared ubyte[0x64] tss; // task state data

// Now, we'll declare helper functions to load this data.

/// Enables interrupt requests.
/// lowest bit set = irq 0 enabled
void enableIrqs(ushort enabled) {
  // the hardware actually expects a disable bitmask
  // rather than an enabled list/ so we'll flip the bits.
  enabled = ~enabled;
  asm {
    // tell the interrupt controller to unmask the interrupt requests,
enabling them.
    mov AX, enabled;
    out PIC1_DATA, AL;
    mov AL, AH;
    out PIC2_DATA, AL;
  }
}


// The interrupt handler structure has a strange layout
// due to backward compatibility requirements on the
// processor. This helper function helps us set it from
// a regular pointer.
void setInterruptHandler(ubyte number, void* handler) {
  IdtEntry entry;
  entry.offsetLowWord = cast(size_t)handler & 0xffff;
  entry.offsetHighWord = cast(size_t)handler >> 16;
  entry.attributes = 0x80 /* present */ |  0b1110 /* 32 bit interrupt
gate */;
  entry.selector = 8;
  idt[number] = entry;
}
```

```
  // Tell the processor to load our new table.
  void loadIdt() {
    DtLocation loc;

    static assert(idt.sizeof == 8 * 256);

    loc.size = cast(ushort) (idt.sizeof - 1);
    loc.address = &idt;

    asm {
      lidt [loc];
    }
  }

  // Load a global descriptor table
  //
  // We don't actually care about memory protection or
  // virtual memory, so we load a simple table here that
  // covers the entire address space for both code and data.
  void loadGdt() {
    GdtEntry entry;
    entry.limit = 0xffff;

    // page granularity and 32 bit
    entry.limitAndFlags = 0xc0 | 0x0f;
    entry.access = 0x9a; // present kernel code
    gdt[1] = entry;
    entry.access = 0x92; // data
    gdt[2] = entry;

    auto tssPtr = cast(size_t) &tss;
    entry.baseLow = tssPtr & 0xffff;
    entry.baseMiddle = (tssPtr >> 16) & 0xff;
    entry.baseHigh = tssPtr >> 24;
    entry.limit = tss.sizeof;
    entry.limitAndFlags = 0x40; // present

    entry.access = 0x89; // a task buffer (we don't use it but do
  prepare it)
    gdt[3] = entry;

    DtLocation loc;
    loc.size = cast(ushort) (gdt.sizeof - 1);
    loc.address = &gdt;

    asm {
      lgdt [loc]; // tell the processor to load it
    }
  }
```

```
// This function initializes the system and enables interrupts,
// setting all handlers, except the keyboard IRQ, to our null
// handler. We'll call it from main.
void initializeSystem() {
  loadGdt();

  foreach(i; 0 .. 256)
    setInterruptHandler(cast(ubyte) i, &nullIh);

  setInterruptHandler(IRQOffset + 1, &keyboardHandler);
  loadIdt();

  enableIrqs(1 << 1 /* IRQ1 enabled: keyboard */);

  asm {
    sti; // enable interrupts
  }
}
```

And here is our new `main` function that watches for the keyboard input:

```
void main() {
  clearScreen();
  //print("Hello, world, from bare metal!");
  initializeSystem();

  while(true) {
    asm {
      sti; // enable interrupts
      hlt; // halt the CPU until an interrupt arrives
      cli; // disable interrupts while we handle the data
    }

    if(gotKey) {
      print("We got a key!");
      // Change the color of the W so we can see a
      // difference on each key press
      ubyte* videoMemory = cast(ubyte*) 0xb8000;
      videoMemory[1] += 1;

      // clear out the buffer
      gotKey = 0;
    }
  }
}
```

You may factor out the helper functions and hardware structure definitions to a separate file if you want. Build the program with the same `make` file as before, then load it with `qemu -kernel my_kernel` in the same way. When it loads, the screen will clear. Press any key and you'll see a message.

How it works...

Interrupt handlers have specific requirements by the hardware. They must leave the stack and all registers in the same state they were found when the method was entered, and unlike normal methods, they must return with the `iret` family of instructions (specifically, `iretd` on 32-bit) instead of the regular `ret` instruction.

D has two important features that help with these requirements without requiring us to write a helper file with a separate assembler: inline assembly and `naked` functions.

A `naked` function is a block of code with no instructions generated by the compiler. It neither prepares a stack frame nor automatically returns at the end of its execution.

 If you want to create a stack frame manually, for example, to use local variables, you may use the `__LOCAL_SIZE` constant provided by the compiler to allocate enough space for your locals.

The other part of complete control is writing the entire interrupt handler in the assembly language, which is made easy thanks to the easy accessibility of D's variables. While we could have used D itself, even in a `naked` function, that would require us to store more registers on the stack to ensure they are preserved correctly. This is doable, but it is unnecessary here because the interrupt handler needs to stay short anyway.

The keyboard handler performs three tasks. First, it reads the byte from the keyboard's I/O port with `in AL, 0x60;`. Then, it stores that value in a global variable for later reference and acknowledges the interrupt by writing `0x20`, the magic number defined by the hardware for acknowledgements, to the programmable interrupt controller's control port. If you forget to acknowledge an interrupt, you won't get any more—the first key press would work, but then all others wouldn't.

Finally, it returns with the special `iretd` instruction after carefully restoring the register we used and cleaning up the stack.

 Be careful not to use `iret` instead of `iretd`. dmd will output the 16-bit opcode instead of the 32-bit opcode we need, causing the processor to fault and reset the computer.

The event loop in `main` is currently written for simplicity and can be improved if written more concurrently and to perform other tasks while waiting. The basic idea is to wait for an interrupt by first ensuring they are enabled with `sti` and then stopping the CPU until one arrives with `hlt`.

Once it arrives, we basically assert a global lock by disabling interrupts with `cli`, ensuring our data won't be changed mid-read (an interrupt can occur after any CPU instruction), and check for new data. If we have a key, we display our message, update the color of the first character cell to see the change on each event, and reset the buffer for the next event.

 We write to `videoMemory`, a pointer, with the indexing operator such as an array. D allows this in the same way as C, with no bounds checking at all.

A better implementation may provide a longer keyboard buffer and shorter lock if it locks at all. After installing an interrupt handler for the system clock and running a task while not doing anything else (although still using `hlt` if there are no tasks to be run), we'd have the beginning of a real operating system kernel.

The rest of the code prepares the hardware to enable our interrupt handler. Although it's necessarily bulky, it doesn't utilize many D features. One notable aspect, however, is the struct alignment and the `static assert` to confirm that the size is correct—this is the real-world application of some code we wrote in *Chapter 7, Correctness Checking*. In this case, the outer align isn't strictly necessary for the code to work, but generally, when going for a specific size, both `align`s are necessary for the size check to pass: the one outside to remove struct padding and the one inside to remove field padding. If we forgot one or the other, there may be unused space in the struct that would confuse the hardware. Better to have strict tests that pass reliably than depend on implementation details of struct padding.

Also note that all the global variables are marked with `__gshared`. D's module-level and static variables are put in thread-local storage by default. Since our operating system has no threads, it also does not support thread-local storage! If we forgot `__gshared`, the code would still compile, but it would corrupt the memory and likely crash our system when we tried to run it. In the bare metal environment, the guideline against `__gshared` doesn't apply—here, you should use it or the `shared` keyword, unless you know you have correctly implemented TLS.

 The `shared` keyword has another potential use on bare metal: it can make up for the lack of a `volatile` statement in D. Since the compiler knows shared data may be updated by somebody else (another thread in most cases, but it could also be updated by other hardware), it treats shared reads and writes as `volatile`. Another alternative is to always perform volatile input and output with inline assembly or functions written in assembly.

12

Web and GUI Programming

In this chapter, we will use third-party libraries to write web and GUI programs with D. We will investigate the following recipes:

- ▸ Creating a dynamic website with `cgi.d`
- ▸ Creating a web API with `web.d`
- ▸ Parsing and modifying an HTML page with `dom.d`
- ▸ Accessing a SQL database
- ▸ Sending an e-mail
- ▸ Writing colored output to the console
- ▸ Getting real-time input from the terminal
- ▸ Working with image files
- ▸ Creating a graphics window to show a TV static demo
- ▸ Creating an OpenGL window

Introduction

D has a growing community of third-party library authors. In this chapter, we'll look primarily at libraries written by me and others. With these libraries, performing web and GUI programming with D can be easy, though they don't do everything. To prepare you to move beyond these limitations, we'll also look at techniques used in library implementation. We will also see practical applications of many of the recipes in this book as well as some new techniques that you may find useful when writing your own code.

I'll make reference to my Github repository throughout this chapter. This repository can be located at `https://github.com/adamdruppe/arsd`.

Creating a dynamic website with cgi.d

My `cgi.d` file is a self-contained module to create dynamic websites that can be accessed over the classic CGI protocol, the SCGI and FastCGI protocols, or by an embedded HTTP server that can be placed behind a reverse proxy—all with the same API for your code to use. The `cgi.d` module provides a `Cgi` class whose API exposes basic interaction with the requesting web browser such as query parameters, file uploads, cookies, HTTP headers, and writing response data.

Getting ready

Download `cgi.d` from `https://github.com/adamdruppe/arsd` and put it in your project's directory. You do not need any other files from the repository nor any other external libraries unless you want to use the FastCGI interface, which requires the C library `libfcgi` to be installed on the system.

For testing, you can use the embedded HTTP server and access it directly from your browser. However, to deploy the application, you'll also want to configure your web server software to use the application. This differs with each server and each protocol.

How to do it...

Let's execute the following steps to create a dynamic website:

1. Import `arsd.cgi`.
2. Write a function that handles each request. It should return `void` and take one parameter; an instance of the `Cgi` class.
3. Inspect request parameters with the properties of `Cgi` such as `get`, `post`, `cookies`, `pathInfo`, and `domain`.
4. Set any cookies and headers needed for your response with the methods of `Cgi` such as `setCookie`, `setResponseContentType`, and others.
5. Send a response with the `write` method of `Cgi`.
6. Mix in the library's generic `main` function with `mixin GenericMain!your_function_here;`.
7. Compile with `dmd.d yourfile.d cgi.d -version=embedded_httpd`.
8. Run the program. It will remain open in the console, ready to serve requests.
9. Open your web browser to `http://localhost:8085/` to see your page.
10. Terminate the server by pressing *Ctrl* + *C* in the console when you are finished.

The code is as follows:

```
import arsd.cgi;

import std.array, std.conv;

// This function does a quick and dirty HTML entity encoding
// to prevent XSS. Typically, I use htmlEntitiesEncode in dom.d
string simpleHtmlEncode(string s) {
  return s.replace("&", "&amp;").
    replace("<", "&lt;").replace(">", "&gt;");
}

void handler(Cgi cgi) {
  // this is the default, so the following line is not
  // necessary. It is here for demonstration purposes.
  cgi.setResponseContentType("text/html; charset=UTF-8");

  string data = "Hello, " ~
    cgi.request("name", "user").simpleHtmlEncode();
  data ~= "<br />\n";
  data ~= "Called from: " ~ cgi.pathInfo.simpleHtmlEncode();
  data ~= "<br />\n";
  data ~= to!string(cgi.get).simpleHtmlEncode() ~ "\n";

  cgi.write(data, true); // all written at once
}

mixin GenericMain!handler;
```

If you go to `http://localhost:8085/foo?name=your+name` in your browser, you'll see the following output:

Hello, your name

Called from: /foo

["name":"your name"]

 The `cgi.d` module also supports a command-line interface in all compiled versions for easier debugging. Call the function with at least two arguments: an HTTP verb and a path. Then, optionally, add other request parameters as `name=value` pairs. For example, `./app HEAD /foo name=test` will print the response, including headers, to `stdout`.

How it works...

The `cgi.d` module abstracts away the details of interacting with the web server protocols by hiding them behind the `Cgi` class and `GenericMain` function.

The constructors of `Cgi` come in two flavours: one understands CGI-like input data with a list of environment variables and a byte stream and the other understands HTTP, with just a byte stream from which the header information must be extracted. Both of these constructors support delegation, allowing the details of each protocol implementation to exist elsewhere (passed to it from `GenericMain`) while reusing the core code.

The data from HTTP headers is organized into `immutable` properties of the `Cgi` class for easy access while prohibiting modification. These properties are `immutable` to discourage using them as global variables due to a bad experience I had with PHP code using the `$_POST` array to perform an action at a distance, making functions very difficult to understand. The `Cgi` properties are meant to represent the HTTP request, not to be a place to stash function arguments and other global data.

Responses are crafted through the methods of the `Cgi` class. The `Cgi` class offers dedicated methods to set various headers including cookies, cache, content type, compression, and others. These methods try to intelligently handle multiple calls, for example, by updating the buffer instead of writing out two contradictory headers.

Response data is written with `cgi.write`. If you send all the data at once, set the second argument to `true`, allowing `Cgi` to optimize the response. For example, a complete response need not be double-buffered or chunked.

Implementation-wise, `Cgi` is a fairly simple class, using few of D's features. The `GenericMain` function is a `mixin template` that simply provides a prepackaged `main` function. The most interesting method, implementation-wise, is `cgi.request`, which uses an implicit compile-time type argument and `std.conv.to` to extract a value from the request parameters. It is a simple template that does little more than call a library function with an error handler, but it is an easy-to-use way to filter input that doesn't match a particular type.

If you use `cgi.request` with an `enum` variable, it will filter input and create a whitelist. The code is as follows:

```
enum Option { value, option, another }
// this will always be one of the valid options,
// regardless of user input
Option option = cgi.request!Option("option");
```

The embedded_httpd version of Cgi has two network server functions. One is used on Linux by default: forks, which creates new processes to handle concurrent requests. The other one is used on all other systems, and it uses Phobos' threads and message passing to achieve the same task. Processes are more reliable because the server can recover from segmentation faults, such as null pointer uses, but aside from on Linux, they come with a performance penalty and do not work correctly at all on Windows. Thanks to D's thread-local storage, both modes are indistinguishable to most user code. To achieve maximum compatibility across all server models, you may want to use lazy initialization of thread-local resources.

See also

▶ http://vibed.org/ is another web application framework for D. The vibe.d module (the name of the entire framework) differs significantly from cgi.d. While cgi.d was inspired by a desire to replace PHP and is very conservative in its approach, vibe.d was inspired by Node.js and innovates with fibers (see *Chapter 10*, *Multitasking*) for asynchronous I/O based scalability with code written in an intuitive, serial manner.

Creating a web API with web.d

My web.d file is an add-on module for cgi.d that utilizes D's reflection and code generation capabilities to automate tasks such as URL routing and JSON and HTML generation from your code.

Getting ready

The web.d file has several dependencies that can be found in my Github repository. You'll need to download each of the files and compile them all together. Download cgi.d, web.d, sha.d, dom.d, and characterencodings.d to your project's directory.

How to do it...

Let's execute the following steps to create a web API:

1. Import arsd.web.
2. Create a class that inherits from ApiProvider.
3. Write the export methods, which implement various functions that you want to expose.
4. Mix in a main function from the library with mixin FancyMain!Your_Class_name;.

5. Compile the program and all dependencies together using any version modifiers you want from `cgi.d` or `web.d`. We can compile with the following command to use the embedded HTTP server and disable the automatic creation of session files:

   ```
   dmd yourfile.d cgi.d web.d sha.d dom.d characterencodings.d
   -version=no_automatic_session -version=embedded_httpd
   ```

6. Access the functions from a web browser, JavaScript, or any other programming language through HTTP.

The code is as follows:

```
import arsd.web;
class Test : ApiProvider {
   export int add(int a, int b) { return a+b; }
   export string sayHello(string name) {
      return "Hello, " ~ name;
   }
}
mixin FancyMain!Test;
```

If you go to `http://localhost:8085/add` or `http://localhost:8085/say-hello`, you will see the automatic form and can fill it out to see the result of the corresponding function. You can see the machine-consumable result by going to `http://localhost:8085/add?a=1&b=2&envelopeFormat=json&format=json`.

How it works...

The implementation of `web.d` was one of my earliest explorations of compile-time reflection and code generation, and as such, its code is not very pretty to look at, but the results are remarkable.

Using `__traits(derivedMembers)`, `web.d` inspects each method in your `ApiProvider` subclass, looking for other compatible types and functions marked with the export protection level (checking with `__traits(getProtection)`).

It recursively scans compatible types, for example, other `ApiProvider` instances, to prepare a tree of URL-mapped functions and objects. The `export` methods anywhere in the tree are made available through the Web by automatically generating a wrapper function for them.

The wrapper function translates an associative array of parameters from the web request into the typed arguments expected by the method. Then, the method is run and the return value is automatically formatted based on an optional pair of URL parameters: `format` and `envelopeFormat`.

The `format` parameter controls the format of the data (for example, `html`, `json`, or `table`) and `envelopeFormat` controls the format of the surrounding metadata (possible options include `html`, which wraps the content in an HTML document for presentation in the browser, and `json`, which is meant for machine consumption). The wrapper function also catches any exceptions thrown by the method and also forwards them to the API client or web browser.

The formatting implementation uses compile-time reflection paired with conditional compilation to automatically handle most types. If the necessary code to support a format does not compile, attempting to use that format will throw an exception at runtime.

The `web.d` module also uses the information it gathers from compile-time reflection to automatically generate HTML forms that can be used as a prototype UI for the functions.

There's more...

The `web.d` module also includes an HTML template engine that extends `dom.d` (which we'll use in the next recipe), an `ApiObject` type to create `RESTful` resources, and web session support that can be file- or cookie-backed. Moreover, `web.d` works well with `html.d`. Also, my Github repository provides methods for HTML sanitization (done via the DOM parser and a whitelist of allowed tags), CSS denesting and macro expansion similar to the SCSS project, and more. However, these modules aren't very well documented at this time, however, so if you want to experiment with them, look at the source code.

Parsing and modifying an HTML page with dom.d

My `dom.d` module is an HTML and XML parser that can understand much of the tag soup found on the Web. Once it parses a document, it provides a JavaScript-style DOM API for easy inspection and manipulation of the document tree.

Here, we'll use the library to extract some meta-information and text from an HTML page, and then modify it and save a local copy to explore its features and implementation, which uses several of the techniques we've learned in this book.

Getting ready

Download `dom.d` and `characterencodings.d` from my Github repository. It has no other dependencies, so you do not need to download any additional files or libraries.

How to do it...

Let's execute the following steps to parse and modify an HTML page:

1. Import `arsd.dom`.

2. Create an instance of the `Document` class.

3. Pass an unvalidated HTML string to the `parseGarbage` method, or if you want strict checks on case and well-formedness, use `parseStrict`. It will throw exceptions when it encounters bad syntax.

4. Get the document title and author meta-information with the `title` property and the `getMeta("author")` method.

5. Extract the first paragraph's text with the `querySelector` or `requireSelector` methods and the `innerText` property. For example, `document.requireSelector("p").innerText;` makes use of the `requireSelector` method and the `innerText` property.

6. Modify all links to add a source parameter with `document["a[href]"].setValue("source", "your-site");`.

7. Replace the inner HTML text of a specific element with `requireElementByID` and `innerHTML`.

8. Get the new HTML as a string with the `toString` method.

9. Compile the program with `dmd yourfile.d dom.d characterencodings.d`.

The code is as follows:

```
import arsd.dom;

void main() {
   auto document = new Document();

   // The example document will be defined inline here
   // We could also load the string from a file with
   // std.file.readText or the web with std.net.curl.get
   document.parseGarbage(`<html><head>
      <meta name="author" content="Adam D. Ruppe">
      <title>Test Document</title>
   </head>
   <body>
      <p>This is the first paragraph of our
      <a href="test.html">test document</a>.
      <p>This second paragraph also has a <a href="test2.html">link</a>.
      <p id="custom-paragraph">Old text</p>
```

```
        </body>
        </html>`);
        import std.stdio;
        // retrieve and print some meta information
        writeln(document.title);
        writeln(document.getMeta("author"));
        // show a paragraph's text
        writeln(document.requireSelector("p").innerText);
        // modify all links
        document["a[href]"].setValue("source", "your-site");
        // change some HTML
        document.requireElementById("custom-paragraph").innerHTML
        = "New <b>HTML</b>!";
        // show the new document
        writeln(document.toString());
    }
```

Running the program will print the following output:

```
Test Document
Adam D. Ruppe
This is the first paragraph of our test document.
<!DOCTYPE html>
<html><head>
                <meta content="Adam D. Ruppe" name="author" />
                <title>Test Document</title>
        </head>
        <body>
          <p>This is the first paragraph of our
          <a href="test.html?source=your-site">test document</a>.
          </p><p>This second paragraph also has a
          <a href="test2.html?source=your-site">link</a>.

        </p><p id="custom-paragraph">New <b>HTML</b>!</p></body>
        </html>
```

 The document's parse functions take an HTML string, and not a filename or URL. If you get exceptions about missing input, make sure that you are sending it the correct input.

How it works...

The `dom.d` module is centered around two primary classes: `Element` and `Document`. The `Document` class includes the HTML parser and methods to set and get meta-information in the formats typically used on websites. The `Element` class represents one node in the document including its child nodes and attributes.

The parser's implementation doesn't use any of D's special features except array slicing, but did need some optimization work. The entity decoder's first draft naively built a new array on every call, which ended up being a performance problem. For the second draft, I rewrote it to scan the string ahead of time—before performing any copying or decoding for the `&` character. If the `&` character wasn't found, it simply returned the original slice. This slice is propagated everywhere it is used, never copied and never reallocated. If one was found, it performed a single copy and modification for that node.

Replacing the original conservative copying implementation with the new slicing and copy-on-write for both the entity encoder and decoder resulted in a major speed improvement in the parser and serialization methods.

In the example, we used the `parseGarbage` method. The Document class' parser includes two branches in every error condition: one that simply throws an exception and one that attempts recovery. The `parseGarbage` method opts for recovery in all conditions and has been tested against hundreds of real-world websites. It can recover from unclosed tags, mismatched tags, improper paragraph nesting, malformed attributes, and mislabeled character sets.

To handle character sets, the `characterencodings.d` implementation uses the Phobos function `std.utf.validate` to check UTF-8 correctness. If this fails, `dom.d` attempts to find a `charset` meta tag or XML prologue and uses that string to ask `characterencodings.d` to translate the data from that character set to UTF-8 for further processing in D. It performs the translation with hardcoded translation tables. If it cannot determine the character set, `parseGarbage` will assume it is Windows-1252 because that is the most common encoding used on unlabeled websites in my experience.

The `Element` class has a number of searching and mutation methods, primarily based on the JavaScript DOM. Search methods include `getElementById`, `getElementsByTagName`, and `querySelector`, all inspired by and substantially similar to—but not exactly identical to—JavaScript. The biggest difference between the `getElementsByTagName` function of `dom.d` and JavaScript's function with the same name is that `dom.d` returns a simple array of elements, whereas JavaScript returns a live node list that is updated as the tree is mutated.

In D, a live node list would be best represented by a range. However, JavaScript's node list violates one of the D range rules: it offers random access that runs in linear time instead of constant time, as required by D's random access ranges. Nevertheless, a live list could be represented by a forward range in D. The `dom.d` module doesn't do this simply because I didn't consider that at the time, and now I am stuck with it for backward compatibility.

However, the `dom.d` module uses a lazy range called `ElementStream` internally for all searching. This range can be retrieved with the `tree` property on `Element`. The `ElementStream` class uses an internal stack to implement an input range over the recursive DOM tree structure, just like we wrote in *Chapter 3, Ranges*.

As `ElementStream` implements the input range protocol, it can be passed to any `std.algorithm` functions just like any other range, including `filter`, `map`, and others.

The `querySelector` method and its partner method, `requireSelector`, parse a CSS selector and retrieve all nodes that match the pattern. The selector syntax is based on that used in JavaScript's `querySelector` function, CSS stylesheets, and the popular jQuery JavaScript library.

The `querySelector` method returns `null` if no matching elements are found. The `requireSelector` method will instead throw an exception, ensuring that it never returns `null`.

The `dom.d` module also provides `querySelectorAll`, which returns an array of elements that match the selector, whereas `querySelector` only returns the first match. The Document class' `opIndex`, which we used in step 6 of the example, calls `querySelectorAll` to populate an `ElementCollection` object.

The `ElementCollection` object's implementation uses `opDispatch` and string mixins to forward subsequent method calls to each element in the collection at once with minimal boilerplate. This allows quick and easy manipulation of a group of elements through their methods. Each wrapped method returns the whole collection, allowing chained calls, as is often seen in jQuery code.

Lastly, the `innerHTML` property and the `toString` method are used to manipulate and retrieve the content HTML strings. The `innerHTML` property always uses the nonstrict parsing options, similar to `parseGarbage`. Both implementations use an `Appender` argument to minimize intermediate allocations as a performance optimization.

There's more...

The `dom.d` module also makes heavy usage of `opDispatch` to access attributes, similar to JavaScript. The `element.attrs.attribute_name`, `element.style.cssRule` and `element.dataset.someValue` all utilize helper objects with `opDispatch` to generate properties that give easy access to attributes. All three collections use the technique we learned in *Chapter 9, Code Generation*, with different string translation rules. The `attrs` collection provides direct access to the underlying associative array. The `style` collection translates from CamelCase to dash-separated names and parses the existing attribute to provide access to all existing rules and recombines them to provide usable HTML.

The `style` collection also uses `alias this` and `opAssign` to enable implicit conversion to and from an attribute string—something JavaScript cannot do! The `dataset` method performs CamelCase to dash-separated conversion and prefixes the attribute with data—for compatibility with HTML5.

See also

> ▶ `https://github.com/opticron/kxml` is another XML library that is better suited to handle large sets of XML data than `dom.d`

Accessing a SQL database

My Github repository at `http://github.com/adamdruppe/arsd` contains a `database.d` interface file and implementation files for MySQL, PostgreSQL, SQLite, and Microsoft SQL Server via ODBC. Here, we'll use them to perform some SQL queries.

Getting ready

Download `database.d` and a driver file (`postgres.d` for PostgreSQL, `mysql.d` for MySQL, `sqlite.d` for SQLite, or `mssql.d` for SQL Server) from my Github.

The drivers also require C libraries. The `mysql.d` file needs `libmysqlclient`, which comes with the MySQL server. The `postgres.d` file needs `libpq`, which comes with the PostgreSQL server. The `sqlite.d` file needs SQLite installed on the system.

Let's also create a test database to use from the program. In our example, we'll use MySQL, so create a MySQL database, user, and data table. The following are the commands you can run in the MySQL console:

```
create database demonstration;
use demonstration
grant all privileges on demonstration.* to 'demo_user'@'localhost'
identified by 'test';
create table info (id integer auto_increment, name varchar(80), age
integer null, primary key(id)) CHARSET=utf8;
```

How to do it...

Let's access a SQL database by executing the following steps:

1. Import the driver module, in our case, `arsd.mysql`.

2. Instantiate the object with target-specific parameters. MySQL takes strings for the hostname, user name, password, and database name. SQLite takes a filename. PostgreSQL and MS SQL both take connection strings with the parameters in them.

3. Issue queries through the `Database` interface by using question marks as placeholders for any data parameters.

4. Process result rows with `foreach` or the range interface. Each column can be accessed by integer positions or by name strings.

The code is as follows:

```
import arsd.mysql;
void main() {
    auto db = new MySql("localhost", "demo_user",
    "test", "demonstration");
    // Add some data to the table
    db.query("INSERT INTO info (name) VALUES (?)", "My Name");
    db.query("INSERT INTO info (name, age) VALUES (?, ?)",
    "Other", 5);

    // get the data back out
    foreach(line; db.query("SELECT id, name, age FROM info")) {
        import std.stdio;
        // notice indexing by string or number together
        writefln("ID %s %s (Age %s)", line["id"],
        line[1], line["age"]);
    }
}
```

Running the program will add data to the table and print the following text. Note how the first ID's age is an empty string; this is how `null` is represented in the result line. The following is the output:

ID 1 My Name (Age)

ID 2 Other (Age 5)

If the program throws an exception, it may be because the database was not properly created.

 Avoid building SQL strings by concatenating user data strings. This is bug prone and may lead to SQL injection vulnerabilities. Instead, always use parameterized queries from the library or prepared statements from the database engine's native API.

How it works...

These files wrap the C APIs from the database vendors to provide minimal, but functional, access to the database servers through an abstracted interface. The `database.d` file will not attempt to transform SQL syntax differences across database vendors, but it will present a uniform interface to issue those queries.

The implementation of `Database.query` is broken up into two parts: first, the public `query` method, which is a variadic template that can take any number and mix of types of arguments; and second, the `queryImpl` method, which is a virtual function implemented by each driver. The split was necessary because templates cannot be virtual and fully generic and convenience functions to accept a variety of data types must be templates.

 Older versions of `database.d` tried to use a runtime variadic function to enable the virtual method to take varying argument types. It worked, but only sometimes—because a runtime variadic function needs to inspect each `typeid` given for a type it supports. Given this limitation, it couldn't succinctly support all types, and passing it an unsupported type will result in a runtime exception instead of a compile-time error! The variadic template and virtual method split solution resulted in shorter, simpler code that will properly support all types at compile time.

The public `query` method loops over its arguments and converts them to an array of `std. variant.Variant`, which is then passed to `queryImpl` for the database engine to use in parameterized queries. Then, each placeholder in your query string—represented by `?` or `?n`, the former pulling the next argument and the latter pulling a specific numbered argument—are replaced by the value of the next argument.

The `query` method returns a `ResultSet` interface, which is an input range of `Rows`. `ResultSet` is also an interface, with different implementations for each database engine. As an input range, it can be checked for data with the `empty` property, the current row retrieved with the `front` property, and the next row retrieved with the `popFront` method. It also works with the `foreach` statement for easily iterating over all the results. It could, in theory, also be transformed with `std.algorithm` like any other input range. However, in practice, you should do filtering and sorting in the database itself with your SQL query.

The `Row` object is a struct consisting of an array of strings and a column name mapping. Thanks to operator overloading, the column values are available through both column name strings and column index integers, similar to how PHP's old `mysql_fetch_array` function works.

Each column is represented by strings primarily for ease of database engine implementation and to keep the interface simple. As strings, all regular string operations can be performed, including checking for null or emptiness with the `length` property or converting them to other types with `std.conv.to`.

When you are finished with the data and database connection, you may let the garbage collector clean them up or you may explicitly destroy them with the global destroy method, which will immediately close the connection.

There's more...

The `database.d` file also includes two helper objects for building queries: `DataObject`, which provides a simple implementation of the active record pattern, and `SelectBuilder`, which helps you build a `SELECT` query by putting together individual components.

The implementation of `SelectBuilder` is very simple: it is simply a collection of string arrays and member variables for `LIMIT` clauses. Its `toString` method concatenates the arrays into the proper order to build a working query. The purpose of `SelectBuilder` is to make modifying, reusing, and creating queries easier than trying to reparse and splice a SQL string.

The code is as follows:

```d
import arsd.database;

void main() {
    auto query = new SelectBuilder();
    query.table = "users";
    query.fields ~= "id";
    query.fields ~= "name";
    query.limit = 5;
    query.wheres ~= "id > 5";
    query.orderBys ~= "name ASC";

    import std.stdio;
    writeln(query.toString());
}
```

That program will print out the following constructed query that could be passed to `Database.query`:

```
SELECT id, name FROM users WHERE (id > 5) ORDER BY name ASC
LIMIT 5
```

`DataObject` uses `opDispatch` properties to get and set data for a query. The getter property returns a string which can be converted to other types with `std.conv.to`. The setter property is a template to take any kind of argument and convert it to strings for use in queries automatically. `DataObject`, like many ORM solutions, may be subject to race conditions on the database and is not appropriate for all situations.

The `database.d` file also includes experimental code generation to create a strongly-typed subclass of `DataObject` based on a `SQL CREATE TABLE` statement. It takes a SQL string and parses it (using several parsing shortcuts) to extract column names and types. Then, it converts them into D properties and mixins as a generated string of D code, like we did in the Duck typing to a statically-typed interface recipe, in *Chapter 9, Code Generation*, to implement the subclass. However, since the parser is tailored to the particular way I wrote those statements at the time, it may not work for you.

Lastly, it also has code that uses compile-time reflection on structs to fill them in with a query. As I find the strings to be generally sufficient for me though, I rarely use this code and, as a result, it is not maintained.

See also

▸ `http://code.dlang.org/packages/ddb` is a native PostgreSQL driver that does not use `libpq` and offers ORM and other advanced functionality

▸ `https://github.com/rejectedsoftware/mysql-native` is a native MySQL driver that does not use `libmysql` and integrates with the `vibe.d` framework

▸ The module `etc.c.sqlite3`, distributed with Phobos, provides bindings to the SQLite C library

Sending an e-mail

Sending an e-mail is possible with the Phobos wrapper of cURL. cURL is a network client library which lets us work with a variety of tasks involving URL, including downloading files through HTTP, uploading files with FTP, and sending e-mail.

Getting ready

cURL is most likely already installed on Posix systems and is installed automatically by the `dmd` Windows installer. However, you may need to ensure you have the 32-bit library installed if you are building 32-bit binaries or the 64-bit library if you are building 64-bit binaries. To change the type of binary you are building, pass `-m32` or `-m64` to dmd.

As `std.net.curl` is a part of Phobos, you do not need to download any additional D libraries to send a basic e-mail with it.

How to do it...

Let's send a basic e-mail by executing the following steps:

1. Import `std.net.curl`.

2. Create an SMTP object, passing it a server URI and including a protocol, for example, `smtp://localhost` or `smtps://smtp.gmail.com:465`. SMTP is a reference counted struct, so do not use the new keyword.

3. Call `smtp.setAuthentication` with your username and password if you need to log in to your mail server.

4. Call `smtp.mailTo(array_of_recipients);`. This array should include all e-mail addresses that will receive the message, including people in the To list, the Cc list, and the Bcc list of recipients.

5. Set `smtp.mailFrom = "your_email_address"`. The `mailFrom` value should not include your name.

6. Set `smtp.message` to the message string, including e-mail headers separated from the body by a blank line.

7. Call `smtp.perform()` to send the e-mail.

8. Link the `curl` library with `pragma(lib)` or the `-L` option to `dmd`.

The code is as follows:

```
import std.net.curl;
pragma(lib, "curl");
void main() {
        auto smtp = SMTP("smtp://localhost");
        smtp.mailTo(["recipient@example.com"]);
        smtp.mailFrom = "sender@example.com";
        smtp.message = "Subject: Hello!\nFrom: Your Name
        <sender@example.com>\nContent-Type: text/plain;
        charset=UTF-8\n\nHey there.";
        smtp.perform();
}
```

If you change the e-mail addresses and mail server to the ones you can actually use, that will send an e-mail with a subject line of `Hello!` and body text of `Hey there`.

If you cannot send e-mail through your mail server, try setting `smtp.verbose = true;` before sending the e-mail. This will cause the library to print debugging information when it runs.

How it works...

There are two common ways for applications to initiate an e-mail: to ask a **Simple Mail Transfer Protocol** (**SMTP**) server to relay it for them or to call a local application (often `sendmail`) to send it for them. Phobos has support for both: it can call a local application with `std.process` or it can talk to a mail relay server with `std.net.curl`, which is what we did here.

The `std.net.curl.SMTP` module is a fairly low-level wrapper around the cURL library's functionality. To use it well, you need to manage the e-mail headers yourself and manage some protocol details such as building the array of all the `mailTo` recipients and putting a plain e-mail address in the `mailFrom` property. These properties are separate from the e-mail headers the end user sees. `std.net.curl` will not parse headers in the message body, nor will it add recipient headers from the properties.

As a result, the `mailTo` property must contain all recipients, including the `To`, `Cc`, and `Bcc` lists. Additionally, the corresponding e-mail headers should be present in the message. Similarly, `mailFrom` should contain your e-mail address while the `From:` header in the message should also be present and include your name for display to the user.

A `Content-Type` header should also be present. E-mails will typically work without these components, but may not appear correctly on the recipient's computer.

The `std.net.curl` module also supports username and password-based SMTP authentication and the `STARTTLS` features often used by e-mail providers. To add your username and password, use `setAuthentication`. To use SSL or TLS, use the `smtps://` protocol in the SMTP constructor as well as the appropriate port for your mail server (typically 465 or 587; check with your provider to be sure). It is written after a colon that follows the server name, for example, `smtps://yourserver.com:465`.

After constructing the message, a call to `smtp.perform()` will connect to the server and send the message. It may throw an exception saying it lost the connection to peer. This is most often caused by bad authentication information or an invalid recipient e-mail address. Be sure that your username is correct and you are sending to valid recipients; check that all addresses in the `mailTo` array are well formed. The `std.net.email` module has a helper function to validate that e-mail addresses are well-formed. You can also check that they have non-zero length and no extra white space.

Finally, to compile the program, we must add `libcurl` to the linker command. The easiest way to do this is to write `pragma(lib, "curl")` in your main file. You may also pass `curl.lib` to dmd on Windows or `-L-lcurl` to dmd on Posix systems.

There's more...

Creating and parsing e-mails can be a complex task due to the need to handle various character encoding rules, message headers, and the **Multipurpose Internet Mail Extensions** (**MIME**) standard for attachments, alternative bodies, and more.

From my Github repository, you can download my `email.d` file. The `email.d` file includes a `EmailMessage` class that permits you to build an e-mail message out of a property list and helper methods without worrying about the specific message format. Once the message is ready, you can call `message.send()` to send it via `std.net.curl.SMTP`. My `email.d` file depends on `htmltotext.d`, `dom.d`, and `characterencodings.d` to automatically convert HTML e-mails to a plain text alternative and parse incoming e-mails with different character sets.

Writing colored output to the console

The `writefln` function has a lot of formatting options for strings, but they always come out with the same default color. How can we create colored text output in D?

Getting ready

Download `terminal.d` from my Github repository to your project's directory.

How to do it...

Let's write colored output to the console by executing the following steps:

1. Import `terminal`.
2. Create an instance of `Terminal` with a linear output type.
3. Set the foreground and background color with the `terminal.color` method.
4. Write text with the `terminal.write`, `terminal.writeln`, `terminal.writef`, or `terminal.writefln` functions. They work the same way as the homonym functions in `std.stdio`.
5. You can flush output with `terminal.flush()` if it isn't done soon enough automatically.
6. Compile the program and `terminal.d` together with `dmd yourfile.d terminal.d`.

The following is the code:

```
import terminal;

void main() {
   auto terminal = Terminal(ConsoleOutputType.linear);
   terminal.color(Color.green, Color.red);
   terminal.writeln("Hello, world!");
}
```

Running the program will print **Hello, world!** in green text on a red background.

How it works...

Writing colored output is carried out differently on a Unix terminal than on the Windows console. On a Unix terminal, colors are set by printing an ANSI escape sequence to `stdout`, and it is the program's responsibility to set it back to normal before termination. On the Windows console, colors are changed with an API function, and the operating system will ensure the next program run sees a consistent state, so you do not have to clean it up manually.

The `terminal.d` module hides these implementation details behind a consistent interface, with the `Terminal` struct performing necessary cleanup work in its destructor.

In an earlier draft of `terminal.d`, I used an array of delegates created in the constructor to roll back changes in the destructor. That was a mistake that led to random crashes because delegates have a hidden internal pointer to the object. Using internal pointers in D's structs invokes undefined behavior because the struct may move at any time without notice, leaving a dangling pointer to the old, now reused memory. While a list of cleanup delegates may look elegant like `scope(exit)`, alas it is bug prone and should not be used with structs.

`Terminal` operates on a unique resource that is modified in its destructor, and it has a disabled postblit to statically prohibit copying the object. Similarly, the default construction is disabled to force the user to call the explicit constructor, giving `Terminal` a chance to run necessary initialization functions and gather information about the terminal's existing state at startup.

Otherwise, the implementation of `Terminal` is pretty unremarkable—it is just a wrapper for operating system and library functionality with its own buffering solution.

See also

▶ `http://code.dlang.org/packages/ncurses` is a binding to the C library `ncurses`, which provides similar functionality to `terminal.d`. For advanced uses, `ncurses` may provide better compatibility with your system.

▶ `https://github.com/robik/consoled` is an alternate D library to provide colored output and other cross-platform console and terminal operations.

Getting real-time input from the terminal

Getting real-time input from the console or terminal can take a fair amount of platform-specific code, quite a bit more than writing out colored output.

Getting ready

Download `terminal.d` from my Github and put it in your project directory.

How to do it...

Let's execute the following steps to get real-time input from the terminal:

1. Import `terminal`.
2. Create a `Terminal` object.
3. Create a `RealTimeConsoleInput` object, passing it a pointer to your `Terminal` object and passing flags for the types of input you need.
4. Use the `input` object's methods.

The code is as follows:

```
import terminal;

void main() {
    auto terminal = Terminal(ConsoleOutputType.linear);
    auto input = RealTimeConsoleInput(&terminal,
    ConsoleInputFlags.raw);
    terminal.writeln("Press any key to exit");
    auto ch = input.getch();
    terminal.writeln("Bye!");
}
```

Now, run the program. It will immediately exit as soon as you press any key without waiting for a full line.

How it works...

By default, text input from the user is line buffered by the operating system. This means your program won't be able to process any of the data the user types until she or he either presses the *Enter* key or signals the end of the file (*Ctrl + D* on most Posix setups and *Ctrl + Z* on Windows). To get real-time input, this line buffering must be disabled.

`RealTimeConsoleInput` is a struct that disables this buffering in its constructor and resets the settings to normal in its destructor. Like `Terminal`, the default constructor and postblit functions of `RealTimeConsoleInput` are annotated with `@disable` to force correct use of the shared resource.

There's more...

The `terminal.d` module also has optional integration with another file in my Github repository, `eventloop.d`. To try it, compile both files together and add `-version=with_eventloop` to the compile command. The `terminal.d` module includes a commented-out demo function to show the usage. The `eventloop.d` module implements a generic event loop through which any kind of message can be passed from any number of sources, identified by type. The goal of the event loop is to allow arbitrary combinations of event-driven libraries, such as a terminal and a GUI window, in a single application.

The implementation of `eventloop.d` passes messages in two parts: a type identifier and a pointer to the data. The type identifier is created by hashing the type's mangled name, which is acquired with `typeof(data).mangleof`. A type's mangled name is guaranteed to be unique across an application because a non-unique name will cause a compile-time name clash error. Alternatively, a handle to `typeid` could have been used. This pair of numbers is sent through an operating system pipe back to the application itself, and it can be handled in a generic event loop as another file descriptor, watched by functions such as `select` or `poll`.

An interesting consequence of this implementation is that pointers to the garbage-collected data cannot be reliably sent as a message. The reason is that the garbage collector cannot see the kernel's pipe buffer. Consider the following: you send a message, then allocate some memory before receiving the message. The allocation triggers a garbage collection run.

As the garbage collector cannot see the pipe buffer, it may not find any reference to the message data and thus believe it is safe to free the data. Then, when the message is read, the pointer is invalid.

To fix this bug, I opted for manual memory management in the event loop's `send` and `receive` functions. When you send a message, it uses malloc to allocate a copy of the message. When the message is received, it frees the memory.

The `eventloop.d` module only contains a Linux `epoll` and self-pipe-based implementation at this time.

See also

▶ The `ncurses` C library also provides real-time input functionality

Working with image files

Reading and writing image files is a way to present visualized results to the user and is also a starting point to write out images to a web browser or GUI window. Here, we'll use my `color.d` and `png.d` or `bmp.d` modules to load an image file, convert it to grayscale, and then write it out to a new file.

Getting ready

Download `color.d` and either `png.d` or `bmp.d` from my Github repository and put them in your project's directory. In the example, we'll use `png.d`. Neither module requires any additional D or C libraries.

How to do it...

Let's work with image files by executing the following steps:

1. Import `arsd.png`.
2. Load the file with `readPng`, passing it a filename. Be sure that the file is already in the PNG format.
3. Use the `getAsTrueColorImage` function to convert the input from whatever PNG format it was saved as into an RGBA array.
4. Manipulate the pixels. Here, we'll convert to greyscale with a simple average-of-components algorithm.
5. Write the new image out to a file with `writePng`.

The code is as follows:

```
import arsd.png;
void main() {
        auto image = readPng("test.png").getAsTrueColorImage();
        foreach(ref pixel; image.imageData.colors) {
                int average = (pixel.r + pixel.g + pixel.b) / 3;
                pixel.r = pixel.g = pixel.b = cast(ubyte) average;
        }
        writePng("test-bw.png", image);
}
```

The following image shows `test.png` after the conversion:

The `bmp.d` module works the same way as `png.d`; however, the functions are named `readBmp` and `writeBmp` instead of Png.

How it works...

The modules we dealt with in this recipe implement the file formats independently and provide a simple pixel buffer interface to the image.

The implementation of `png.d` builds on top of the lazy file input ranges Phobos provides to give a lazy input range of PNG data. This implementation was tricky because the Phobos `byChunk` range provides a fixed number of bytes, whereas the PNG file format is made out of a stream of variable sized bytes. To bridge the gap, I wrote a `BufferedInputRange` object with additional consume methods which manage variable sized chunks.

Underneath the `readPng` and `writePng` convenience functions, `png.d` offers both low- and mid-level access to the PNG data structures. The low-level functions provide access to the individual chunks that make up the file, the precise pixel format stored in the file, the palette, and so on. The mid-level functions provide input ranges of PNG file chunks and `RgbaScanlines`. The range of `RgbaScanlines` offers a potential hook to use the image data with `std.algorithm` and other lazy generic transformation functions.

See also

▸   `http://code.dlang.org/packages/cairod` is a binding to the Cairo drawing library, written in C and used by major projects such as GTK. Cairo has significantly more functionality and quality than my library, though it isn't as lightweight.

▸   `http://blog.thecybershadow.net/2014/03/21/functional-image-processing-in-d/` is a blog post by Vladimir Panteleev where he discusses his library, which takes the idea of using ranges of images and runs with it.

Creating a graphics window to show a TV static demo

My `simpledisplay.d` file is a module to create and interact with a simple window, enabling easy graphics display. On Windows, it wraps the Win32 GDI API, and on other systems it uses Xlib for broad compatibility with minimal dependencies.

Getting ready

Download `simpledisplay.d` and its dependency `color.d` from my Github.

How to do it...

Let's execute the following steps to create a graphics window:

1. Import `simpledisplay`.

2. Create an image to use as your pixel drawing buffer.

3. Create a `SimpleWindow` object with the image's size.

4. Create an image to use as your buffer.

5. Create and run an event loop with `window.eventLoop`.

6. Pass `25` as the first argument to `eventLoop` to request a 25 millisecond timer.

7. Pass a delegate that takes no arguments to serve as the timer handler. In this function, fill the image with random white and black pixels, get a painter with `window.draw`, and draw the image to it with `painter.drawImage`.

8. Pass a delegate that takes a `KeyEvent` argument to serve as a key handler. Call `window.close` to close the window and exit the loop when you receive the key to exit.

9. Implement the pausing functionality by making the timer delegate a return call if paused and changing the `pause` flag in the key handler.

10. Compile the program with `dmd yourfile.d simpledisplay.d color.d`.

The code is as follows:

```
import simpledisplay;

void main() {
  bool paused;
  auto image = new Image(256, 256);
  auto window = new SimpleWindow(image.width, image.height);
  window.eventLoop(25,
    () {
      if(paused) return;
      import std.random;
      foreach(y; 0 .. image.height)
      foreach(x; 0 .. image.width)
        image.putPixel(x, y, uniform(0, 2) ?
        Color.black : Color.white);
      auto painter = window.draw();
      painter.drawImage(Point(0, 0), image);
    },
    (KeyEvent ke) {
      if(ke.key == Key.Space)
```

```
        paused = !paused;
    if(ke.key == Key.Escape)
        window.close();
    }
  );
}
```

Running the program will pop up a window with random white noise, similar to static on an old TV set, as shown in the following screenshot:

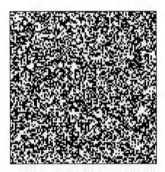

As you hold the Space bar, the animation will temporarily stop, and releasing the Space bar will cause it to resume.

How it works...

The `simpledisplay.d` module includes the necessary operating system function bindings and some cross-platform wrapping to enable the easy creation of a graphics window with no outside dependencies except `color.d`. It doesn't even use Phobos. You may notice improved compile times because neither file imports the standard library.

The implementation uses `mixin` templates to provide the different code for each platform. If I write this again, I will *not* use this approach—it resulted in code duplication and difficulty in maintenance. However, this approach does have one potential saving grace: it can be used to separate the operating system implementations into entirely different modules, which may become more maintainable. I didn't do this because I wanted the file to just work when downloaded individually. The `color.d` module eventually became a requirement—without it, the image modules and windowing module will both need to declare separate structures to hold a color, leading to silly incompatibilities between them. Even if two structures in different modules have exactly the same layout, they are considered separate, incompatible types (unless you use an adapter or a `cast`). However, while the ideal of one standalone file did not work, I still wanted to stay as close to it as possible and opted for one large `simpledisplay.d` file that covers all platforms.

Another challenge of the implementation was mapping window procedures of the operating system level back to the `SimpleWindow` object of D's class. The window procedures must match a specific signature and calling convention to be callable by the operating system (or, in the case of X11, the event loop must work with window IDs from the X server, which similarly leaves no room for the injection of a D class).

To solve this, I used an associative array of window handle/ID to window class mappings. The constructor of `SimpleWindow` creates the window and stores the native window handle in a static associative array that leads back to itself. Similarly, the destructor of `SimpleWindow` removes itself from this map. When a window handle comes through the event loop, the associative array is used to get the class instance and forward the message to it to be processed.

The event loop of `SimpleWindow` uses an array of delegates that are matched on argument types, inspired by `std.concurrency`. This is implemented with a `foreach` loop and `__traits(compiles)`; it loops over its arguments and attempts to assign them to the event handling delegates. If it succeeds, it accepts the handler. If not, a static assert is used to issue a compile-time error.

Finally, `simpledisplay.d` also supports the following two forms of drawing:

▸ Drawing directly to a window or image using the operating system functions
▸ Writing straight to a local image's pixels

To draw to the window, a `draw` method that returns a `Painter` struct is used. The painter retains a reference to the window for use with native API functions and has a destructor to automatically swap buffers and clean up resources when it goes out of scope.

Do not use `draw` before entering your event loop unless you surround the code in braces to ensure the painter goes out of scope before entering the loop. Otherwise, its destructor will not fire until program termination!

To draw directly to an image, the implementation tries to achieve efficiency by using a `final` class and shared memory on X11, when available. The `final` class provides a ~10 percent speed boost over a regular class because it contains no virtual functions, which can be a performance bottleneck on modern CPUs. The shared memory obviates image copying to and from the display server on the network-transparent X protocol, saving a significant amount of time. All this is done transparently to the user.

An interesting consequence of the shared memory approach, however, is the requirement to ensure cleanup tasks are always performed. As the resource is shared across processes, the operating system will not automatically release the shared memory handles when your program terminates. Thus, a signal handler must be installed to handle SIGINT when the user presses _Ctrl + C_. This is the same situation that was discussed in the _Getting real-time input from the terminal_ recipe. If you fail to do this, it may make your X server difficult to use because the number of possible shared memory handles is limited.

See also

▸ `http://code.dlang.org/packages/derelict-sdl2` provides dynamic bindings to SDL, the C Simple Directmedia Layer library used by several graphics applications

▸ `http://code.dlang.org/packages/gtk-d` provides an object-oriented wrapper for GTK, a cross-platform GUI toolkit

Creating an OpenGL window

My `simpledisplay.d` module also supports the creation of OpenGL contexts. It uses an older version of OpenGL but covers the basic functionality, and the same principle can be used to add other OpenGL functions. Here, we'll create a colorful spinning pyramid.

Getting ready

Download `simpledisplay.d` and `color.d` from my Github repository and put them in your project folder. On Windows, you must also acquire `opengl32.lib` and `glu32.lib` from my Github repository.

How to do it...

Let's create an OpenGL window by executing the following steps:

1. Import `simpledisplay`.

2. Create a new `SimpleWindow` object, passing `OpenGlOptions.yes` to the constructor.

3. Set `window.redrawOpenGlScene` to a delegate that will be called to draw your scene. This function should use the `gl*` family of functions to do the drawing and should not have to swap the OpenGL buffers. For our spinning pyramid, this function will set up our matrix, set up our viewport, and enable depth testing. Then, draw the pyramid.

4. Call `window.eventLoop` with a timeout and a timeout handler function (a delegate with no arguments) that calls `redrawOpenGlSceneNow` to draw your new frame.

5. Compile with `dmd yourfile.d simpledisplay.d color.d` on Posix. On Windows, also add `-version=with_opengl` to the compile command.

The code is as follows:

```
import simpledisplay;

void main() {
```

```
    auto window = new SimpleWindow(512, 512, "OpenGL Demo",
OpenGlOptions.yes);

    float f = 0.0;
    window.redrawOpenGlScene =  {
      glMatrixMode(GL_PROJECTION);
      glClearDepth(1.0f);
      glEnable (GL_DEPTH_TEST);
      glDepthFunc(GL_LEQUAL);
      glViewport(0,0,window.width,window.height);

      // clear the screen
      glClearColor(0,0,0,0);
      glClear(GL_COLOR_BUFFER_BIT | GL_DEPTH_BUFFER_BIT | GL_ACCUM_
BUFFER_BIT);

      glLoadIdentity();
      glRotatef(f, 1, 0, 0);
      f += 4.5;

      glBegin(GL_TRIANGLES);
      // base of the pyramid
      glColor3f(1, 0, 0); glVertex3f(0.5, -0.5, 0);
      glColor3f(0, 1, 0); glVertex3f(0, 0.5, 0);
      glColor3f(0, 0, 1); glVertex3f(-0.5, -0.5, 0);

      // the other three sides connect to the top
      glColor3f(1, 1, 1); glVertex3f(0, 0, 0.5);
      glColor3f(0, 1, 0); glVertex3f(0, 0.5, 0);
      glColor3f(0, 0, 1); glVertex3f(-0.5, -0.5, 0);

      glColor3f(1, 0, 0); glVertex3f(0.5, -0.5, 0);
      glColor3f(1, 1, 1); glVertex3f(0, 0, 0.5);
      glColor3f(0, 0, 1); glVertex3f(-0.5, -0.5, 0);

      glColor3f(1, 1, 1); glVertex3f(0, 0, 0.5);
      glColor3f(1, 0, 0); glVertex3f(0.5, -0.5, 0);
      glColor3f(0, 1, 0); glVertex3f(0, 0.5, 0);

      glEnd();
    };


    window.eventLoop(50,
      delegate () {
        window.redrawOpenGlSceneNow();
      });
}
```

Running the program will open a window with an animated spinning pyramid. The following is one frame from it:

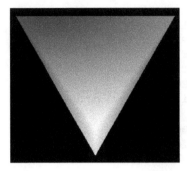

How it works...

The `simpledisplay.d` module also includes bindings to OpenGL 1.1. It uses a delegate to redraw the scene so that it can automatically handle cases where your window was covered partially and exposed without needing you to work the whole message loop. The delegate is bracketed by code that prepares the OpenGL context, binding it to the correct window and then swapping the buffers when it is finished—automatically displaying your frame.

OpenGL is disabled by default on Windows because the necessary library files are not bundled with DMD. I created these libraries by running `implib`, the tool from Digital Mars, on the `opengl32.dll` and `glu32.dll` files—as we learned about in *Chapter 1, Core Tasks*. On 32-bit Windows, the creation or conversion of import libraries is often necessary because DMD uses an old format that is no longer common. This limitation has been solved for 64-bit Windows.

See also

> ▶ `http://code.dlang.org/packages/derelict` has the Derelict library, which is used by many games programmers in D. It contains more up-to-date bindings than `simpledisplay.d`.

Addendum

This appendix will list short tips and tricks that didn't fit into any particular theme for the other chapters:

- ▶ Compiling D for ARM/Linux Raspberry Pi
- ▶ Running D on bare metal ARM
- ▶ Using the exponentiation operator
- ▶ Getting a stack trace without throwing an exception
- ▶ Finding more information about D

Compiling D for ARM/Linux Raspberry Pi

Raspberry Pi is a small, low-cost computer that uses an ARM processor and the Linux operating system.

Getting ready

If you don't own a Raspberry Pi, you can emulate the hardware with QEMU. The process is described at `http://xecdesign.com/qemu-emulating-raspberry-pi-the-easy-way/`.

How to do it...

To compile D for an ARM/Linux Raspberry Pi, we need to execute the following steps:

1. Download the **GNU D compiler** (**GDC**) cross-compiler from `http://gdcproject.org/downloads/`. The header gives the platform you are on. The table lists the targets. The target for Raspberry Pi is **arm-linux-gnueabi**.

2. Compile the program. The command-line arguments of GDC that are based on the `gcc` compiler differ significantly from `dmd` in the following manner:

   □ The output file will always be called `a.out` unless you specify a new name with the `-o` option.

   □ You must always include the `.d` file extension when passing source files to the compiler.

   □ Many of D's additional compile options need to be passed with `-f` and may have different names. For example, `-fno-bounds-check` works in the same way as `-boundscheck=off` on `dmd`. Refer to the GDC documentation for more info, or download the `gdmd` helper script that converts the flag syntax for you.

3. Copy the executable to your Raspberry Pi.

4. Run the program.

 You can also download a native compiler for the Pi which runs directly on it and produces programs for it. The bottom of the GDC download page has a native compiler for ARM.

The code is as follows:

```
import std.stdio;
void main() { writeln("Hello, ARM!"); }
gdc hello.d -ohello
./gdc
```

The output is as follows:

```
Hello, ARM!
```

How it works...

GDC combines the D language portions of `dmd` (the dmd frontend) with the code generation portions of `gcc` (the gcc backend) to create a portable compiler with mature code generation. With GDC, D code can be generated for every target `gcc` supports.

Code generation is only half the story to using D. Using it on a new platform also requires that the runtime library be ported. The GDC team successfully ported the runtime to Linux on ARM with all tests passing in 2013 and 2014, enabling the full language and standard library on that platform. Most D code and libraries will now work on ARM/Linux targets such as Raspberry Pi.

There's more...

Android and iOS systems often have ARM processors too, but they do not run a standard Linux operating system. In the case of Android, it also does not have linker support for thread-local variables which D will have to emulate. Work is in progress towards porting the library to these operating systems and adding support to the language to enable direct access to Objective-C APIs to facilitate better integration on Apple systems.

See also

  ▶   http://wiki.dlang.org/LDC is the LDC compiler, a D compiler based on the LLVM compiler backend. It also has growing support for ARM targets.

Running D on bare metal ARM

By combining the GDC ARM compiler with the stripped runtime concept we used in *Chapter 11, D for Kernel Coding*, we can also run D on a bare metal ARM board. Going from this concept to a working program will take a lot of work, but we will get started with a "hello world" program.

Getting ready

Get an emulator such as QEMU and the GDC cross-compiler targeting ARM. The same cross-compiler for Raspberry Pi that we used previously will work here too. Also, copy the minimal object.d from *Chapter 11, D for Kernel Coding*, to a new folder for the ARM project.

How to do it...

To run D on bare metal ARM, we need to execute the following steps:

1. Create a startup.s file that sets up the stack, calls the D function, and then endlessly loops. The code is as follows:

```
.global _start
_start:
  LDR sp, =stack_top   @ prepare a stack
  BL _d_run_main       @ call our D entry point
  B .                  @ endlessly loop
```

2. Create a linker script, `linker.ld`, which puts the startup code at the beginning of the file and reserves stack space. The code is as follows:

```
ENTRY(_start)
SECTIONS
{
  . = 0x10000;
  .startup . : { startup.o(.text) }
  .text : { *(.text) }
  .data : { *(.data) }
  .bss : { *(.bss COMMON) }
  . = ALIGN(8);
  . = . + 0x1000; /* 4kB of stack memory */
  stack_top = .;
}
```

3. Modify `object.d` to add an ARM version which calls `_Dmain` and loops with regular D code instead of inline assembly. The code is as follows:

```
void _d_run_main() {
        version(ARM) {
                _Dmain();
                while(true) {}
        }
}
```

4. Write a `hello.d` file that says hello by writing to the serial port's memory address. The code is as follows:

```
enum serialPort = cast(shared(uint)*) 0x101f1000;

void printToSerialPort(string s) {
        foreach(c; s)
                *serialPort = c;
}

void main() {
        printToSerialPort("Hello world from D!\n");
}
```

5. Create a `Makefile` that assembles `startup.s`, compiles `object.d` and `hello.d` with exceptions disabled and the release mode flag turned on, links it together with the linker script, and then converts the output to a binary image. The code is as follows:

```
all:
        arm-gdcproject-linux-gnueabi-as -mcpu=arm926ej-s -g
startup.s -o startup.o
```

```
        arm-gdcproject-linux-gnueabi-gdc -frelease -fno-exceptions
-c -mcpu=arm926ej-s -g object.d -o object.o
        arm-gdcproject-linux-gnueabi-gdc -frelease -fno-exceptions
-c -mcpu=arm926ej-s -g hello.d -o hello.o
        arm-gdcproject-linux-gnueabi-ld -T linker.ld hello.o
startup.o object.o -o hello.elf
        arm-gdcproject-linux-gnueabi-objcopy -O binary hello.elf
hello.bin
```

6. Run the program using `qemu-system-arm -M versatilepb -m 128M
   -kernel hello.bin -sdl`.

In the serial console view of QEMU (press *Ctrl + Alt + 3* to switch to it), you'll see the "hello world" message.

How it works...

Bare metal code for ARM computers follows the same basic principles as for x86 PCs, and the D code to get you started is substantially similar. The biggest difference is the use of the GDC compiler instead of `dmd`, because GDC can generate code for ARM targets and `dmd` cannot.

GDC also does not support inline assembly syntax of `dmd` or `naked` functions (though the `gcc` backend does support `naked` functions for ARM targets, so support for that may be added later). Instead, GDC supports inline assembly based on the `gcc` syntax, which uses strings of assembly code with input, output, and destroyed register specifiers.

Other significant differences between `dmd` and GDC will only become apparent if exceptions are enabled, and since we disabled them for the minimal runtime, we didn't have to worry about that here.

Of course, x86 and ARM hardware is significantly different in regards to details such as memory mapped addresses, but the principle is the same: use a pointer to the correct address to communicate. Here, we used a pointer to the UART0 serial port and wrote our string to it, saying hello.

See also

▶ `http://gcc.gnu.org/onlinedocs/gcc/Extended-Asm.html` explains the inline assembler syntax of `gcc`, which is also used by GDC.

Using the exponentiation operator

D has a built-in exponentiation operator: the `^^` operator.

How to do it...

In order to use the exponentiation operator, we need to execute the following steps:

1. Write an expression with the `^^` operator.
2. Make one or both arguments floating point if you want a floating point result.

The code is as follows:

```
int a = 2^^3; // a == 8
float b = 2.0 ^^ 3.0; // b == 8.0
auto c = 2 * 2 ^^ 3; // c == 16
```

How it works...

The exponentiation operator is first subject to constant folding and is then rewritten into a call to the `std.math.pow` library function to perform the operation. The result follows the regular arithmetic type rules of the D language, so the `int` arguments yield an `int` result and the `float` arguments yield a `float` result.

The operator also follows the usual arithmetic order of operations, so it has higher precedence than multiplication, as seen in the third example line.

The choice of `^^` for the operator was driven by the desire: to look like ASCII math without being confusing in the context of the D programming language. The two other major competitors, `^` and `**`, were rejected because they conflict with existing operations inherited by C: `^` is the bitwise XOR operator in both C and D, while `**` is currently parsed as multiplication of a dereferenced pointer. While the lexer could be changed to make it into a new operator, this could potentially lead to silent breakages when porting C code to D, which D tries to avoid. (D doesn't mind breaking C code, but it prefers it to be a compile error whenever possible instead of code that compiles the same then acts differently.)

Thus, `^^` was chosen, and it is visually similar to how exponentiation is often written in ASCII text (2^3 for example), without being in conflict with any existing C or D code.

Why isn't `^^` used for Boolean XOR in the same way that `||` is Boolean OR and `&&` is Boolean AND? It is because Boolean XOR already has an operator: `!=`. If you write out the truth tables for is-not-equal, you'll find they are an exact match for a hypothetical Boolean XOR!

Getting a stack trace without throwing an exception

When debugging, it may be helpful to get a stack trace without changing the flow of execution. Throwing an exception will get you a stack trace, but it will also terminate the program. How can we extract the stack trace without actually unwinding the call stack?

How to do it...

To get a stack trace without throwing an exception, we need to execute the following steps:

1. Import `core.runtime;`.
2. Call `defaultTraceHandler()` to get an instance of `Throwable.TraceInfo`.
3. On Posix systems, wrap the call to `defaultTraceHandler` in four functions to ensure relevant data is not cut out by `druntime`.
4. Return or print `trace.toString()`.

The code is as follows:

```
string getStackTrace() {
  import core.runtime;

  version(Posix) {
    // druntime cuts out the first few functions on the trace because
they are internal
    // so we'll make some dummy functions here so our actual info
doesn't get cut
    Throwable.TraceInfo f4() { return defaultTraceHandler(); }
    Throwable.TraceInfo f3() { return f4(); }
    Throwable.TraceInfo f2() { return f3(); }
    Throwable.TraceInfo f1() { return f2(); }
    auto strace = f1();
  } else {
    auto trace = defaultTraceHandler();
  }

  return trace.toString();
}
```

We can test the function by calling it inside another program. The value this function returns matches the stack trace seen when an exception is printed.

 You may have to compile with debug information turned on (dmd -g -debug) to get file and line information about your call stack.

How it works...

When an exception is thrown in D, the trace handler is called to gather information about the call stack. When the exception is printed with `toString`, it also calls `trace.toString` to add the stack trace to the message.

The trace handler is also available outside of exceptions by importing `core.runtime`. It works the same way and provides the same string without modifying the program's execution state. The only tricky part is on Posix. The trace handler ignores the first several lines of the result because they are typically functions internal to `druntime`. Since we're using the handler outside of the `druntime` context, this behavior would cut off relevant information!

As a work around, we wrap the call to `defaultTraceHandler` in several dummy functions so they are removed by the handler's truncation instead of information we actually care about.

Generating the stack trace string is an expensive operation, so only use it as a debugging tool. A full stack trace used to be immediately generated any time an exception was thrown. This proved to be an enormous performance problem, so the code was changed. Now, a snapshot of the stack trace is taken immediately, but resolving it into a string with function names is done lazily upon a call to `toString`. The result is about a 1000 times speedup of exceptions thrown and caught inside the application.

Finding more information about D

Searching for D information on the Web can be difficult. If you have a question, how can you get help?

How to do it...

To find more information about D, we need to execute the following steps:

1. Check the documentation at `http://dlang.org/`. Navigation is easier if you have an idea where to look: the Phobos functions are organized by module and the language features are organized by the type of item: expressions, statements, and so on. Generally, if you are looking for something which returns a value, it can be found under **Expressions** or **Functions**. Other language constructs can be found under **Statements** if a specific page for it cannot be found on the sidebar. The web page contents are also included in the `dmd` zip download in `dmd2/html` for offline viewing or searching (for example, with `grep`).

2. Try searching the web with the terms `D programming language` (optionally in quotes) or `dlang` in your query.

3. Search the wiki at `http://wiki.dlang.org/` for your topic.

4. Search or ask on Stack Overflow using the D tag (`http://stackoverflow.com/questions/tagged/d`).

5. Ask in the D.learn forum at `http://forum.dlang.org/`. No question is too trivial or too complex to ask the group.

6. Join the #d chat room on the server `irc.freenode.net`. Use an IRC client to log in, or use the web client `https://webchat.freenode.net/`. In the chat, you can ask a bot for definitions or links by typing `?some_term` or ask the other people in the room normally. Just jump in and ask; there is usually at least one person active who will be willing and able to help.

7. If all else fails, read the source. The complete source is available on Github at `https://github.com/d-programming-language` or in the `dmd` zip file under `dmd2/src`.

 If you write an article on D, use the complete D programming language term in the header so search engines will help other people find it.

How it works...

The preceding tips may help you find answers to questions on your own, and if that fails, the D community is active and generally friendly. Don't hesitate to stop by the forums or chat room to ask us anything. We know a lot of projects and links in our brains that aren't easy to find on the open Web and are often willing to work with you to find solutions to novel problems too.

Index

output range
about 58
creating 66-68

P

package
URL 53
pair function 123
parallel data
processing, with std.parallelism 267-269
parallelism module
URL 269
parseGarbage method 306
platform-specific code
writing 189-191
playRound function 46
popFront property 64
post-conditions
verifying 181-183
pre-conditions
verifying 181-183
processes
creating 271-273
process module
URL 274
program
modules, adding to 8-10
properties
generating, opDispatch used 252-254
pure functions side effects
avoiding 180, 181
put method 51

Q

QEMU
URL 280
querySelector method 307

R

RAII
using 136
Random access ranges 58
random numbers
generating 44-47

ranged integer
creating 140-145
range interface
putting, on collection 72-75
ranges
Bidirectional ranges 58
Forward ranges 58
Output ranges 58
Random access ranges 58
searching 85
sorting 82, 83
storing, as data member 80, 81
used, for implementing algorithm 58-61
readln method 47
readOctalString function 235
readSet function 39
real-time input
obtaining, from terminal 316-318
reference counted object
making 119, 120
reference semantics
struct, creating with 138, 139
ref function 25
registerType function 219
regular expressions
searching with 49-51
release method 134
requireSelector method 307
Resource Acquisition Is Initialization. *See* **RAII**
runtime polymorphic ranges
using 79, 80
runtime type information
extending 219-222

S

scope guards
used, to manage transactions 123, 124
SearchPattern parameter 212
server
creating 39
sigaction function 273
single-locking singleton
exploring 274, 275
slicing 14
spawn function 266

Thank you for buying
D Cookbook

About Packt Publishing

Packt, pronounced 'packed', published its first book "*Mastering phpMyAdmin for Effective MySQL Management*" in April 2004 and subsequently continued to specialize in publishing highly focused books on specific technologies and solutions.

Our books and publications share the experiences of your fellow IT professionals in adapting and customizing today's systems, applications, and frameworks. Our solution based books give you the knowledge and power to customize the software and technologies you're using to get the job done. Packt books are more specific and less general than the IT books you have seen in the past. Our unique business model allows us to bring you more focused information, giving you more of what you need to know, and less of what you don't.

Packt is a modern, yet unique publishing company, which focuses on producing quality, cutting-edge books for communities of developers, administrators, and newbies alike. For more information, please visit our website: www.packtpub.com.

About Packt Open Source

In 2010, Packt launched two new brands, Packt Open Source and Packt Enterprise, in order to continue its focus on specialization. This book is part of the Packt Open Source brand, home to books published on software built around Open Source licences, and offering information to anybody from advanced developers to budding web designers. The Open Source brand also runs Packt's Open Source Royalty Scheme, by which Packt gives a royalty to each Open Source project about whose software a book is sold.

Writing for Packt

We welcome all inquiries from people who are interested in authoring. Book proposals should be sent to author@packtpub.com. If your book idea is still at an early stage and you would like to discuss it first before writing a formal book proposal, contact us; one of our commissioning editors will get in touch with you.

We're not just looking for published authors; if you have strong technical skills but no writing experience, our experienced editors can help you develop a writing career, or simply get some additional reward for your expertise.

C++ Application Development with Code::Blocks

ISBN: 978-1-78328-341-5   Paperback: 128 pages

Develop advanced applications with Code::Blocks quickly and efficiently with this concise, hands-on guide

1. Successfully install and configure Code::Blocks for C++ development.

2. Perform rapid application development with Code::Blocks.

3. Work with advanced C++ features including code debugging and GUI toolkits.

CryENGINE Game Programming with C++, C#, and Lua

ISBN: 978-1-84969-590-9   Paperback: 276 pages

Get to grips with the essential tools for developing games with the awesome and powerful CryENGINE

1. Dive into the various CryENGINE subsystems to quickly learn how to master the engine.

2. Create your very own game using C++, C#, or Lua in CryENGINE.

3. Understand the structure and design of the engine.

Please check **www.PacktPub.com** for information on our titles

www.ingramcontent.com/pod-product-compliance
Lightning Source LLC
Chambersburg PA
CBHW062052050326
40690CB00016B/3068